YORKSHIRE WALKS

6 DALES
30 WALKS

Published by Sigma Leisure – an imprint of
Sigma Press, Stobart House, Pontyclerc, Penybanc Road, Ammanford, Carmarthenshire SA18 3HP.

British Library Cataloguing in Publication Data
A CIP record for this book is available from the British Library.

ISBN: 978-1-85058-992-1

Typesetting and Design by: Sigma Press, Ammanford.

Cover photograph: Malham Cove © John Burland

Photographs: © John Burland unless stated otherwise.

Maps: © Ron Scholes M.Ed, Adv. Dip. Ed, FRGS, Chartered Geographer

Printed by: Akcent Media

YORKSHIRE WALKS

6 DALES
30 WALKS

John Burland

FOREWORD

Despite being born a Yorkshireman, the first three decades of my life were mostly spent further south and I did not really discover the Dales until being commissioned to photograph *James Herriot's Yorkshire* in 1979. I was completely taken aback by the savage beauty of the remoter valleys and totally in awe of the farmers and lead miners from centuries past who worked above and below ground in all weathers to eke a hard fought living from the region's natural resources. The gaunt shells of long abandoned farmsteads speak volumes about the harsh realities of hill farming in an era ruled by technology and automation. The National Park authorities and other conservation bodies are sometimes accused of being over protective of the countryside that we are often guilty of taking for granted, but without their input and land management, parts of the dales and moors would be in a far more parlous state.

When first becoming acquainted with the Dales, I soon realized that although the roads and high passes that link the Dales' communities provided a means of covering a lot of ground in a short space of time, it was only when the car keys were safely pocketed and one set out on foot that the true character of this glorious part of Yorkshire revealed itself.

This book is perfect reminder that the Yorkshire Dales comprise so much more than the main tourist and walking destinations of Swaledale, Wensleydale and Wharfedale. When Wainwright originally conceived the Coast to Coast route, his avowed intention was to show those people who love being out and about in the wild country and National Parks of the north just what could be achieved with a bit of pre-planning and map reading.

Many of the expeditions detailed in John Burland's *6 Dales – 30 Walks* will tempt even the most lethargic ramblers to dust off their boots and sally forth amidst some of England's finest countryside.

Derry Brabbs
Nidd, North Yorkshire

ACKNOWLEDGEMENTS

There are a number of people for whom I owe a debt of gratitude in producing this book about the Yorkshire Dales. Firstly, my late parents for taking me in my youth to many of the places mentioned in this book and introducing me to walking these broad acres, as they are often known. Also, to David Hodgson and my late friend Alex Miller who were the Outdoor Pursuits Instructor and Venture Scout Leader in the 9thAiredale Scout Group from Horsforth when I was Scout Leader there in the 1970s and early 1980s who assisted me whilst taking groups of youngsters on many of these walks.

I have been offered much help during the preparation of the book itself from Mark Allum the Recreation Manager for the Yorkshire Dales National Park Authority and I must thank him particularly for allowing use of some of the details from their website which has added depth to the details of a number of these walks, as well as the introduction and geology sections of the book.

I have walked most of these walks on my own but also a number with my wife Vivienne and I must take this opportunity to thank her for her companionship on some of the shorter walks and for her encouragement during the preparation of the book. Most importantly she has put up resolutely with my absences during weekends when I have been out walking these routes over the last couple of years.

Jim Chapman from Guiseley has helped me in the preparation of the book by test walking some of the routes and I must express my thanks and gratitude to him for his sterling work in checking detail for me on the walks.

Additionally, Ron Scholes, another good friend from The Wainwright Society has provided sketch maps for each of the walks in the book and thanks must be given to him for his attention to detail in this respect.

Finally, I must thank my son Matthew whose expert knowledge of English and History has been invaluable during the proof reading stages of the book.

CONTENTS

INTRODUCTION

Yorkshire is often referred to as "God's own County" and those of us who were privileged to be born 'a Tyke' would wholeheartedly agree. Whilst not wishing to decry those parts of the county to the south and east of my home town of Leeds, it is the area to the north and north-west of England's third largest city that stands out particularly from a walker's point of view. This is the area usually entitled 'The Dales'.

The Yorkshire Dales is a special place: it has outstanding scenery; a range of wildlife habitats and a rich cultural heritage. It is a fantastic outdoor arena for recreation as well as peaceful relaxation and a haven for wildlife. The Dales National Park was established in 1954, and covers an area of 680 square miles (1,762 square kilometres) in the north of England, straddling the central Pennines and the counties of North Yorkshire and Cumbria.

Easily accessible from the industrial conurbations of West Yorkshire and Lancashire, the Yorkshire Dales has for many years been an attractive walking area for the many thousands of people from these two major areas of population and far beyond as well.

The Yorkshire Dales National Park is one of the most important areas of the United Kingdom for its rich and diverse wildlife heritage and has the largest area of nationally and internationally important habitats of any National Park. This ranges from the wildflower rich hay meadows and pastures in the dale bottoms, through to the moorland fringe with its rush pastures so important for wading birds and the windswept uplands with their open heather moorland and blanket bog, to the unique limestone pavements. Many of the habitats are more common in some parts of the National Park than others and occur together where conditions suit them. For example, calcareous grassland, limestone pavement and upland mixed ashwoods are typical of areas where Carboniferous limestone occurs and are concentrated in the Craven District of the Park.

The Yorkshire Dales is home to a wide range of species. Many of these are rare or scarce nationally and this is the last stronghold for many plants and animals. Many species are adapted to certain conditions and these lead to a wide diversity of plants and animals in the Yorkshire Dales, ranging from the lime-loving plants and invertebrates of the limestone country to the breeding birds of the moorland and moorland fringe. The habitats and species found in the countryside are often closely linked with the underlying geology of the area along with natural processes and human influence.

The dales of the Yorkshire Dales National Park are well recognised internationally for the traditional agricultural landscape of hay meadows and pastures divided up by drystone walls. It is this landscape and its flower-rich meadows which attract the majority of people to visit the National Park. The most species rich of these grasslands have been managed in a consistent low intensity manner for decades. Little or no inorganic fertiliser will have been applied; meadows will have been cut once a year and pastures grazed lightly with a summer resting period. This type of management has lead to the development of diverse and species-rich flower meadow and pastures. The cranesbill meadows are internationally recognised. However, grassland habitats in the dales are generally more intensively managed than other habitats and are particularly vulnerable to changes in farming practices such as the use of artificial fertilisers and silage-making.

The interaction of people with nature through history has produced a landscape of remarkable beauty, distinctive character and immense interest in the Yorkshire Dales that is cherished and enjoyed by the nation. These special qualities have been recognised as worth conserving for the enrichment of us all, and are valued by millions of people in this country and world wide.

The area straddles the Pennines, the backbone of England. Geology and natural processes have been the fundamental force behind the creation of this familiar landscape and of the variety found within it. They are quite literally the bedrock of the Yorkshire Dales and have numerous dramatic and impressive features. The Yorkshire Dales is an expansive area of hill country that rises in the Millstone Grit-capped Three Peaks area to over 2,300 feet (700 metres). Rivers have cut deep valleys (dales) of which there are over 20 named examples, each distinctive in character.

The south of the National Park displays one of the best examples in Britain of classic limestone (Karst) scenery, with its crags, pavements and extensive cave systems. The area's northern landscape is equally striking. Its valleys with distinctive stepped profiles, the product of differential weathering of the Yoredale Series, are separated by extensive moorland plateaux. Spectacular waterfalls – such as Hardraw Force with its 90 foot (27 metre) single drop (the largest in England), the famous series of Aysgarth Falls, Cautley Spout with a broken drop of 600 feet (180 metres); Thornton Force with its geological unconformity, and numerous cascading streams – bring movement and sound to the many different individual valleys.

There are six major rivers that rise in the Yorkshire Dales. From west to east these are: The Ribble, The Aire, The Wharfe, The Nidd, The Ure and The Swale. The majority of these have subsidiary rivers flowing into them and a number of the walks in the book will have their starting points in some of these smaller Dales. Of these six rivers, five of them flow in an easterly or south-easterly direction to eventually join with one another to form the River Ouse which runs through York, the original county town of Yorkshire. Only The Ribble, however, forsakes its Yorkshire gathering grounds of the Three Peaks area and source at Ribblehead, and flows instead through Lancashire to emerge in the Irish Sea at Royal Lytham St. Annes.

In this book I have chosen five of what I class as the 'Best Walks' from each of these six Dales. Some of you will agree with my choices, others may disagree and think that walks you have completed in these areas are better. To term anything 'best' is always subjective; we all have our own opinions of what is 'the best'. It would indeed be a sad world if everyone agreed on everything. The weather conditions, time of year and many other factors may affect one person's opinion compared with another's, but I have tried to pick out, for any readers who have not walked in this delectable part of the country, what I think are some of the finest areas in which to walk. The walks vary from shorter easier walks to those that are much longer and harder and I have tried in the introduction to each to grade them accordingly.

One major thing to bear in mind whilst walking in the Yorkshire Dales are the weather conditions as many of the different dales have their own micro-climates and the weather can change considerably from one dale to the next or even within a short section of a dale itself. It is always useful to check with local sources before setting out as many dalesfolk know from signs and wind directions what the weather is likely to be.

I would express caution in some of the limestone areas especially after rain as the rocks beneath your feet can often be slippery. As the famous Alfred Wainwright used to comment, "Watch where you're putting your feet!"

J D Burland
Otley

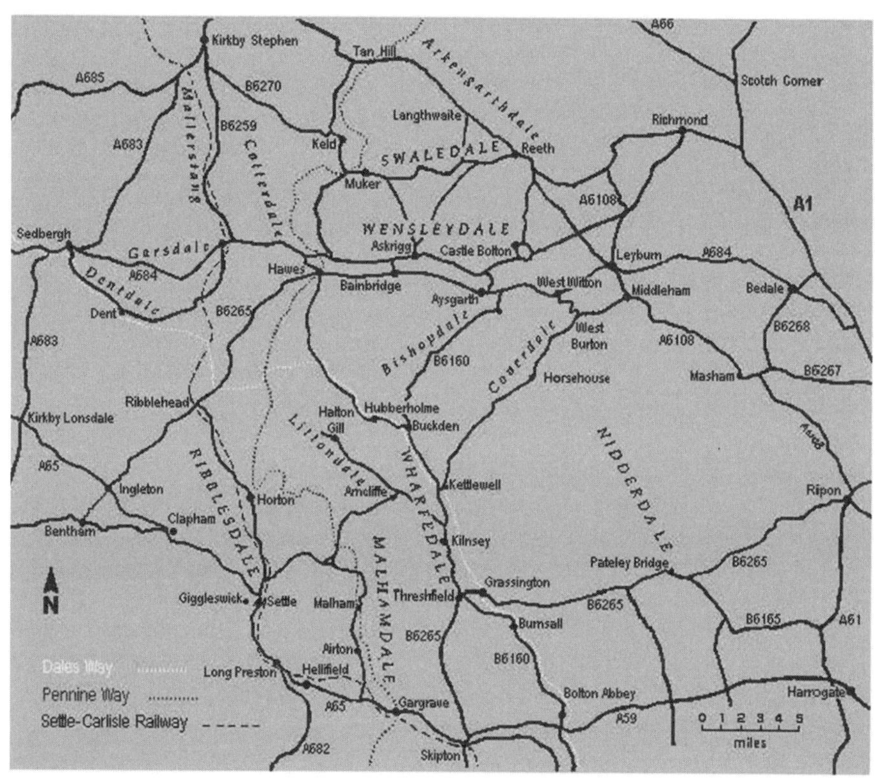

Map courtesy of the Yorkshire Dales Public Transport Users Group

GEOLOGY OF THE YORKSHIRE DALES

The spectacular scenery of the Yorkshire Dales is a direct result of the area's unique geology – predominantly carboniferous limestone (including Great Scar Limestone and the 'Yoredale Series' of layered limestones interspersed with shales and sandstones), capped on the higher fells by Millstone Grit.

Much of what is now known as the Yorkshire Dales lies on an area roughly defined by the underlying Askrigg Block, bordered to the south and west by the Craven Fault (which marks an approximate boundary with Bowland and Pendle to the west and south-west, and Brontë Country to the south-west and the south). To the north and north-west the Askrigg Block is bordered by the Dent Fault (which runs along Dentdale marking a natural boundary with the much older Silurian and Ordovician rocks of the Howgill Fells to the north). To the east the rocks overlaying the Askrigg Block dip below more recent sediments which form the valley floor of the Vale of York and the Vale of Mowbray.

Because much of the Yorkshire Dales is limestone country, there are many caves and potholes in the area. There are also many spectacular karstic limestone features on the surface, including cliffs and gorges such as Malham Cove and Gordale Scar near Malham, as well as limestone pavements (which were formed by the scouring action of glaciers on the bedrock). The layered structure of the Yoredale Series in particular is conducive to the formation of fine waterfalls such as Hardraw Force and Aysgarth Falls in Wensleydale.

Other kinds of limestone features found in the dales include reef knolls (conically shaped and fossil rich hills which formed as coral atolls in the shallow waters of an ancient prehistoric sea). Fine examples of these kinds of reef knolls (which generally run along the southern edge of the Craven Fault) can be found on Scosthrop Moor above Settle, in the southern part of Malhamdale and perhaps most famously at the Cracoe Reef Knolls (which lie between the villages of Rylstone and Cracoe and Burnsall in Lower Wharfedale).

In the most northern of the Yorkshire Dales the geology sees the intrusion of the Whin Sill, an igneous dolerite rock. Mineral deposits are relatively common in the dales, and in days gone by lead mining was a common source of employment: veins having been worked primarily on Grassington Moor, Greenhow Hill and also in Arkengarthdale and Swaledale. In fact, several of today's 'honeypot' dales villages (including Grassington and Pateley Bridge) originally grew up to service this old industry.

Today the miners have all gone, but limestone and other types of rock present in the dales are sought after by the construction industry, and despite the environmental damage incurred by open cast extraction there are actually several large scale quarries operating even within the boundaries of the national park.

SAFETY

The routes described in this book vary considerably in length and difficulty. Some of the shorter and easier routes should be safe for most people at any time of the year and under most weather conditions provided the walkers are reasonably equipped and are sensibly behaved. However, some of the longer and more difficult walks are in areas where weather conditions can change rapidly, even on good summer days, and walkers should be well equipped with correct clothing, food and emergency items such as a torch, survival bag, whistle etc. More details of this are given below.

In Mountain Hill and Moorland Areas

You should carry sufficient equipment for the length of the expedition and the worst weather conditions possible. Below is the minimum required:

Clothes: Clothing should be of several layers, the base layer of wicking materials to distribute moisture, one or more mid layers of lightweight fleece materials for warmth plus an outer layer, which is windproof and waterproof (preferably breathable), including over-trousers.

Boots: Suitable sturdy walking boots or trainers with a good grip, appropriate for the season in which you are walking.

Backpack: A sturdy pack with good comfortable harness and external straps for compression and attachment of additional equipment. The size of the pack will depend on the length of the expedition and anticipated weather conditions. A waterproof liner is recommended.

A full checklist of equipment you should consider for some of the full day walks would be:

- Waterproof and windproof jacket and trousers
- Fleece and spare fleece
- Hat / gloves / scarf
- Emergency bivouac bag
- Whistle
- Head torch (+ spare batteries)
- Map and compass
- Food (including extra high energy foods)

- Water (and warm drink in winter)
- Sun cream
- First aid kit
- Sunglasses
- Walking poles (your knees will last longer if you use these)

In Old Mining Areas

Abandoned mines may be dangerous to anyone who attempts to explore them without proper knowledge and safety training. Old mines are often unsafe and can contain deadly gases. Standing water in mines from seepage or infiltration poses a significant hazard as the water can hide deep pits and trap gases below the water. Additionally, since weather may have eroded the earth and rock surrounding it, the entrance to an old mine in particular can be very dangerous. Old mine workings, caves, etc. are commonly hazardous simply due to the lack of oxygen in the air, a condition in mines known as blackdamp. The simple advice whilst walking in old mining areas is to keep away from entrances, shafts, etc.

Weather Forecasts

Mountains can be inhospitable and dangerous places for the ill prepared. From one hour to the next, from one hill to the next, they can exhibit a dramatic variation in weather conditions. Whether it's a well-planned expedition or a spur of the moment decision to go to the hills, it is important to check the forecast. For the Yorkshire Dales area there is an excellent website available through the Met Office:

http://www.metoffice.gov.uk/loutdoor/mountainsafety/yorkshiredales/ yorkshiredales_latest_weather.html

The Countryside Code

Five sections of The Countryside Code are dedicated to helping members of the public respect, protect and enjoy the countryside:

- Be safe, plan ahead and follow any signs
- Leave gates and property as you find them
- Protect plants and animals and take your litter home
- Keep dogs under close control
- Consider other people

USEFUL INFORMATION

Public Transport in the Yorkshire Dales

There are many bus services within the Yorkshire Dales which run throughout the year. These are supplemented by extra services during the Summer period, which mainly operate on Sundays and Bank Holidays from Easter or May Day weekends until mid-October.

The main Dales areas covered by the all-year services are:

- Grassington and Buckden in Upper Wharfedale from Skipton and Ilkley
- Malham from Skipton and Gargrave
- Settle from Skipton, Ingleton and Clitheroe
- Bolton Bridge in Wharfedale from Skipton and Harrogate
- Pateley Bridge in Nidderdale from Harrogate
- Fountains Abbey from Ripon
- Bedale and Leyburn in Wensleydale from Ripon and Richmond
- Hawes in Wensleydale from Garsdale (on Settle-Carlisle railway)
- Hawes and Leyburn in Wensleydale from Bedale and Northallerton
- Keld and Reeth in Swaledale from Richmond

Accommodation

Where possible I have included details of nearby accommodation in the Appendix at the end of the book. However, this is only correct at the date of publishing (2015) and it is best to check in advance before leaving home regarding availability. This is only a limited selection of the accommodation in each of the areas and local tourist information centres and the Internet are good sources of up to date information.

Maps

The following maps cover the area of the Yorkshire Dales in this book

Ordnance Survey 1:25000 Explorer Maps 7 Sheets)

OL2	Yorkshire Dales – Southern and Western areas
OL21	South Pennines
OL30	Yorkshire Dales – Northern and Central areas
288	Bradford & Huddersfield
297	Lower Wharfedale & Washburn Valley

298   Nidderdale
304   Darlington and Richmond

Explorer Maps are ideal for the walker as they show all rights of way.

Ordnance Survey 1:50000 Landranger Maps (5 Sheets)
        92 – Barnard Castle & Richmond
        98 – Wensleydale & Upper Wharfedale
        99 – Northallerton & Ripon
        103 – Blackburn & Burnley
        104 – Leeds & Bradford

Landranger Maps show all public rights of way, are very widely used, and are usually easily obtainable from bookshops or may be borrowed from Public Libraries in the area.

THE ROUTES

Areas: 1 – Ribblesdale, 2 – Airedale, 3- Wharfedale, 4 – Nidderdale, 5 – Wensleydale, 6 - Swaledale

Area	Details	Distance in Miles	Distance in Km	Ascent in Feet	Ascent in Metres	Time in hours	Start GR	Map	Grading
1	Ribblehead	5	8	330	100	2.5	765792	OL2	Easy
1	Ingleton Falls	5	8	700	210	2 hrs	694732	OL2	Moderate
1	Penyghent	6	10	1500	450	3.5 hrs	809725	OL2	Strenuous
1	Attermire	5.5	9	900	270	3.5 hrs	819636	OL2	Moderate
1	Cattrigg Force	5	8	525	160	2 hrs	821672	OL2	Easy
2	Malham's Big 3	8.5	14	1300	400	4 hrs	901629	OL2	Strenuous
2	Five Rise Locks	4	7	500	160	1.65 hrs	108392		Easy
2	Nappa Cross	6	9.8	1200	360	2.75	900627	OL2	Moderate
2	Top Withens	6.5	10	650	200	2.5 hrs	029373	OL21	Moderate
2	Hetton & Winterburn	7	11.5	800	250	3 hrs	961588	OL2	Moderate
3	Ilkley Moor	4.5	7	450	130	2.5 hrs	117477	OS297	Moderate
3	Simon's Seat	9	14.5	1000	300	4 hrs	051572	OL2	Strenuous
3	Linton from Burnsall	6	9	500	150	3 hrs		OL2	Easy
3	Mosedale	12	19	1000	300	5 hrs	002640	OL2	Strenuous
3	Otley Chevin	5	8	1000	300	2.5 hrs	203454	OS297	Moderate
4	Brimham Rocks	8	13	950	290	4 hrs	173645	OS298	Moderate
4	Scar House	7.5	12	900	275	4 hrs	101734	OS298	Moderate
4	Knaresborough	4	6	200	60	1.5 hrs	349570	OS298	Easy
4	Yorke's Folly	4	6.5	350	110	2 hrs	159657	OS298	Easy
4	Greenhow Mines	6	10	1200	360	3 hrs	128634	OS298	Moderate
5	Aysgarth & Bolton Castle	7	11	330	100	3 hrs	013887	OL30	Moderate
5	Hawes & Hardraw	5	8	430	130	2 hrs	875898	OL30	Easy
5	Semerwater	5	8	850	260	2 hrs	921875	OL30	Moderate
5	Middleham	7	11.5	500	150	2.5 hrs	127878	OL30	Easy
5	West Burton	4	6.5	400	120	1.5 hrs	017867	OL30	Easy
6	Gunnerside Gill	9.4	15	1600	490	4 hrs	951982	OL30	Strenuous
6	Keld & Kisdon	7.5	12	800	240	4 hrs	892012	OL30	Moderate
6	Booze	5	8	650	200	2 hrs	005024	OL30	Easy
6	Reeth	5.5	9	500	155	2 hrs	039993	OL30	Easy
6	Willances Leap	6.5	10	500	155	3 hrs	171015	OS304	Moderate

NOTES ON
THE ROUTE DESCRIPTIONS AND MAPS

Difficulty

The routes have been selected to give a wide variety in both terms of distance and ascent. This was done deliberately to add as much variety to the book as possible and to encourage all types of walkers to use the book. For the sake of both interest and safety, details of the degree of difficulty is given at the beginning of each walk. The time to complete the walk has also been given taking into account distance and ascent and this has been based on Naismith's Rule (see below). However, roughness of the terrain can take its toll, as can the level of difficulty for route-finding, and the time may needed to be adjusted accordingly.

The measure of difficulty has been based on three factors. (i) The distance involved, (ii) the amount of ascent on the walk, and (iii) the type of terrain. The walks have been divided into three catagories – Easy, Moderate and Strenuous. These are not intended to be rigid categories but are merely a guide to the difficulty of the walk. A 'typical' walk within each category would be as follows:

Easy – A short walk of up to 5 miles (8km) over good paths with no real route finding difficulties. Some climbing may be involved but mostly over gradual slopes with only short sections of difficult ground.

Moderate – A longer walk of up to 10 miles (16km) or of greater difficulty mostly over good paths but perhaps with some sections less well defined. Some summits of hills may be reached necessitating climbing over steeper and rougher ground.

Strenuous – Walks of over 8 miles (13+ km) often with prolonged spells of climbing or shorter walks with much more difficult terrain. More difficult from a route finding point of view and also containing more rough paths and scrambling.

Distance

Distance has been given in both miles and kilometres. These are 'map-miles' and take no account of the amount of climbing involved.

Ascent

These figures are given in both feet and metres.

Naismith's Rule

The usual method of calculating the times for walks is based on the rule devised by William W. Naismith, a Scottish mountaineer, in 1892. This allows, for the normal walker, one hour for every 3 miles (5km) plus a further 30 minutes for every 1,000 feet (300m) of ascent.

Car Parks

All the walks start at a car park or suitable parking place. Details of these with a grid reference are given at the start of each walk. Please do not park in other areas where you may block gates or other access for the local community.

Route descriptions

As well as the usual left and right turns at junctions, stiles, etc. I have also included directions based on the usual compass bearings. These are as follows:

North – 0 degrees
East – 90 degrees
South – 180 degrees
West – 270 degrees

North-east – 45 degrees
South-east – 135 degrees
South-west – 225 degrees
North-west – 315 degrees

The Maps

The sketch maps have all been drawn by my good friend from the Wainwright Society, Ron Scholes. These are purely an outline of the route with villages and other points of interest marked on them. They are an addition to, but not a substitute for, the Ordnance Survey maps recommended for each route. Please note that because the distances of the walks vary, so the scales of the maps vary accordingly. Some of the longer routes are on a smaller scale to the other shorter routes in the book in order to include the complete route. The maps are similar to those found *Pennine Journey* by David Pitt for whom Ron kindly supplied the maps as well.

Features of Interest

Some particular features of interest are included in both the description of the route and also on the map itself.

Access

As far as is known the routes described either: (i) use public rights of way, (ii) cross areas where there is a current access agreement, (iii) use a concessionary path or (iv) cross land which is privately owned but has been opened to the general public through regular use.

Nevertheless, it is necessary to emphasise that walkers have an obligation to behave properly when using footpaths or crossing areas of moorland so that no damage is caused or nuisance given to other people. Also, it should be noted that the access to areas could change over time. If diversions are marked, often to allow a particularly eroded area to recover, these should be followed implicitly.

RIBBLESDALE INTRODUCTION

Ribblesdale is the most westerly of the Yorkshire Dales whose river (the Ribble) drains into the Irish Sea and not the North Sea, as is the case with all of the other dales we will be looking at in the book. Ribblesdale runs in a southerly direction from Ribblehead between the high fells of Ingleborough and Pen-y-Ghent (two of the area's famous 'Three Peaks') through Horton in Ribblesdale, Stainforth and Langcliffe and onto the market town of Settle.

South of here the landscape becomes gentler as the Ribble meanders out of the Yorkshire Dales and along the Ribble Valley. It then passes between the moors of Bowland and Pendle Witch country en route to Preston and the Irish Sea, which it joins between Lytham St. Annes and Southport.

The Ribble begins at the confluence of Gayle Beck and Cam Beck near the famous viaduct at Ribblehead, in the shadow of Whernside, the highest of the Yorkshire Three Peaks, 2415 feet (736 metres) high. These two becks that form The Ribble have many smaller becks or gills joining them.

The Ribble Way is a long-distance footpath which follows the river for much of its course. This footpath was opened on 1st June 1985. It follows the valley of the River Ribble from the estuary at Longton near Preston in Lancashire to its source above Ribblehead, a distance of approximately 70 miles (113 km).

The area is famous for the twenty-four arched Ribblehead Viaduct, which carries the Settle-Carlisle Railway Line. The first stone was laid by William H. Ashwell, the contractor's agent, on 12th October 1870. The viaduct stands 104 feet (31.7 metres) high, has 24 arches and spans 440 yards (402 metres). This will be visited in Walk 1 in this section of walks.

From the viaduct another side valley heads off to the west to Chapel le Dale where the River Doe emerges from the limestone rocks and joins up with Kingsdale Beck (whose source is also high on Whernside's slopes) and Swilla Glen at Ingleton to form the River Greta. This area is still within the Yorkshire Dales National Park and includes the famous Pecca Falls and Thornton Force and is typical of much of the limestone scenery in these parts. We will visit these during Walk 2.

Horton-in-Ribblesdale is a small village about 5 miles (8km) downstream from Ribblehead being most famous as a traditional starting (and finishing) point for climbing Yorkshire's famous Three Peaks. The Pennine Way long distance footpath and the Pennine Journey also pass through the village. Additionally, the area is famous for caving and potholing, with Alum Pot and the Long Churn cave system just to the north, near the hamlet of Selside, and

Hull Pot and Hunt Pot on the western side of Pen-y-ghent (which we will visit during Walk 3).

Stainforth is the next village downstream, 3 miles (5km) from Horton-in-Ribblesdale and is visited particularly for its nearby waterfalls of Stainforth Force and Catrigg Force (visited on Walk 5). Catrigg Force is an absolute gem. The waterfall is hidden from view in a small secluded copse one mile upstream of Stainforth village. The main waterfall (there is a series of smaller ones in the copse further down) has a vertical drop of about 20 feet (6 metres) into a lovely step pool. The walk to the Force is easy along a bridleway from the village.

Settle is often referred to as 'The Gateway to the Dales' and since its bypass was built the town now lies just off the main A65 linking Leeds and the Lake District. Above the town's market square towers the dominant limestone cliff of Castleberg Crag, and the spectacular limestone outcrops and caves of Warrendale Knots, Jubilee Cave, Victoria Cave and Attermire Scar (visited in Walk 4). Settle is also the start of the forty-two mile Six Dales Hike, which has an annual walking competition over its route each September.

Ribblehead Circular

This first walk in Ribblesdale is around the Ribblehead Viaduct area, a short circular walk along the lower slopes of Whernside and through the fields to the south with some magnificent views of nearby Ingleborough and also in the distance Pen-y-Ghent, which is the subject of walk 3 in Ribblesdale.

Distance	**5 miles (8km)**
Ascent	**330 feet (100m)**
Time	**2½ hours**
Grading	**Easy**
Suggested Map	**OS Outdoor Leisure 2 – Yorkshire Dales – Southern & Western**
Starting point	**Grid Reference: SD 765792**
Parking	**At junction of the B6255 and B6479 near Ribblehead Viaduct**
How to get there	**Take the B6479 from Settle which itself is reached by the B6480 from the main A65 Skipton to Kendal road**
Terrain	**Mainly farm tracks and good footpaths throughout**

Ribblehead Viaduct

The viaduct is a Grade II listed building and a Scheduled Ancient Monument. It is 440 yards (400 m) long, and 104 feet (32 m) above the valley floor at its highest point. It is made up of twenty-four arches of 45 feet (14 m) span, with foundations 15 feet (4.6 m) deep. The north end of the viaduct is 13 feet (4.0 m) higher in elevation than the south end and it lies across Batty Wife Moss.

Ribblehead Viaduct was designed by the engineer John Sydney Crossley. The first stone was laid on 12th October 1870 and the last in 1874. Over a thousand navvies were employed in the building of the viaduct. They also erected shanty towns on the moors for themselves and their families. The shanty towns were named after victories of the Crimean War, posh districts of London (which was done sarcastically), and Biblical names. During the construction there were many deaths from industrial accidents and a number of smallpox epidemics; meaning that the church graveyard at Chapel-le-Dale had to be extended to bury the resultant bodies. A total of one hundred navvies were killed during the construction of the viaduct.

Ribblehead Viaduct is highly impressive at all times of the year. In summer it can be a busy place, visited by walkers ascending Whernside and the others of the three peaks and also by many day trippers who stop for refreshment and wait for trains to cross the viaduct. There are plenty of lay-by spaces near the junction of the Ingleton to Hawes road with the Horton in Ribblesdale road. There are information boards near to this junction about the viaduct and the Yorkshire Dales National Park Authority has also produced a podcast to guide walkers round the site.

Train on viaduct and Three Peaks walkers

The Walk

From the parking place by the two road junctions, cross the road and take the track by the sign towards the viaduct. Turn right and follow the track for about ¼ mile (400m). At this point it turns under the viaduct, but **do not turn left at this point.** Instead, continue forward following the Whernside track which you can see straight ahead of you. There is an information board here about the viaduct and on the way back, at the end of the walk, you will see a monument to the building of the viaduct as you pass underneath this magnificent structure.

The walk now continues forward parallel with the railway line which is high above you to your left. When you reach the Three Peaks signboard keep walking forwards, still following the Whernside sign. You will soon reach a wooden stile, cross this and continue ascending until you reach the railway signal. Here you will see a railway arch to your left. Take the tunnel underneath this and the look out for the public bridleway sign and continue straight forward.

At the end of the arch go through a gate, now heading downhill and follow the track down towards the stream. You then need to head towards the farm buildings at Winterscales by bearing left. Pass through a gate between the buildings and onto the humpback bridge. Here you will see a group of large limestone boulders on the left.

Continue along the lane crossing over two cattle grids, then through a wooden gate by a barn, and onwards through a metal gate, leading between the farm buildings at Ivescar. Pass through firstly another metal gate and then immediately afterwards go through a waymarked wooden gate. Go over a small bridge comprised of railway sleepers and when you reach the sign to Scar End you need to bear to the right. Cross the next three fields, passing through a series of gates and continue ahead to reach the farm buildings at Broadrake.

Turn left by the farm and set off down the farm track until it bends to the right and becomes a tarmaced section. Go across the cattle grid and turn sharp left continuing by the side of the fence and onto a track heading for a ladder stile. This is a well defined track which goes across the fields to reach a stream bed which can be dry in the summer. Jump across this, and keep heading forward along the track which eventually meets a road near to the cattle grid. When you have crossed the cattle grid, turn left and follow the road which then heads back up towards Ivescar. Go over the bridge that crosses Winterscales Beck. At this point you have a magnificent view of the viaduct in front of you with Plover Hill and Pen-y-Ghent off to the right.

When the road divides ahead take the turning to the right. Pass through a gate, heading towards the viaduct. At the next gate turn right again and cross

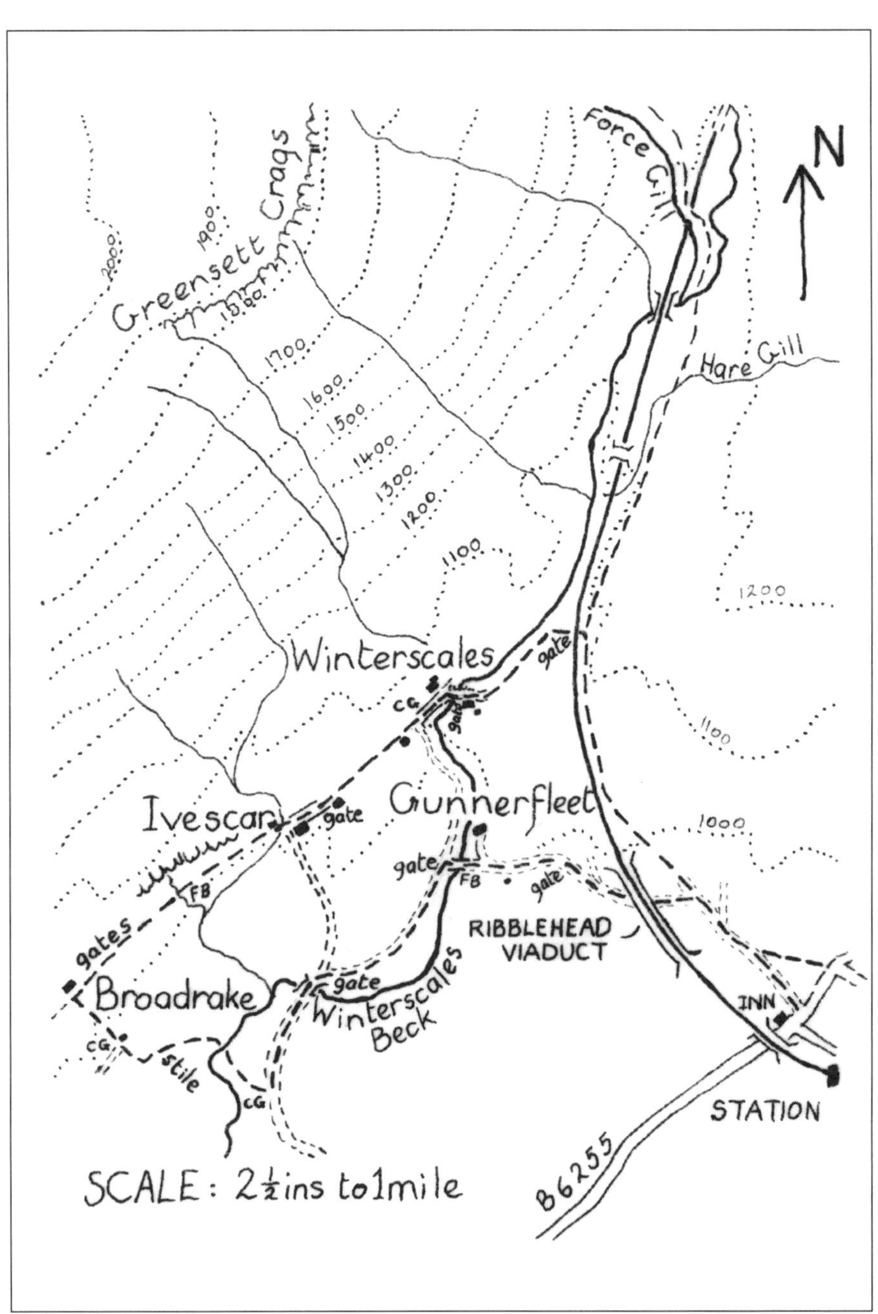

Greensett Crags
2000
1900
1800
1700
1600
1500
1400
1300
1200
1100
Force Gill
Hare Gill
1200
1100
1000
Winterscales
CG
gate
gate
gate
Ivescar
gate
Gunnerfleet
gate
FB
FB
gate
RIBBLEHEAD
VIADUCT
gates
Broadrake
gate
Winterscales
Beck
CG
stile
CG
INN
STATION
B6255
SCALE: 2½ins to 1mile
N

over the footbridge near to the farm buildings at Gunnerfleet Farm. Continue ahead passing through two more gates and then follow the track heading towards the viaduct. Go underneath the viaduct itself and here you will see the monument stone giving much information about the building of the viaduct. From here continue on the track towards the road and your parking place (unless of course you came by train from Settle or Carlisle to Ribblehead Station).

There is usually a refreshment van parked at Ribblehead, certainly at weekends and most times during school holidays, but if not sustenance can be found at The Railway Inn, some 200 yards (180m) up the road to the right.

Track by railway, Simon Fell in the background

Ingleton Falls

The famous Ingleton Waterfalls Trail that we are about to follow on this walk offers some of the most spectacular waterfall and woodland scenery in the North of England. The trail is 4.5 miles long (8 km) and leads you through ancient oak woodland and magnificent Yorkshire Dales scenery via a series of stunning waterfalls and geological features.

Distance	**5 miles (8km)**
Ascent	**700 feet (210m)**
Time	**2 hours**
Grading	**Moderate**
Suggested Map	**OS Outdoor Leisure 2 – Yorkshire Dales – Southern & Western**
Starting point	**Grid Reference: 694732**
Parking	**National Park Visitor Centre car park**
How to get there	**Ingleton is on the main A65 Skipton to Kendal road**
Terrain	**Good paths throughout although there are some steep sections by some of the falls but these are well stepped. Boots definitely recommended**

Ingleton

Ingleton is famous for walking, hiking and caving and is a thriving tourist attraction. The River Doe and the River Twiss join together in the town to form the source of the River Greta.

Throughout history, the Romans, Celts, Vikings and Normans have all left their mark on Ingleton and its surrounding area. The village nestles at the foot of Ingleborough – probably the most easily recognised of the Three Peaks due to its flat summit. Nearby are a number of caves popular with tourists – White Scar Caves, Ingleborough Cave and Gaping Gill. Here, the 365 ft (111m) cavern can be visited by tourists on bank holidays when a winch is set up to take the public down to this underground wonderland. For more experienced cavers, the area has a labyrinth of challenging potholes and caves. This is due to the 300 million year old limestone rock of the area, which has gradually been dissolved by groundwater.

The village of Ingleton has a history going back to the Iron ages, when a fortress existed on top of Ingleborough. Written by local historian and author, John Bentley, *The Ingleton History Trail* shows something of the industrial archaeology and other features of Ingleton's past. Ingleton can boast the first Hoffman kiln, still visible in Mealbank quarry, and the site of a conservation park for the millennium. Cotton mills were once also in abundance, powered by a water mill, of which there is now little trace, but signs of the mill races are still to be found near the playground by the river.

There are a number of 16th century buildings in Ingleton, and remnants of an agricultural past can be found in places like the village square. The old

Ingleborough

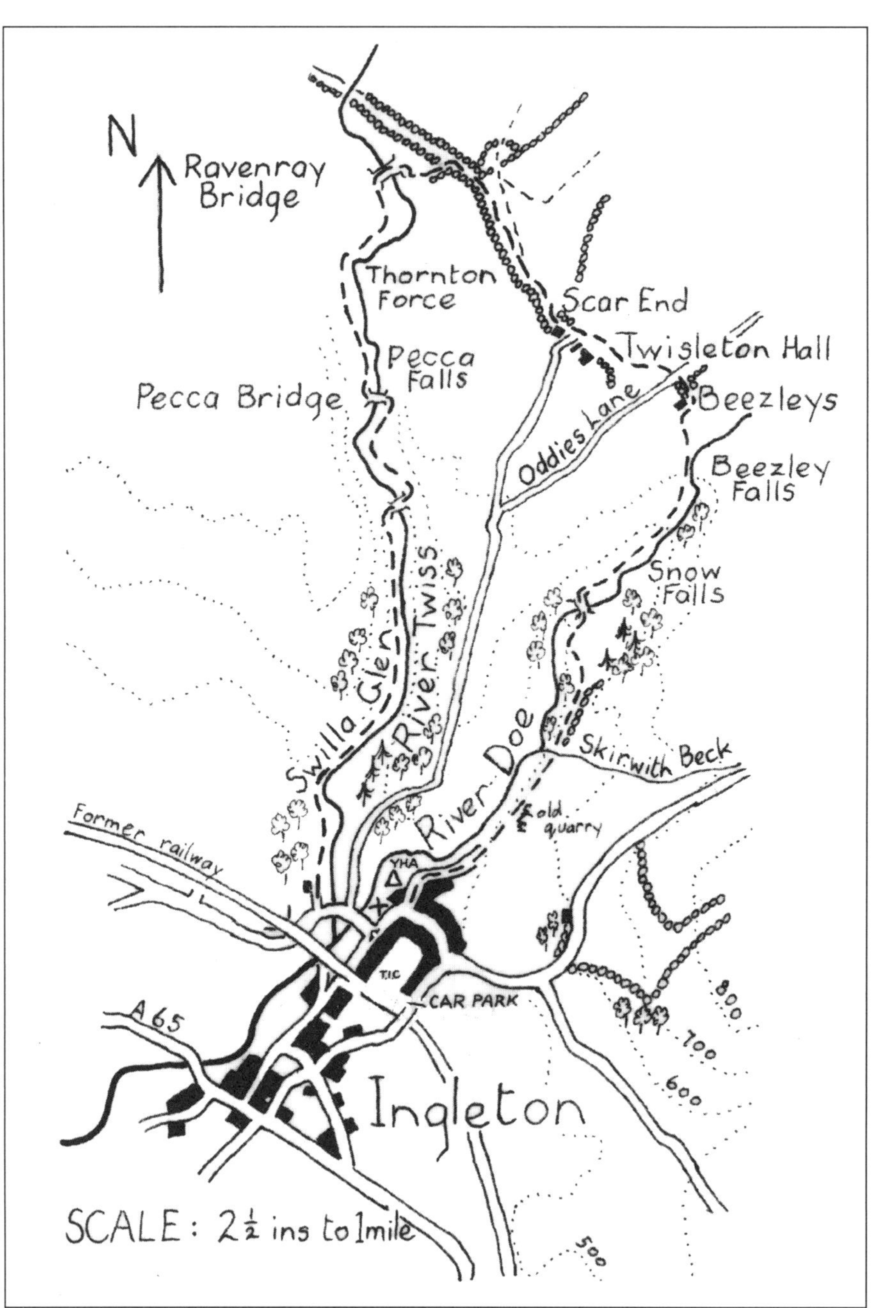

N
Ravenray Bridge
Thornton Force
Pecca Falls
Pecca Bridge
Scar End
Twisleton Hall
Beezleys
Beezley Falls
Oddies Lane
Snow Falls
Swilla Glen
River Twiss
River Doe
Skirwith Beck
old quarry
Former railway
YHA
T.I.C
CAR PARK
A65
Ingleton
500
600
700
800
SCALE: 2½ ins to 1 mile

bullring, where animals were baited and slaughtered in bygone years, is still visible in the tarmac. The Church of St. Mary's has one of Ingleton's oldest relics, the 800 year old Norman font, found in the river during the last century.

Mary Doyle, the mother of Sir Arthur Conan Doyle, lived in Masongill, a small hamlet nearby, and the man himself would have been a regular visitor to the area, as were other poets such as Thackary, who visited Masongill House many times. A brass in the church commemorates the death of one Randall Hopley Sherlock, brother of the Reverend Sherlock (vicar of Ingleton), struck by lightning at Ingleton station. And with the area below the prominent viaduct that crosses the valley in the village called the Holmes (Holme Head etc.), one can only speculate about the origin of the name of a certain detective!

The Walk

Alfred Wainwright said of this walk in his *Walks in Limestone Country* guidebook: "Surely, of its kind, this is the most delightful walk in the country? And not only delightful: it is interesting and exciting and captivating and, in places, awesome. Here Nature, always bountiful, has been lavish indeed: charming rivers, sparkling waterfalls, wooded ravines, sinister pools and gorges all combine to present a pageant of unexcelled beauty and grandeur. Here loveliness walks abreast. This is Ingleton's showplace, attracting crowds of visitors in summer, but better enjoyed in the quiet of winter, when one can wander in wonderland undisturbed and enchanted".*

There are a number of parking places in the centre of Ingleton, either the main car park in the town, one by the entrance to the falls or others on the outskirts. From the town centre look for the 'Waterfalls Walk' signs, which will take you downhill and across the river to the entrance to the falls. Go through the car park, pay the admission fee (currently £5 per head or £11 for a family of 2 adults and up to 3 children), and go through two kissing gates. The path goes downwards then ascends a set of steps. In the table of walks I have classed the walk as 'moderate'

Pecca Falls

rather than 'easy' because even though it is only five miles in length there are quite a number of sets of steps throughout the walk. Cross over Manor Bridge and continue upstream, now with the river on your left, for about ½ mile (800m) towards Pecca Bridge.

On the outward leg of the walk we are following the River Doe and on the return journey we will be coming down the valley of the River Twiss (derived from Twistleton). Wainwright wrote this of the two rivers: "Of the two glens the more frequented and westerly one containing the Doe is the more charming and lovely; the eastern one, however, much the grander and more romantic, the greater volume of water of the Greta (Twiss) restlessly pounding the black walls of the gorges beneath a canopy of trees".*

When you reach the bridge, cross it and turn right bringing you back on to the left bank of the stream. Continue to follow the path for ¼ mile (400m) as it climbs uphill to reach Thornton Force. During his 'Pennine Journey' walk in 1938, Alfred Wainwright described Thornton Force as follows: "I stood on the rocky bluff overlooking the Force and could feel the ground trembling at the thunderous roar of the river as it leaped clear in a boiling cloud of spray…It was pure white; a surging raging turbulence of sparking crystals".**

The path now winds slightly away from the stream and goes up another set of steps to firstly pass the waterfall, and then pass Raven Ray before it takes you over Ravenray Bridge, and up even more steps, to a kissing gate on to Twisleton Lane.

Thornton Force

Beezley Falls

Turn right along the rough lane. Go through two gates, after which the track becomes metalled. Walk past the farm buildings at Scar End, following the 'Waterfalls Walk' signs. Go over a gated stone stile and along the track, then though a kissing gate and on to a road (Oddies Lane) that leads back down to Ingleton. However, rather than follow the road back to the village we head instead towards the Glen of the River Twiss.

Go straight across the road, following the sign to Skirwith. Follow the path as it bends right at Beezleys, still following the

Former quarry workings

'Waterfall Walk' sign. Go through a gate, and then enter into another wooded area. The path passes firstly Beezley Falls and then down Baxengill Gorge and Yew Tree Gorge to the Rival Falls and Snow Falls. There are disused quarries on the other side of the River Twiss that you are now following downstream. A little further down, take a path to the left on to a footbridge with a good view of the deep and narrow Baxenghyll Gorge. Continue to follow the path, which takes you to another footbridge over Skirwith Beck near Cat Leap Fall.

Cross the bridge, go through the kissing gate, and then follow the path as it bends, at one point almost down to the river level, then going away from the water into trees. The path eventually brings you though former quarry workings. Continue through a hand gate on to a lane. Beyond the gate follow the lane that soon re-enters Ingleton.

Bear right, through the houses and back into the centre of the village, bearing left to pass under the railway viaduct and back to the town centre. There are a number of cafés, restaurants and The Wheatsheaf, Craven Heifer and Three Horseshoes Inn where refreshment can be sought at the end of the walk.

* From *Walks in Limestone Country* by Alfred Wainwright published by Frances Lincoln Ltd, copyright The Estate of A. Wainwright 1970, Reproduced by permission of Frances Lincoln Ltd.

** From *A Pennine Journey: The Story of a Long Walk in 1938* by Alfred Wainwright published by Frances Lincoln Ltd, copyright The Estate of A. Wainwright 1986, 2004, Reproduced by permission of Frances Lincoln Ltd.

RIBBLESDALE WALK 3
Pen-y-ghent from Horton

This walk is the most strenuous of our walks in Ribblesdale climbing from the village of Horton to the summit of Pen-y-ghent 2,277 feet (694m) high and then returning via the Pennine Way with a short detour to Hull Pot, the largest single hole in England.

Distance	**6 miles (10km)**
Ascent	**1500 feet (500m)**
Time	**3.5 hours**
Grading	**Strenuous**
Suggested Map	**OS Outdoor Leisure 2 – Yorkshire Dales – Southern & Western**
Starting point	**Grid Reference: SD809725**
Parking	**Car park in Horton or roadside parking**
How to get there	**Take the B6479 from Settle which itself is reached by the B6480 from the main A65 Skipton to Kendal road. Horton is 6 miles from Settle. Trains from Settle and Carlisle also travel through Horton on a regular service**
Terrain	**Good paths throughout but a steep ascent up to the summit of Pen-y-ghent. Boots definitely recommended**

Horton in Ribblesdale

Horton in Ribblesdale was established in the 12th century when the church of St. Oswald was built in the village, and was under the control of the Diocese of York. Nowadays it is part of the Diocese of Bradford and the church itself is well worth a visit whilst you are in Horton. In its parish records it includes the recording of deaths in 1597 caused by a plague which took 74 deaths, compared with only 17 the previous year.

One of the main reasons people have heard of Horton in Ribblesdale is due to the fact that the famous Yorkshire Three Peaks walk starts and finishes in the village, usually by clocking in and out at the Penygent Café. The Three Peaks walk is an endurance challenge of 26 miles, including 5,000 feet of ascent and descent over the mountains of Pen-y-Ghent, Whernside and Ingleborough all to be completed in less than 12 hours. This challenge attracts thousands of walkers each year. There is also an annual fell race over this course which has taken place for sixty years with the exception of one year when the outbreak of foot and mouth disease meant it couldn't take place.

The Pennine Way, Pennine Journey and Ribble Way long-distance footpaths also pass through the village and the region is very popular for cavers and potholers, with Alum Pot and the Long Churn cave system just to the north of the village, and Hull Pot and Hunt Pot on the western slopes of Pen-y-Ghent, which we will visit on the return leg of the walk.

St. Oswald's Church, Horton

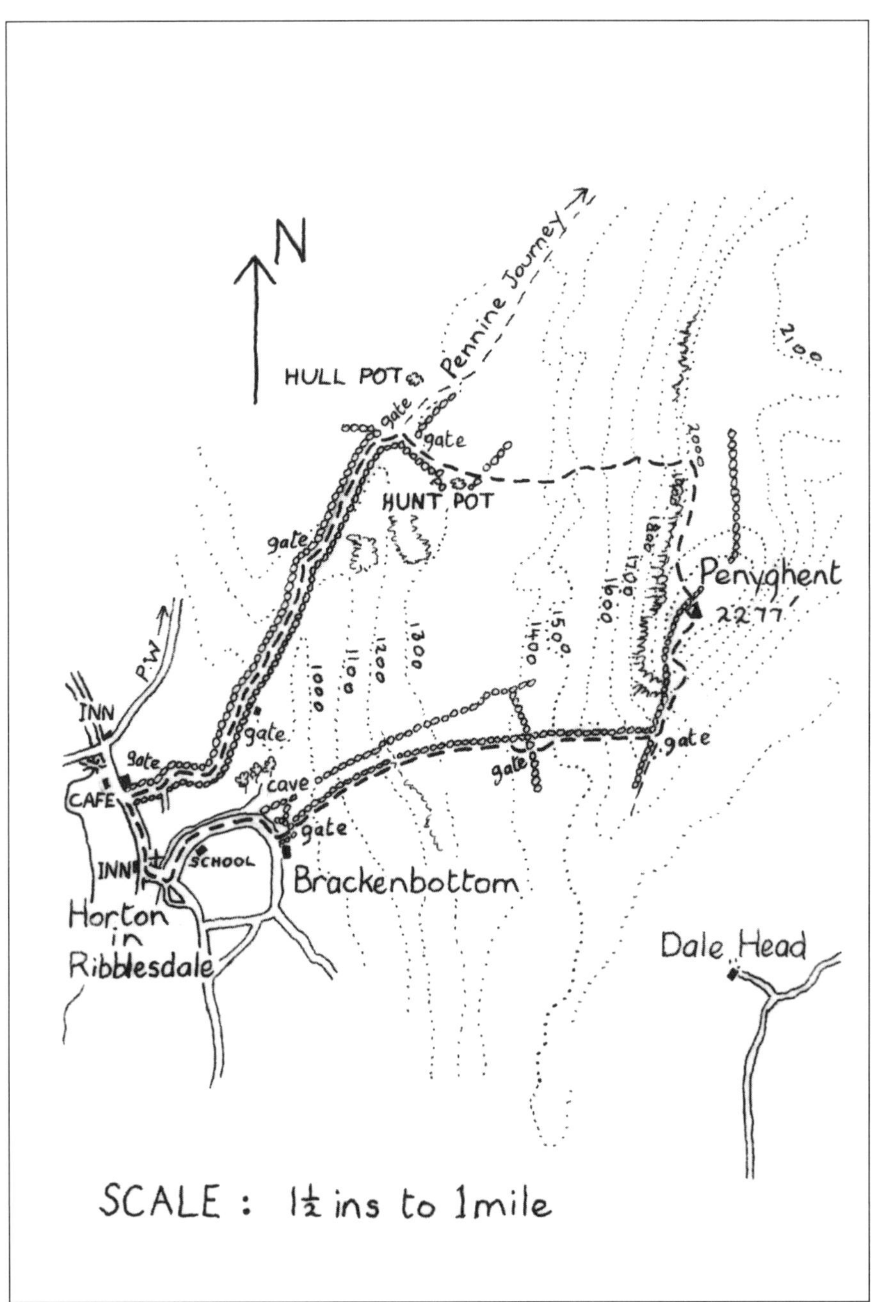

N
HULL POT
HUNT POT
Pennine Journey
2100
2000
1900
1800
1700
1600
1500
1400
1300
1200
1100
1000
Penyghent
2277
gate
gate
gate
gate
gate
gate
gate
gate
P.W.
INN
CAFE
INN
SCHOOL
cave
Brackenbottom
Horton
in
Ribblesdale
Dale Head
SCALE : 1½ ins to 1mile

The village has two pubs, The Crown Hotel and The Golden Lion, a village store as well as a café and tea rooms. The village post office that was previously located in the village store is now located in the Crown Hotel and is only open on Monday afternoon and Thursday morning.

The Walk

The walk starts from the centre of Horton and heads towards St. Oswald's Church. The Church is well worth visiting either at the start of the walk or when you return later in the day. It has a complete Norman nave, south door and tub-font and is the most complete of the Norman churches built in the Yorkshire Dales after the Norman Conquest and the Harrying of the North that followed. The square tower was built sometime later. The lichgates to enter the churchyard are roofed with huge slabs of Horton slate.

After crossing the bridge by the church you then walk along the lane past the Primary School and then Nether Close to Brackenbottom Farm. From Brackenbottom Farm you need to follow the footpath by the wall sides while climbing steadily towards Brackenbottom Scar. Throughout this section of the walk Pen-y-Ghent sometimes is in view, but sometimes disappears behind the walls.

At the area of Brackenbottom Scar for the more dedicated climber there is always the classic 'Red Pencil Direct' climb which is classed as 'severe'. After Brackenbottom Scar the southern face of Pen-y-ghent looms large ahead and at Gavel Rigg the spectacular face is at its most imposing. The climb now becomes very much steeper with two sections to the final climb, the first onto Pen-y-ghent's snout and the second onto its brow. Both of these involve a little easy scrambling but it is never difficult.

It is usually at this point that the wind from the west first hits you as until now you have been relatively sheltered. In the Cumbric language 'Pen' presumably meant hill or head, but 'ghent' is more obscure. It could be taken to be edge or border. The name 'Pen-y-ghent' could therefore mean Hill on the border. Alternatively, it could be mean 'wind' or 'winds' – from the closest Welsh language translation as 'gwynt'. Thus it might mean simply 'Head of the Winds'. This is well born out at this point on the walk.

After the climb you now reach the summit of Pen-y-Ghent at a height of 2277 feet (694m), 138 feet (42m) lower than Whernside and 95 feet (29m) lower than Ingleborough, the final summit of the three peaks trio. It was announced in July 2011 that future walkers on the Three Peaks Walk will be able to keep their feet dry thanks to a cash boost from the European outdoors industry. An alternative route to the notorious bogs of Black Dubb Moss will be developed for walkers and runners on the route.

The moss, between Pen-y-Ghent and Ribblehead, is one of the worst sections on the 24-mile (39km) route, but an alternative over Whitber Hill to the south has been developed with a €30,000 grant from the European Outdoor Conservation Association, a group of businesses in the European outdoor industry that raises funds to put directly into conservation projects worldwide.

A spokesperson for the Yorkshire Dales National Park Authority said at the time: "Much of the route is a sustainable walking surface catering for the high numbers of visitors. But, on the section between Pen-y-Ghent and Ribblehead through High Birkwith, most walkers use a route over Horton Moor and Black Dubb Moss. The route has become badly eroded and the topsoil has been washed away, causing significant damage to internationally important peat habitat. An alternative, though little used, route over Whitber Hill passes over drier ground and uses mainly existing paths but needs some development work and, subject to the landowners' agreement, it will also be developed as an alternative shorter route over Whitber Hill and walkers will be encouraged to use it." The bid was put together by the Yorkshire Dales Millennium Trust with the national park authority.

Pen-y-ghent

From the summit of Pen-y-Ghent there are two tracks, one heading north towards Plover Hill, the route of the Three Peaks Walk and Race, and another north-west to the edge of the escarpment. It is the latter that we need to take but if you go wrong initially it matters not as within ¼ mile (400m) there is a turning on the left to drop down to this track (presumably created by many people previously going astray at this point). Following the correct track north-westwards from the summit you drop down towards Pen-y-ghent Side and Pen-y-ghent

Hull Pot

Needle, a small broken limestone edge that stands proud on the western slope. One day it will fall and that will be a sad occasion as it has been visited here by many thousands of walkers over the years. After ¼ mile (400m) the track makes a turn left and descends sharply following the Pennine Way route for ½ mile (800m) to Hunt Pot. At this point it is possible to make a planned detour to the nearby Hull Pot, the single largest hole in England. Continue past Hunt Pot for a couple of hundred yards and at a junction of four tracks, where you need to turn left to head downhill to Horton Scar and the village, turn right instead and head north for a couple of hundred yards where you will see Hull Pot on your right. If you have never been to Hull Pot before you must not miss the opportunity. It is superb with two sunken waterfalls within the Pot.

Return back to the junction and now continue straight ahead following the Pennine Way once again, going past Stot Rakes and Skell Gill Pasture on the right and down past Horton Scar on your left. The track brings you out in the village opposite the Pen-y-Ghent café, where refreshments are available and liquid refreshment (their fine mug of Yorkshire Tea) makes a fitting end to one of Ribblesdale's finest walks.

RIBBLESDALE WALK 4
Attermire Scar from Settle

This walk explores the area to the north-east of the market town of Settle. From the town it climbs up Banks Lane towards Jubilee Cave. It then visits Victoria Cave and Attermire Scar and Cave before returning past Sugar Loaf Hill and Stockdale Lane back to Settle.

Distance	5.5 miles (9km)
Ascent	900 feet (270m)
Time	3.5 hours
Grading	Moderate
Suggested Map	OS Outdoor Leisure 2 – Yorkshire Dales – Southern & Western Areas
Starting point	Grid Reference: 819636
Parking	Settle Market Place
How to get there	Settle is reached by the B6480 from the main A65 Skipton to Kendal road
Terrain	Good tracks. Some slightly boggy sections near Victoria Cave, some minor road walking for the last mile

Settle

Settle is often referred to as 'The Gateway to the Dales' and 'The 'capital' of Upper Ribblesdale' and since its bypass was built the town now lies just off the main A65, linking Leeds and the Lake District. The railway from Leeds to Carlisle (but often referred to as the 'Settle to Carlisle' line) starts its climb from here up through Horton to Ribblehead and onwards to Dent. Above the town's market square towers the dominant limestone cliff of Castleberg Crag, and beyond that (but mostly out of view from the town) Scosthrop Moor and the spectacular limestone outcrops and caves of Warrendale Knots, Jubilee Cave, Victoria Cave and Attermire Scar. Settle is also the start of the forty-two mile Six Dales Hike, which has an annual walking competition over its route each September.

Fifty years ago I read a children's book by Eileen Fiddler about a group of youngsters who were evacuated to Settle during the war. One of them asked, "Why is it called Settle?" Another replied, "Because people have always settled down here". This stuck with me but looking up details of the name, Settle is of Anglican seventh century origins, its name being the Angle word for settlement. So in effect the children's story book was right!

A Market Charter was granted to the town in 1248. The market square developed and the main route through the medieval town led to Giggleswick, where the parish church was located and for many years the inhabitants of Settle had to walk the two miles there to worship. The first recorded mention of a bridge over the Ribble was in 1498.

The first railway arrived in Settle in 1875 when the Settle to Carlisle Railway was built, opening firstly to goods traffic and then to passengers the following year. In the late 18th century cotton spinning became the main employment in the town and Bridge End Mill was converted from corn milling to cotton spinning.

New town museum

Above the town is the imposing Castleberg Cliff and Victoria Cave. The imposing entrance to Victoria Cave is artificial, the result of man's efforts to gain easier access to the large cavern discovered by the curiosity of a dog and its master in1837 – the year of Queen Victoria's coronation, hence the name – the original place of entry, which is high up on the left, being an opening recessed in the rocks. No other cave has told its story so well, or so graphically illustrated it by visual evidence, by a collection of relics from the cave on display in the museum in Settle.

Attermire Scar

The name Attermire is derived from Otters Mere, a flat tract of marshy ground below the scar, once a tarn but used in the 1970s as a rifle range. The cave in

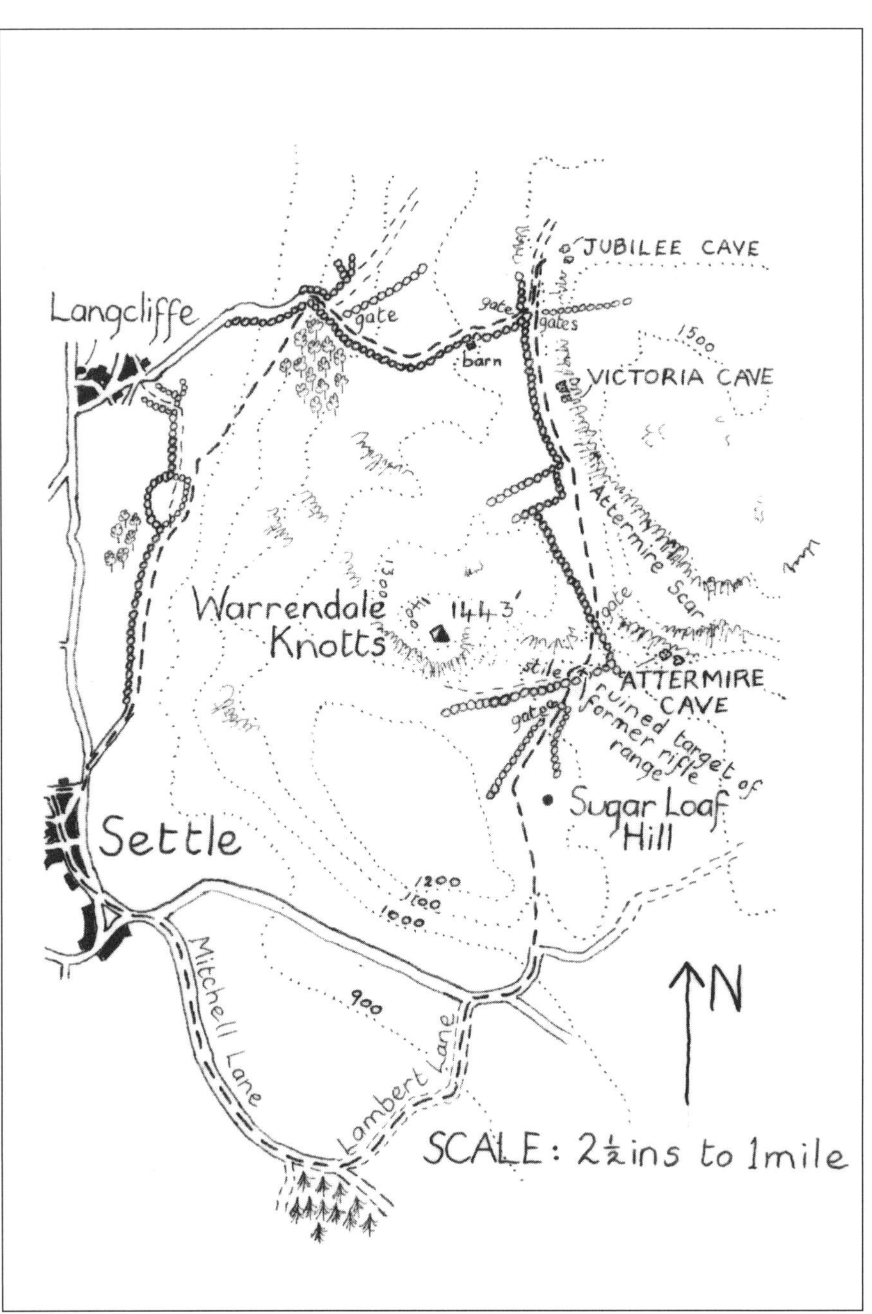
Langcliffe
JUBILEE CAVE
gate
gate
gates
1500
barn
VICTORIA CAVE
Attermire Scar
Warrendale
Knotts
1443
1300
gate
stile
ATTERMIRE
CAVE
gate
ruined target of
former rifle
range
Sugar Loaf
Hill
Settle
1200
1100
1000
900
Mitchell Lane
Lambert Lane
N
SCALE: 2½ins to 1mile

Attermire Scar

the scar is high in the cliff face and is reached along a grassy terrace. Care is needed near the entrance area. It is an interesting cave: a high winding passage is followed by a long crawl into a lofty chamber containing a pool and can be undertaken quite easily by an active and determined explorer.

Limestone escarpments, often known locally as scars, usually take the form of long cliffs fissured horizontally in layers or bedding planes and vertically in cracks and gullies, often revealing the of pressures quite noticeably. Warrendale Knotts however does not conform to this pattern, having the shape of isolated tors greatly eroded and sheltered like crumbling fortresses, the tops having a serrated outline that makes the group very distinctive and readily identifiable from long distances.

The Walk

This walk, although only 5½ miles in length is classed as moderate due to the ascent involved. However, the majority of this is in the first mile or so, after which it is a fairly level walk along the ridge by the caves before the descent back to Settle. I would, however, advise caution when crossing some of the scree slopes near the caves and would mention that if you go into the caves themselves then suitable footwear, a torch and possibly the wearing of a hard hat is advisable.

From the centre of Settle the route takes us first of all up Constitution Hill which is located to the left of the Shambles, which is a large building at the rear of the Market Square. It is a steep climb up Constitution Hill as is the following climb. At the brow of the hill at the top of Constitution Hill there is a track off to the right which ascends steeply. Follow this to a gate which you pass through and then follow the wall. The ground continues to rise but is less steep at this point. Continue ascending and on your left you will see a beech wood. Follow this track now up to the Malham Road. At this point you can see all the Three Peaks of Whernside, Ingleborough and Pen-y-Ghent.

After a matter of a few yards turn right along a cart track and over a cattle grid, keeping the wall on your right. Shortly, you reach a metal gate and if you wish to visit the Jubilee Caves you need to turn left and climb up to these at this point. The caves have two entrances: Albert Cave which has an iron gate in front of it and Wet Cave. Return down to the gate and go through a kissing gate on the left and continue on the track as far as Victoria Cave (GR838651).

Victoria Cave

From the cave continue on the track below Attermire Scar and then cross a stretch of open moorland to reach a ladder stile on your right. Cross the wall at this point, descend slightly and bear right where you will see the ruined target of a shooting range. Pass this and after 50 yards (45m) cross the wall on the left using the stone stile. Bear right at this point to continue between two walls rising up the hillside to a gate. Pass though the gate and you will notice Sugar Loaf Hill on your left. Sugar Loaf Hill is comprised of two different types of rock: Bowland Shale at the bottom and then limestone nearer the summit. When it was formed 300 million years ago the reef limestone grew in tropical seas on the edge of the 'Bowland Basin' and was then shifted on top as a result of shifting of the faults and plates.

Continue past Sugar Loaf Hill and pick up a limestone track which continues south-eastwards to Stockdale Lane. Like the first part of our walk, Stockdale Lane is another steep climb out of Settle as competitors taking part in the Six Dales Hike are all too well aware as they encounter this in the first mile of the walk. However, we are now going to be descending down the road rather than climbing up it so it is much easier. Turn right onto the road and then after about 100 yards (90m) Lambert Lane leads off to the left. Follow this downhill, bearing right, until you reach a tarmac section of road – Mitchell Lane. Follow this down through Upper Settle, along Victoria Street, past the folly (an impressive 17th century building which is now the town museum) and back into the Market Square.

There a several good restaurants and cafés in Settle for refreshment at the end of the walk, including the famous Naked Man Café which dates back to 1663.

Catrigg Force and Langcliffe

This is a delightful walk from the picturesque village of Stainforth up to Catrigg Force and then across pastureland before descending to the neighbouring village of Langcliffe. The walk returns on part of the Ribble Way alongside the river passing Stainforth Force before returning to Stainforth village.

Distance	**4.5 miles (8km)**
Ascent	**525 feet (160 metres)**
Time	**2 hours**
Grading	**Easy**
Suggested Map	**OS Outdoor Leisure 2 – Yorkshire Dales – Southern & Western Areas**
Starting point	**Grid Reference: 821672**
Parking	**Stainforth Village car park (or can park and start at Langcliffe)**
How to get there	**Take the B6479 from Settle which itself is reached by the B6480 from the main A65 Skipton to Kendal road. Stainforth is 1½ miles from Settle**
Terrain	**Good tracks throughout. Can be boggy after rain on the section by Upper and Lower Winskill**

Stainforth

Stainforth is located by the side of Stainforth Beck as it rushes to join the adjacent River Ribble. The village provides the starting point for many tracks across the moors to the east, once important monastic routes for trade, which originally crossed the beck at first on the stone ford and later by the 14th

Stepping stones at Stainforth

century bridge. Stainforth's name actually derives from the 'stony ford' which linked two settlements half a mile apart on opposite banks of the Ribble. The walk follows one of these ancient ways, the walled Goat Lane, as far as the path down to Catrigg Force.

The route then heads over the pastures above Stainforth Scar to Upper and Lower Winskill before dropping down to Langcliffe. Notable residents or former residents of this village include authors Leah Fleming and Marina Fiorato, plus writer, broadcaster and folk singer Mike Harding.

From here the walk follows the Ribble Way alongside the river heading northwards where towards the end of the walk we will pass another waterfall, Stainforth Force, where the Ribble passes over a series of limestone steps in tumultuous cascades. Just above is an attractive humpback bridge leading to Little Stainforth. The bridge was a vital link on a packhorse route between Lancaster and Ripon.

This short 4½ mile walk was one chosen by Alfred Wainwright for his *Walks in Limestone Country* book (Walk No 29) and he described it thus: "The

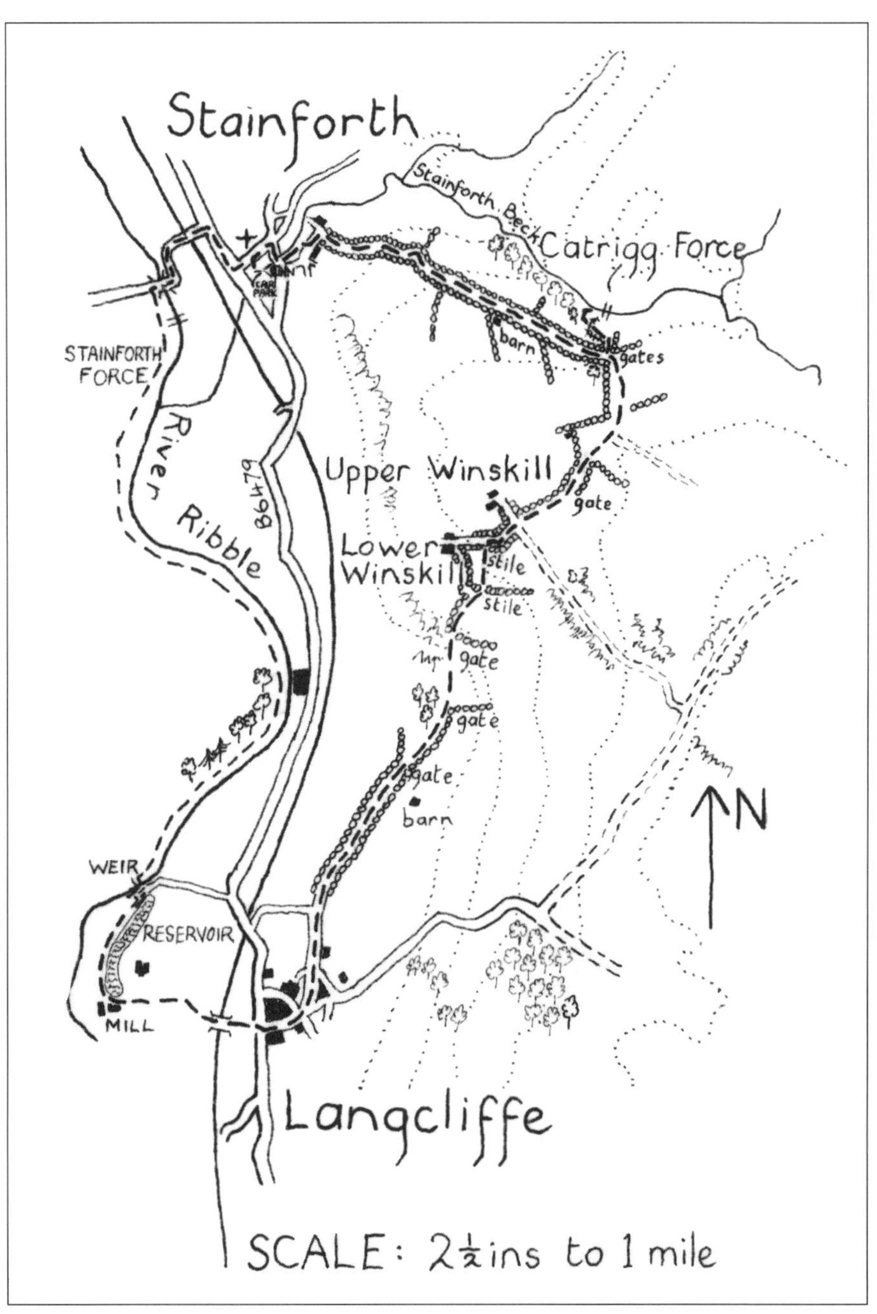

Stainforth
Stainforth Beck
Catrigg Force
CAR PARK
barn
gates
STAINFORTH FORCE
River Ribble
B6479
Upper Winskill
gate
Lower Winskill
stile
stile
gate
gate
gate
barn
WEIR
RESERVOIR
MILL
Langcliffe
N
SCALE: 2½ ins to 1 mile

Ribble's loveliest bridge and Craven's finest waterfall are featured in this beautiful walk".*

The Walk

The walk starts from the car park in the centre of Stainforth. Turn right, then right again, where you see the sign for Settle. Cross over the bridge, go left through a gap in the wall and then follow the beck to an open area of ground. Go through the white posts here and turn left. Go to the right of the green, then turn right and go up the stony uphill lane (Goats Lane) for approximately ¾ mile (1.2km) until you reach a gate and a ladder stile. At this point if you wish to visit Catrigg Force, take the smaller gate to the left. Afterwards, return to the same point. Catrigg Force is a double waterfall of 60 feet in a very lovely setting. Its older name, sometimes still used, is Catrigg Foss. This spectacular waterfall, hidden in a wooded valley, was one of the favourite places of the composer Edward Elgar, who regularly stayed with his friend Dr Charles Buck in nearby Settle. Elgar would walk here, perhaps mulling over his latest work as he did so.

Catrigg Force

Go over the ladder stile. The track here bends to the right. Go over a stone stile in the wall, then turn right, signed for Winskill. Note that on some maps the property is still marked as Upper Winskill. The path here bears left to join a track. Go over a stile and continue along the track until you reach the farmhouses. At this point go straight ahead over a stile signed to Stainforth and Langcliffe. As the track bends to the right, go left over a stile, again signed to Langcliffe.

Cross the field until you reach a stone stile, and then turn right immediately afterwards, to follow the path downhill. After a short walled section, the path descends to a gate, and then bears left as you get halfway down the hill, to

* From *Walks in Limestone Country* by Alfred Wainwright published by Frances Lincoln Ltd, copyright The Estate of A. Wainwright 1970, Reproduced by permission of Frances Lincoln Ltd.

descend to another gate. Follow the path to a final gate after which the lane becomes walled. As you approach the village at the crossroads of paths, go straight on and down into Langcliffe's main street.

Langcliffe is a most delightful village set around the village green. In addition to its picturesque cottages it also boasts a beautiful 17th century Hall, its 'Big Tree' and a fountain. On the wall in the village is a tablet of 'The Naked Woman' (once an inn) and the date 1660. Near to the village are a number of Hoffman Kilns used for lime burning.

Even though most of this area is underlain by various types of limestone, the cool and wet climate renders the soils more acidic than might be expected in limestone areas. In turn, this acidity sours the grass and reduces the grazing potential of the pastures. One effective way of reducing – or neutralising – acidity is by liming the soil, spreading burnt lime in powder form over the pastures and allowing rain water to wash the lime into the soil. This process reduces sourness; it stimulates the activity of minibeasts and decomposers within the soil, and promotes plant growth. Ergo, the farmer is happy. The value of liming soil was known in at least the 16th century (possibly earlier) and increasingly so in the two succeeding centuries. By the time of the great Enclosure Movement, when hills and fells were carved up into a network of walled fields, liming was an accepted aspect of best practice in upland farming.

Every parish in the limestone Dales witnessed the building of limekilns, some isolated, others close to tracks. It is virtually impossible, in the absence of documentary evidence, to date these field kilns but it is valid conjecture to suggest that many were put up during the enclosure process. Nine such kilns have been identified across the Langcliffe parish, five close to tracks that were once important roads, four remote from any obvious access line. Only three of the nine have survived more or less intact: the rest have had their stone robbed out for use elsewhere and, for some, only the tell-tale hollow remains.

To continue the walk from Langcliffe to Stainforth turn right in the village itself and walk down to the main road. Cross the road and go through a gap in the wall on your right. Follow the footpath over the railway footbridge heading down towards the river. When the path ends, go towards the mill and just before the buildings take a path to the right, going behind the mill and alongside the millpond. Go through a gate and continue along the pond side and through a stone stile to reach a gate on the left by a group of houses.

Go through the gate and turn right between the rows of cottages. When the row ends, just before the post box, go left over the footbridge over the River Ribble. At the end turn right, beside the weir, to reach a stone stile with a sign for Stainforth. Follow the riverside path, going over a series of stiles (six in total) to a caravan site. Before you reach the caravan site you will have had a reminder that this is still limestone country when, totally unexpectedly, a tributary gushes out of the ground near to the path.

Take the track to the right of the caravan site, following the riverside path, which leads past Stainforth Force to arrive at the humpback Stainforth Bridge. In the 1670s, Samuel Watson replaced the ford at Stainforth by a packhorse bridge. The elegant arch of Stainforth Bridge has spanned the Ribble for over three centuries originally serving the packhorse traffic on an old highway linking Lancaster and York. New routes and much heavier traffic have now made the bridge redundant. However, the bridge is now preserved by the National Trust and it remains as a graceful ornament of mellowed stone in perfect harmony with its sylvan surroundings.

Just downstream from Stainforth Bridge the River Ribble thunders down a series of limestone steps and into a dangerous whirlpool known as Stainforth Force creating a beautiful small waterfall just west of the village. As the waterfall is so close to the village and also on the Ribble Way it is a well visited

Return along the Ribble

beauty spot, and like many others close to roads and villages it is a favourite spot for family picnics. The waterfall begins as a series of small cascades followed by a final slightly larger one of approximately 4 feet.

To conclude the walk, from Stainforth Bridge, go through a stile on to the lane, turn right over the bridge and follow the narrow lane as it bends and climbs to the main road. Here turn right and then take the second turning left back to the car park.

A suitable watering hole at the end of the walk is the Craven Heifer Hotel. The pub caters for visitors and villagers alike providing a family friendly atmosphere in which to enjoy a thirst quenching fine cask ale, light snack or filling home cooked meal.

AIREDALE INTRODUCTION

The River Aire is 71 miles (114 km) in length and rises at Malham Tarn, flowing underground to Aire Head, near Malham, in North Yorkshire, and then flows through Gargrave and Skipton. The river then enters West Yorkshire where it passes through the former industrial towns of Keighley, Bingley, Saltaire, and Shipley before passing through Leeds and onto Castleford which is the confluence of the Aire and Calder. Just downstream of the confluence was the ford where the ancient British road used by the Romans crossed the river on its way north to York. The river re-enters North Yorkshire near Knottingley and in its lower reaches forms part of the boundary between North and East Yorkshire.

The River Aire empties into the River Ouse at Airmyn: 'myn' being an Old English word for 'river mouth'. The name Aire possibly derived from Brythonic Isara, meaning 'strong river'. The Aire could also have been the winwœd or winwæd written about in Old English, from the Old English elements 'winnan' or 'win' ('strife', 'fight') and wæd ('shallow water', 'ford'), however others have proposed that it is actually the Went (also called the 'wynt' in Old English).

The area we are interested in as walkers is that north and west of Shipley, but that is not to say that there are not interesting walks in the lower reaches of the Aire – they are just less dramatic from a walking point of view.

The first few miles of the river's life are quite extraordinary from a geological point of view. As mentioned above, the river rises at Malham Tarn which is England's highest freshwater lake. The tarn level was raised by Lord Ribblesdale in the 19th century by means of a dam and sluice gate at the southern end of the tarn. Malham Tarn drains at Tarn Foot into a small stream known as Malham Water that soon disappears into the limestone at Water Sinks, approximately ½ mile (800 metres) to the south. The water then reappears not – as was originally thought – at the base of Malham cove, but at Airehead Springs (1 mile south of Malham) where it is joined by Gordale Beck. This is often referred to as the source of the River Aire but scientific dye tests have proved that the water emerging here actually originates from Malham Tarn. These experiments with dyes have now shown that two separate streams go underground at different locations, cross paths without mixing behind the cliff, and re-emerge a mile or so apart. This shows the complexity of the system of caves behind the cliff, which is thought to be around 50,000 years old. Divers have so far explored over 2 miles (1.6 km) of cave passage entered from the base of the cove.

Malham Tarn House stands to the north of the Tarn, built by Walter Morrison to replace Lord Ribblesdale's hunting lodge. It is now used by the Field Studies Council as a learning centre with accommodation for ninety people and five workrooms. It provides courses from primary school level right up to degree level in Biology, Geography and cross curricular studies in Geography and Science, Geography and History, as well as Geography Environment and Conservation. The tarn itself lies largely over Silurian slates covered with thick glacial drift and marl deposits. The tarn basin was dammed by a gravely moraine during the retreat of ice, the Devensian glaciations, c.10, 000 years ago. Prior to the silting up and mire development in the west, Malham Tarn was originally twice its present size. Surrounding the tarn is a Karstic limestone landscape of predominately Carboniferous age.

Malham Cove is a natural limestone formation 1 mile (1.6 kilometres) north of Malham village. A well-known beauty spot, it is a large, curved limestone cliff at the head of a valley, with a fine area of limestone pavement at the top. On the west side of the 260 foot (80 metre) high cliff face are about 400 irregular stone steps: these form part of the route of the Pennine Way and lead to an uneven limestone pavement at the top. Originally, a large waterfall flowed over the cove as a glacier melted above it. The cove, along with nearby Gordale Scar, was featured in an episode of the BBC TV series *Seven Natural Wonders* as one of the natural wonders of Yorkshire. The cove was also featured in the film *Harry Potter and the Deathly Hallows Part 1* as one of the places that Harry and Hermione travel to. The scenes were filmed in November 2009.

Gordale Scar is a dramatic limestone ravine 1 mile or 1.5 km north-east of Malham. It contains two waterfalls and has overhanging limestone cliffs over 100 metres high. The gorge was formed by water from melting glaciers. The stream flowing through the scar is Gordale Beck, which on leaving the gorge flows over Janet's Foss waterfall before joining with Malham Beck two miles downstream to form the River Aire. Janet is said to be the Queen of the Fairies and is reputed to live behind the waterfall.

One of the walks that follows takes the walker to all three locations of Gordale Scar, Malham Tarn, and Malham Cove. Another location covered on one of the walks is the Five Rise Locks at Bingley. As the name implies, a boat going up the lock is lifted in five stages. The 5-rise is the steepest flight of locks in the UK, with a gradient of about 1:5 (a rise of 59 feet 2 inches (18.03 metres) over a distance of 320 feet (97.5 metres). Barry Whitelock, the current lock keeper, after being based here for the past twenty years, is now almost synonymous with the flight. Barry was awarded an MBE (Member of the Order of the British Empire) in the 2006 New Year Honours List for "Services to Inland Waterways in the North". The structure is Grade I listed.

Whilst not on the Aire itself, but forming part of its catchment area, we also visit the Howarth moors with its association to the Brontë sisters and their writings, much of which was done whilst sitting on these high places above the village where their father was parson at the Church of St. Michael.

AIREDALE WALK 1
Malham's Big Three

This walk visits the three famous features in the Malham area – Gordale Scar, Malham Tarn, and Malham Cove. It is a walk of contrasts, with the walk starting through riverside pastures followed by limestone scrambles at Gordale Scar and then moorland over to Malham Tarn before returning back across the limestone clints above Malham Cove.

Distance	8.5 miles (14km)
Ascent	1300 feet (400m)
Time	4 hours
Grading	Moderate
Suggested Map	OS Outdoor Leisure 2 – Yorkshire Dales – Southern & Western
Starting point	Grid Reference: SE900627
Parking	Malham Visitor Centre Car Park
How to get there	Malham is located at the end of a minor road which is signed from the A65 between Skipton and Settle
Terrain	Riverside path initially and then rougher walking over limestone moorland followed by a steep descent on a stepped path to Malham Cove

The walk starts from the Information Centre car park in Malham village (GR900627), which is very popular in summer and at weekends and therefore parking is at a premium at these times. Far better, if you can, to visit either midweek or out of the main season and enjoy the peace and tranquillity that the area has to offer. The village of Malham is clustered around Malham Beck over which is a stone bridge in the centre of the village. Slightly south of the main bridge is a small footbridge, which should be used to cross the beck onto the eastern side. Follow the track across two fields until you reach a sign pointing to the left for Janet's Foss. This is a good track that follows Gordale Beck across half a dozen fields to enter an ash wood and reach the fabulous Janet's Foss waterfall. The wood is carpeted with wild garlic, which is very pungent in the spring.

The steep path to the left of the waterfall goes up to Gordale Bridge where you will see a sign on the left to Gordale Scar, approximately half a mile away at GR 915641. Gordale Scar cannot be seen until you round

Janet's Foss

the corner at the end of the track and is a sight that takes the breath away even if you have visited this particular spectacle before. It contains two waterfalls and has overhanging limestone cliffs over 100 metres high. The gorge was formed by water from melting glaciers over eleven thousand years ago at the end of the ice age. A right of way leads up the gorge, but requires some mild scrambling over tufa (a variety of limestone, formed by the precipitation of carbonate minerals from ambient temperature water bodies) at the lower waterfall. By following the yellow spots on the rocks the route to the top of the Scar is achieved and at the top you need to turn left and head in a north-westerly direction.

However, for the faint hearted who feel that the scramble over these rocks is beyond their capabilities, they can return to Gordale Bridge and turn right into the field by the sign to Malham Tarn. Once at the top of the field by the wall turn sharp right and follow across a grassed area to a small gate in the wall. The path then winds up the hillside (New Close Knotts) and as you ascend splendid views of Gordale Scar can be seen across to the right. The track now descends slightly and at a stile in the wall joins up with the track from Gordale Scar.

This track continues in a north-westerly direction for a further mile until another stone stile is reached. At the stile turn right and follow it to Street Gate approximately 200 yards away. Street Gate is the first of the checkpoints on the Six Dales Hike annual walking competition and is one that I have

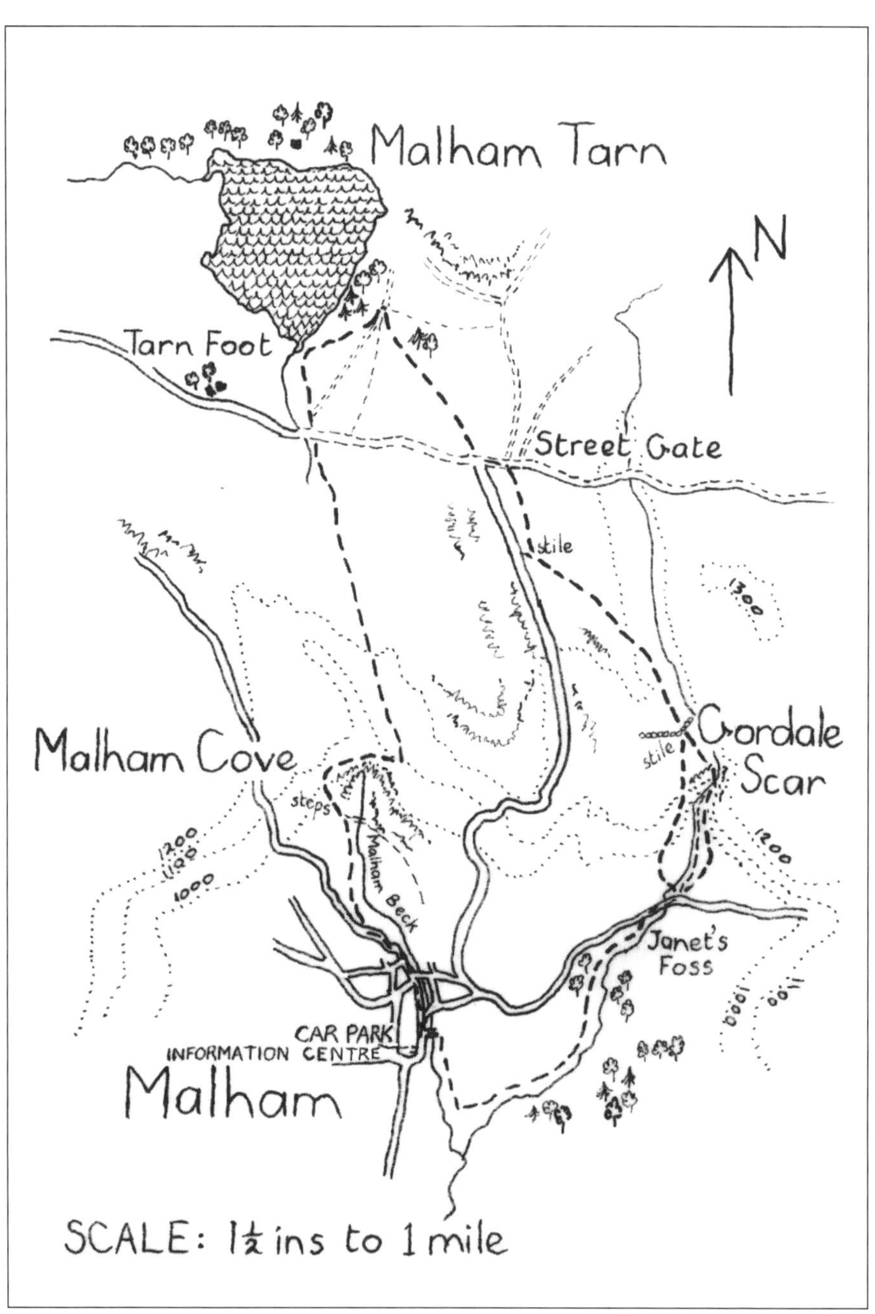

Malham Tarn
N
Tarn Foot
Street Gate
stile
1300
Malham Cove
stile
Cordale Scar
steps
1200
1100
1000
Malham Beck
1200
Janet's Foss
1100
CAR PARK
INFORMATION CENTRE
1100
Malham
SCALE: 1½ ins to 1 mile

manned many times over the years. It is six miles from the start of the walk at Settle and when the current record of 7 hours 29 minutes for the 42 mile distance was set in 1985, the team from the Horsforth Fellandale Club reached this point in 58 minutes. If you have time to spare it is worth passing through the gate to the green lane beyond – the start of Mastiles Lane leading to Kilnsey. Here you will find a monastic cross base on the left. Along the monastic roads, it was customary to place 'crosses' at prominent points, partly to stand as landmarks pointing the way and partly as a symbol of consecration or dedication to the service of the church. The crosses were often a rather plain stumpy shaft, either roughly squared or bevelled to a rough octagon, and set in a socket cut into a large base block. This base was sometimes only a rough boulder but in other cases it was squared-up and tooled. A total of five crosses are in the Malham Moor area with only the bases remaining in most cases.

At the signpost at Street Gate follow the sign for Arncliffe, drop down a dip in the landscape bearing slightly left by the wood of Great Close Plantation at which point the sight of Malham Tarn half a mile away appears. Head still

Clapper Bridge near the Cove

along the tack in a north-westerly direction to reach the tarn. One of the friends of Walter Morrison who built the tarn was the author Charles Kingsley who used his stays here as an inspiration for his book *The Water Babies* published in 1863.

A natural upland lake brought to the surface by the north craven fault, Malham Tarn lies on a floor of older (400 million years old) impervious Silurian slate covered with thick glacial drift and marl deposits. It has a surface area of around 150 acres, average depth is approximately 2.4 metres and the maximum depth is around 4.4 metres. The tarn basis was dammed by a moraine from the retreat of the Devensian ice-sheet from the last ice age and prior to silting and mire development the tarn was originally twice its present size.

The inflow waters have passed through lime-rich soil, and the one outflow stream flows out for a short distance before sinking into the carboniferous limestone when it reaches the line of the north craven fault and re-emerges further down at Airehead Springs. In 1791 the level of the tarn was raised by approximately four feet (1.2m) with the construction of the dam and weir at tarn foot by Lord Ribblesdale. Thus the previous shore-line and beach is now a drowned landscape and has also resulted in the erosion of tarn moss, a raised bog to the west of the tarn which has grown out at the mouth of the tributary streams coming off Fountains Fell. The tarn was granted to Fountains Abbey and its medieval monks by William de Percy in the 12th century, with all its fishing rights – the tarn has a reputation for its excellent trout. It also harbours a varied population of water birds – curlews, mallards, and greater crested grebe among them – protected in a sanctuary on the western shore.

Head south to the exit of the tarn at Tarn Foot and turn right onto the road. Here, after about 100 yards there is a sign on the opposite side of the road marked 'Pennine Way to Water Sinks'. Here, because of the change of the underground rocks from impervious slates to carboniferous limestone, the stream disappears and a dry valley is followed for a mile along the Pennine Way track to the grikes, clints and limestone pavements on the top of Malham Cove. Here, because of the absence of water, we encounter a 'dry waterfall' and one can only imagine what this must have looked like when water was actually pouring over the edge of Malham Cove. It is 260 feet high, roughly the same as that at Niagara Falls. Describing the cove in 1779, Adam Walker said, "This beautiful rock is like the age-tinted wall of a prodigious castle; the stone is very white, and from the ledges hang various shrubs and vegetables, which with the tints given it by the bog water gives it a variety that I never before saw so pleasing in a plain rock."

Malham Cove

Head to the right along the top of the limestone pavement to reach a set of constructed stone steps descending down to the bottom of the cove. Here there is a good track crossing a clapper bridge of large stone slabs before a gentle rise to the Cove Road, which is then followed back down to Malham village where a good pint awaits you at the Buck Inn or Lister Arms. Opposite the Buck Inn are the premises of the female blacksmith Annabelle Bradley (**www.annabellebradley.co.uk**) who has provided the metal chandeliers in the Inn. The Malham Smithy was bequeathed to the Parish Church by artist and blacksmith Bill Wild, and has ever since been leased out by the Church as a traditional blacksmiths workshop. In February 2007, Annabelle Bradley was given the opportunity to work from the Malham Smithy and continues to this day keeping this beautiful Yorkshire Dales village heritage alive. The smithy was featured in 2011 in the ITV series *The Dales*. There are a couple of tea shops in the village serving food and drink. Meals are also available at the aforementioned Buck Inn and the Lister Arms.

AIREDALE WALK 2
Bingley's Five-Rise Locks

Although this is a relatively short walk it is an extremely beautiful one visiting one of the major engineering feats in Yorkshire. Bingley Five-Rise Locks is a staircase lock on the Leeds and Liverpool Canal at Grid Reference SE107399. As the name implies, a boat going up the lock is lifted in five stages. In effect the five-rise consists of five locks connected together with (as always with a staircase) no intermediate 'pounds': The lower gate of each chamber forms the upper gate of the chamber below. There are therefore five chambers, and six gates (the top and bottom gates and four intermediate gates).

Distance	**4 miles (7km)**
Ascent	**500 feet (160m)**
Time	**1.65 hours**
Grading	**Easy**
Suggested Map	**OS Explorer 288 – Bradford & Huddersfield**
Starting point	**Grid Reference: SE108392**
Parking	**Bingley Town Centre**
How to get there	**Bingley is located on the A650 between Bradford and Keighley**
Terrain	**Urban footpaths followed by a small wooded section and then return along the canal side**

As the Leeds Liverpool canal is a wide canal, the chambers are 14 feet (4.3 m) wide, and each 'gate' consists of two half-gates, 'hinged' from opposite sides of the canal. Each half gate is slightly more than 7 feet (2.1 m) wide, so that the two halves close in a 'V' shape (pointing 'upstream'). Water pressure on the 'uphill' side of the gate thus keeps it tightly closed until the water levels on either side are equal, when the gate can be opened and the boat moved to the next chamber.

The five-rise is the steepest flight of locks in the UK, with a gradient of about 1:5 (a rise of 59 ft 2 in (18.03 m) over a distance of 320 ft). The intermediate and bottom gates are the tallest in the country. Because of the complications of working a staircase lock, and because so many boaters (both first-time hirers and new owners) are inexperienced, a full-time lock keeper is employed, and the locks are padlocked 'out of hours'. Barry Whitelock, the lock keeper, after twenty years based here is now almost synonymous with the flight. Barry was awarded an MBE (Member of the Order of the British Empire) in the 2006 New Year Honours List for "Services to Inland Waterways in the North". The structure is Grade I listed.

Five-Rise Locks opened on 12 March 1774 and was a major feat of engineering at the time. When the locks and therefore the canal from Gargrave to Leeds were opened in 1774 a crowd of 30,000 people turned out to celebrate. The first boat to use the locks took just 28 minutes and the whole first trip was described in a newspaper of the time – the *Leeds Intelligencer*.

Five-Rise Locks

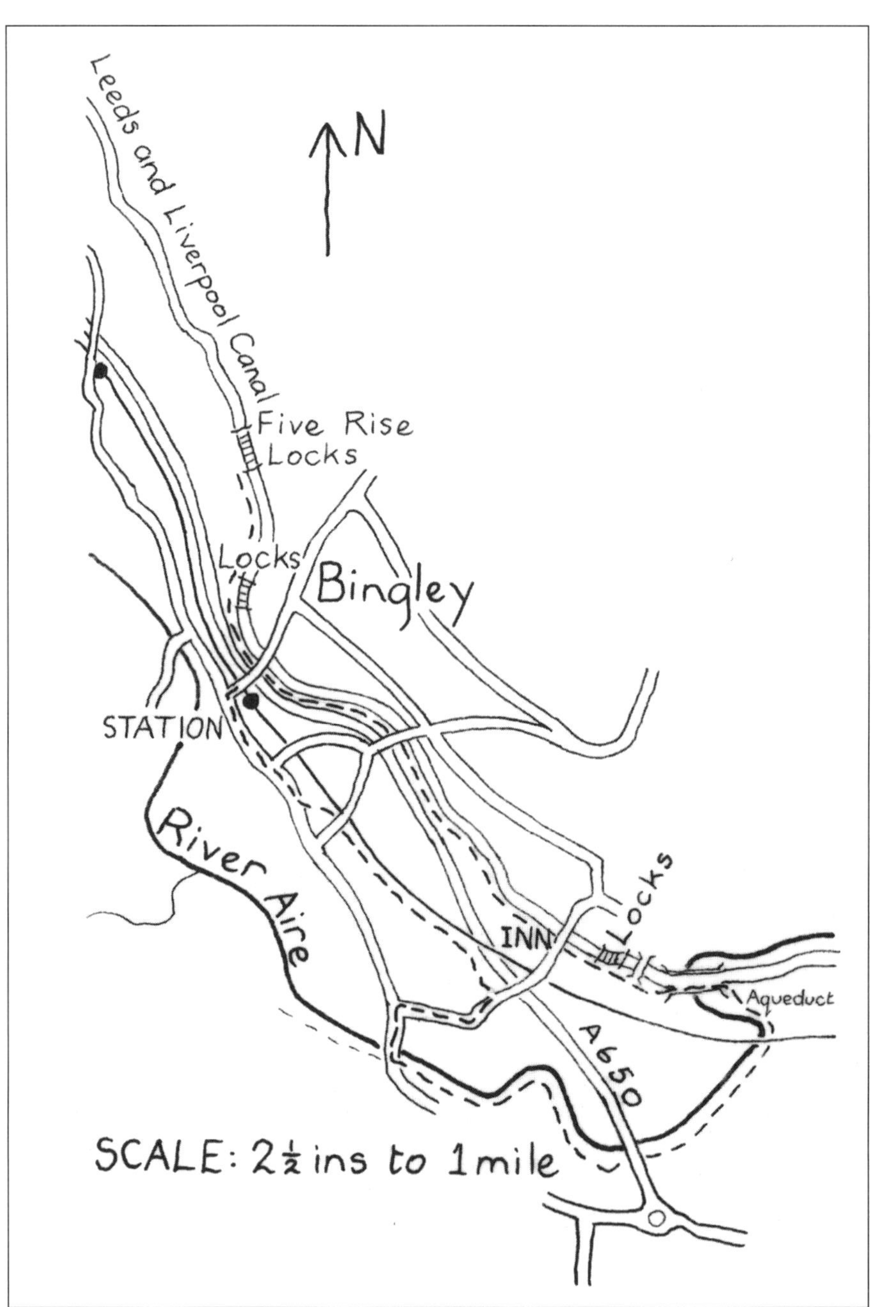

Leeds and Liverpool Canal
N
Five Rise Locks
Locks
Bingley
STATION
River Aire
INN
Locks
A650
Aqueduct
SCALE: 2½ ins to 1 mile

They said at the time, *"From Bingley to about 3 miles downwards the noblest works of the kind are exhibited viz: A five fold, a three fold and a single lock, making together a fall of 120 feet; a large aqueduct bridge of seven arches over the River Aire and an aqueduct and banking over the Shipley valley. This joyful and much wished for event was welcomed with the ringing of Bingley bells, a band of music, the firing of guns by the neighbouring Militia, the shouts of spectators, and all the marks of satisfaction that so important an acquisition merits"*. The smaller Three-Rise opened at the same time just a few hundred metres further down.

The 'flight' is a major tourist attraction in the area. Most boats that pass through attract a lot of attention especially at weekends where there may be a crowd of thirty people or more watching a boat go up or down. The staircase underwent extensive restorative maintenance in 2004, 2006 and again in 2012 when the lock gates and paddles were replaced.

In 2004 the Bingley Relief Road opened. One of the most expensive parts of the construction involved moving a 150 metre stretch of the canal. The £47.9 million road stretches from Crossflatts to Cottingley, threading through

Looking down the locks

Bingley between the railway and the canal. The construction included the removal of Treacle Cock Alley pedestrian tunnel and the Tin Bridge, which have been replaced by the Three-Rise Bridge, and the Britannia Bridge.

Bingley

The market town of Bingley appears in the Domesday Book of 1086 as 'Bingheleia'. Bingley is thought to have been founded around a ford on the River Aire. This crossing gave access to the villages of Harden, Cullingworth and Wilsden on the south side of the river. As well as being located on the River Aire, Bingley is also on the Leeds to Liverpool Canal. It also boasts a railway station and is on the main line from both Bradford and Leeds, and is 7 miles (11km) from Leeds Bradford International Airport.

Like most towns of the West Riding, Bingley prospered during the Industrial Revolution. The Bingley section of the Leeds and Liverpool Canal was completed in 1774, linking the town with Skipton, as well as with Bradford via the Bradford Canal. Several woollen mills were built and people migrated from the surrounding countryside to work in them. Many came from further afield such as Ireland, especially in the wake of the Irish potato famine. The railway and its goods yard were constructed bringing further trade. During this period the villages of Gilstead and Eldwick became conurbated with Bingley. The Bingley Building Society was founded in this period.

The Damart Factory

The Beeching Axe demolished the Bingley goods yard, though the station which recently celebrated its centenary, still serves trains to Leeds, Bradford, Skipton, Morecambe and Carlisle. The textile mills have largely been closed. The Damart mill still stands and trades in textiles, specialising particularly in thermal wear. Since 1995 the tannery, Bingley Mill & Andertons have been converted into flats.

The Walk

Our walk commences at the station car park in the centre of Bingley. Head out of the car park and walk up to the road, turn left, pass the Magistrates Court and then turn left down a bridleway. Go along beside the railway line and after leaving the housing pass a school on your right. Follow the path as it bears right and becomes a road; continue on the right past the Bradford & Bingley Sports Fields, and at the end of Wagon Lane join the main road and turn left.

Cross over the river and turn left down a small flight of steps into what appears at first to be a garden. This route is the Millennium Way and the path then follows the river where a canoe slalom course has been installed. Enter into a small wood and go under a new large road bridge and over a stream on stepping stones. Go up a short rise where the path is between two high walls, then out into the open by the river and under the railway bridge. Bear left at a junction and then right where a small path leads down to the river. The path then climbs slightly until you join the Woodland Walk, which brings you up onto the canal towpath.

Turn left over an aqueduct. The towpath then detours around the canalside buildings. At the end rejoin the towpath and continue up the canal, **do not cross the bridge**. This is now Dowley Gap locks with the Fisherman's Pub beside bridge numbered 205.

The new main road has been taken through on your left, which created a number of problems during the construction and has resulted in a rather noisier stretch here. Walk as far as the Bingley Three-Rise Locks.

When you reach the Three-Rise Locks the Five-Rise is just 300 yards further, so within five minutes by following the towpath, the walk takes you there. There is a small café here which is usually open (especially at weekends). Rettrace your steps downhill to Three-Rise and along the canal. Turn left, just before the railway, and then walk down the steps to the car park to find your vehicle or use the train if you have travelled to Bingley this way initially.

Nappa Cross from Malham

The route on this walk takes us from the Information Centre out of the village and up to the summit of Pikedaw Hill and Nappa Cross. This is an area steeped in history and the return part of the route is one that was trod by the Monks of Fountains Abbey in the Middle Ages.

Distance	**6 miles (9.8 km)**
Ascent	**1200 feet (360m)**
Time	**2¾ hours**
Grading	**Moderate**
Suggested Map	**OS Outdoor Leisure 2 – Yorkshire Dales – Southern & Western**
Starting point	**Grid Reference: SE900627**
Parking	**Malham Visitor Centre car park**
How to get there	**Malham is located at the end of a minor road which is signed from the A65 between Skipton and Settle**
Terrain	**Good paths over the limestone moorland. If visiting Malham Cove on the return leg there is a steep descent on steps down to the Cove**

Malham

Malham in the last census is listed with a population of approximately 150. However, this small resident population is out of all proportion to the number of visitors that the village receives each year, which run into the tens of thousands. They visit the area to appreciate the surrounding countryside, well known for its limestone pavements and other examples of limestone scenery. The village hosts an annual agricultural and horticultural show on the

Saturday before the August Bank Holiday. This is known as the Malham Show and has competitions for everything from Lego models to fell running. Another major annual event is the Malham Safari, where the villagers, and particularly the local school, build sculptures around the village. This event attracts many tourists and stalls are put up on the green.

Mentioned in the Domesday Book as 'Malgun', Malham has been a place of settlement for at least a thousand years. The village is probably much older though, and traces of Iron Age boundaries are still visible today. A century ago, Malham was a place of mills and mines. Nowadays, however, hill farms and tourism are the main activities.

Malham is a very popular walkers' destination and the rise in tourism over recent years has led to some deterioration of the area's surrounding paths as tourists cause pockets of erosion, a process often called 'footpath erosion'. The footpaths in the area are maintained and managed by the Yorkshire Dales National Park Authority and a programme of footpath improvements is underway to tackle this problem. Please therefore, wherever possible, stick to directed paths in the area to minimise this erosion problem. The long-distance path of the Pennine Way passes through the village before heading up past Malham Cove to Malham Tarn (See walk 1 in the Airedale section).

In the village itself there is a National Park Information Centre and a large car park, which is the starting point of this walk. There is also some roadside parking on the entrance to the village but this is limited and particularly at weekends is usually all taken early in the day.

As a tourist area, there is much accommodation available both catered and self catering. Details of these are to be found in the Appendix at the end of the book.

The Walk

From the car park take the walled track at the western end of the car park and walk north along the track that runs parallel with the main street of the village. Turn left at the first junction (Grid ref. SD 899629) to walk west and then north-west between dry stone walls. At the next junction (Grid ref. SD 896631) fork left. You now pass a number of field barns and the walk starts to take on a distinctive Yorkshire Dales feel. Leave the track just before it bends left and follow a clear path across pastures.

The ascent steepens with Pikedaw Hill rising to your right. If you have the energy then a sharp ascent will take you to the summit cairn from where there are excellent views across Malhamdale and surrounding countryside. The cairn is in a magnificent position at the head of Malhamdale, overlooking the lowlands of Craven. Like the cairn on Sheriff Hill above Malham Cove, it is

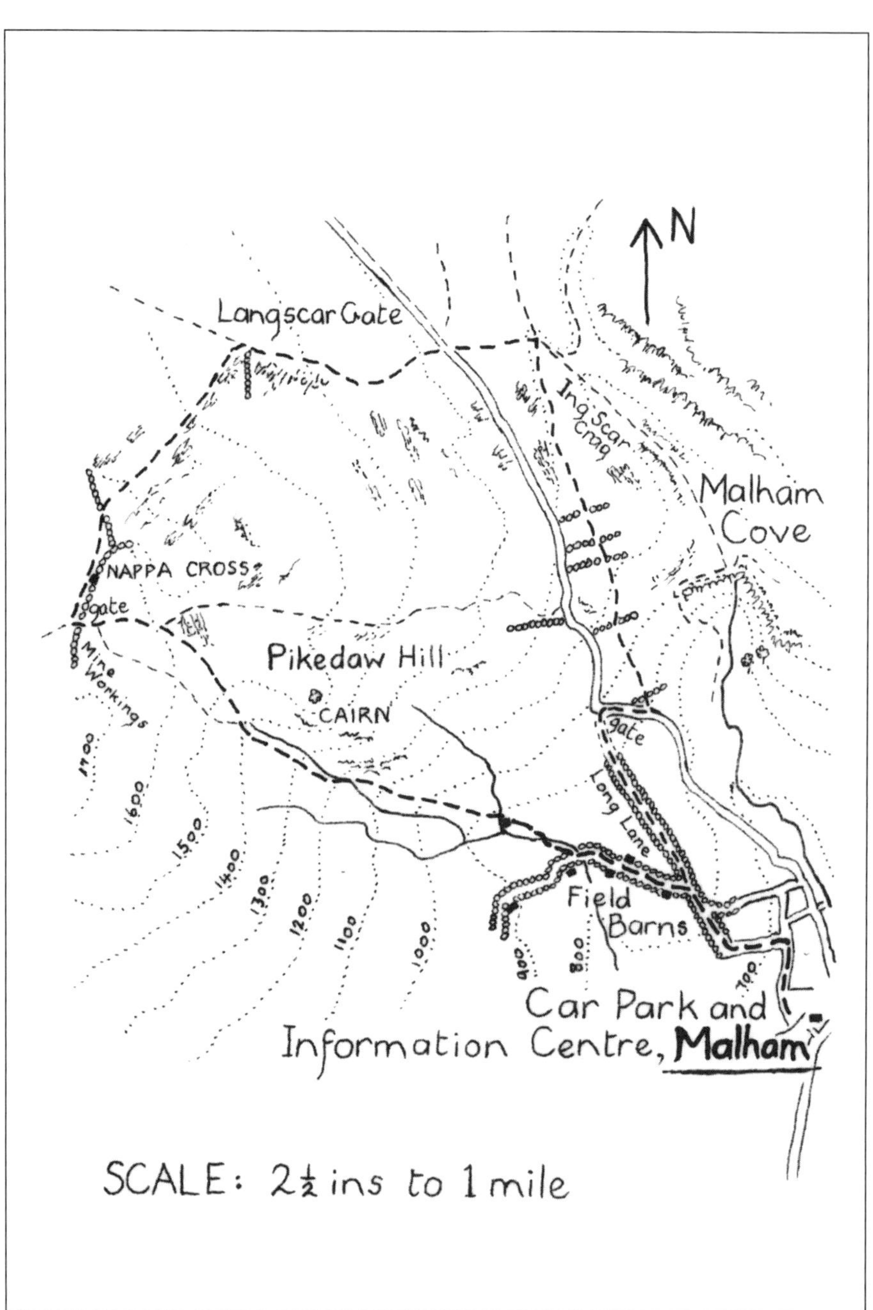

N
Langscar Gate
Ing Scar Crag
Malham Cove
NAPPA CROSS
gate
Mine Workings
Pikedaw Hill
CAIRN
1700
1600
1500
1400
1300
1200
1100
1000
900
800
700
gate
Long Lane
Field Barns
Car Park and Information Centre, Malham
SCALE: 2½ ins to 1 mile

situated on the edge of the great plateau which lies behind Malham. Built on top of a natural limestone knoll, the turf covered mound is approximately 15 metres in diameter and 1.5 metres high, surmounted by a tall narrow modern walker's cairn.

Partial excavation of the site revealed a burial accompanied by an iron spearhead, which means that the cairn was definitely in use during the Iron Age. Whether it was initially constructed earlier than this is not known, but it is common for large burial cairns like this one to have their origins in the Bronze Age and attract other burials and depositions later on. On the west side of the cairn a natural band of limestone pavement runs up to the knoll on which the cairn is situated, and this appears to have been enhanced by the addition of stones, giving the effect of a low bank. The cairn is a Scheduled Monument, and protected by law. It is an offence to disturb the site. From the summit, passing evidence of old mine workings you reach a wall (Grid ref. SD 874640). Go through the gate and turn right to follow the path alongside wall northwards. Almost immediately you pass the restored Nappa Cross on your right.

Limestone escarpments

You have now reached the monastic trade route used by the monks of Fountains Abbey. Their principal grange in Wharfedale was at Kilnsey and they often travelled to Settle via their Malham Moor properties and sheep farms. It was a very busy route, frequented by the monks themselves, abbey servants, messengers and, of course, flocks of sheep and herds of cattle. Even after monastic times, the route was followed by traders with their packhorses laden with wool, salt, iron and coal heading for the market at Settle. Today it is still one of the

Limestone clints

finest foot routes over the Wharfe/Aire/Ribble watersheds. Along the monastic roads, it was customary to place 'crosses' at prominent points, partly to stand as landmarks pointing the way, and partly as a symbol of consecration or dedication to the service of the church. The crosses were often a rather plain stumpy shaft, either roughly squared or bevelled to a rough octagon, and set in a socket cut into a large base block. This base was sometimes only a rough boulder but in other cases it was squared-up and tooled. A total of five crosses are in the Malham Moor area with only the bases remaining in most cases. From Nappa Cross, the path gently descends across limestone moor to reach a junction of paths and tracks (Grid ref. SD 881649). Turn right (east) and follow the track to reach a road.

Go straight across and continue in the same direction on a signed footpath. After a short way you reach a complex path junction (Grid ref. SD 891649). Do not descend into the dry valley. Instead turn right on a clear path that crosses a limestone pavement above the valley. This leads easily across grass, soon offering an excellent view of Malham Cove to your left. The path then descends through pastures to reach a road (Grid ref. SD 895637). Turn right (uphill) to where the road swings right. Here you go left through a gate and cross a field. This path leads into a walled lane (Long Lane) that will lead you back to the start by the Malham Visitor Centre.

For those who wish to visit or revisit Malham Cove, there is a path on the left before the descent to the road mentioned above which will lead you to the steps on the western side of the Cove which should be descended down into the Cove itself. From here there is a good track back into the village itself.

Whichever final route you take, you will end up back in the village where there are tea rooms or a welcoming pint at the Buck Inn or Lister Arms to slake your thirst after what will have hopefully been a most enjoyable walk.

Opposite the Buck Inn are the premises of the female blacksmith Annabelle Bradley (**www.annabellebradley.co.uk**) who has provided the metal chandeliers in the Inn. The Malham Smithy was bequeathed to the Parish Church by artist and blacksmith Bill Wild, and has ever since been leased out by the Church as a traditional blacksmiths workshop. In February 2007, Annabelle Bradley was given the opportunity to work from the Malham Smithy and continues to this day keeping this beautiful Yorkshire Dales village heritage alive. The smithy was featured in 2011 in the ITV series *The Dales*. There are also a couple of tea shops in the village serving food and drink; meals are also available at the aforementioned Buck Inn and the Lister Arms.

Malham Cove

AIREDALE WALK 4
Top Withens

This walk takes in the moors above Howarth visiting Top Withens, reputedly the location used by Charlotte Brontë as inspiration for her novel 'Wuthering Heights'.

Distance	6.5 miles (10 km)
Ascent	650 feet (200m)
Time	2.5 hours (3 hours plus if visiting the village of Haworth afterwards)
Grading	Moderate
Suggested Map	OS Outdoor Leisure 21 – South Pennines
Starting point	Grid Reference: SE025364
Parking	Penistone Hill Country Park car park
How to get there	Haworth is located on the B6144 which is accessed from the main A629 Keighley to Halifax road
Terrain	Heather moorland with a final mile of road walking from Stanbury village back to the car park

Haworth and the Brontës

Haworth is located amongst the Pennine foothills, 3 miles (4.8 km) south-west of Keighley and 10 miles (16 km) west of Bradford. The surrounding areas include Oakworth and Oxenhope. The walk starts about a mile above Haworth but it is only a 15 minute walk (5 minute drive) from here to the village at the end of the walk for those who wish to visit the village and the Brontë Parsonage.

Haworth is first mentioned as a settlement in 1209. The name possibly referring to a 'hedged enclosure' or 'hawthorn enclosure'. The name was recorded as 'Howorth' on a 1771 map. One of the modern events organised by the Haworth Traders' Association is 'Scroggling the Holly' – an annual holly gathering event which has no traditional basis. The name, sometimes claimed to have its origin in the local dialect, is also a modern invention. It takes place each November in the village. At the start of the festive season bands and Morris men lead a procession of children in Victorian costume, who follow the Holly Queen up the cobbles to her crowning ceremony on the church steps. The newly crowned Holly Queen unlocks the church gates to invite the spirit of Christmas into Haworth. Father Christmas then arrives bringing with him glad tidings and Christmas cheer to all.

In Haworth itself there are tea rooms, souvenir and antiquarian bookshops, restaurants, pubs and hotels (including the Black Bull, where Branwell Brontë's decline into alcoholism and his opium addiction allegedly began). Haworth is a good base for exploring Brontë Country, while still being close to the major cities of Bradford and Leeds. Haworth railway station is part of the Keighley and Worth Valley Railway, an authentic preserved steam railway. Haworth and Haworth railway station have been used as settings for numerous period films and TV series, including *The Railway Children* (starring Jenny Agutter), *Yanks* (starring Richard Gere and Vanessa Redgrave), and Alan Parker's film version of Pink Floyd's *The Wall* (starring Bob Geldof).

The 43 miles (69 km) long Brontë Way, which we will follow for part of our walk leads past Lower Laithe Reservoir, Stanbury to the Brontë waterfalls, the Brontë Bridge and the Brontë Stone Chair in which – it is said – the sisters took turns to sit and write their first stories. It then leads out of the valley and up on the moors to Ponden Hall (reputedly Thrushcross Grange in Emily Brontë's *Wuthering Heights*) and Top Withens, a desolate ruin which was reputedly the setting for the farmstead Wuthering Heights.

The village of Howarth is synonymous with the Brontë sisters who were born in Thornton, on the outskirts of Bradford, but wrote most of their novels while living at the Haworth Parsonage (which is now a museum owned and maintained by the Brontë Society), when their father was the parson at the adjacent Church of St. Michael and All Angels. In the 19th century, the village and surrounding settlements were largely industrialised, which put it at odds with the popular portrayal in *Wuthering Heights*, which only bore resemblance to the upper moorland that Emily Brontë was accustomed to.

The sisters, Charlotte (born 21 April 1816), Emily (born 30 July 1818), and Anne (born 17 January 1820), are well known as a trio of sibling poets and novelists. They originally published their poems and novels under male pseudonyms, following the custom of the times practised by female writers. Their stories immediately attracted attention for their passion and originality.

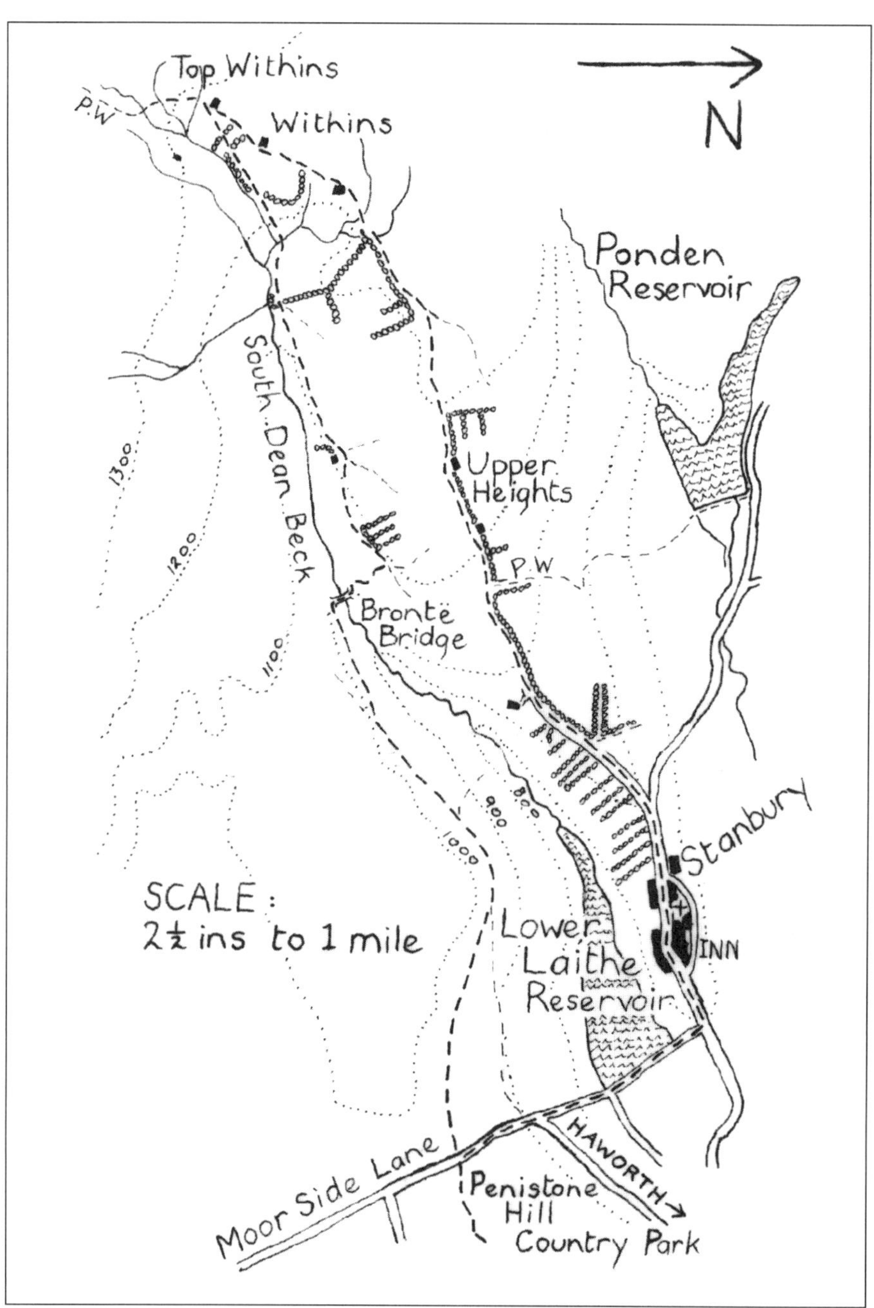

N
Top Withins
Withins
P.W
Ponden
Reservoir
South Dean Beck
1300
1200
1100
Upper
Heights
P.W
Brontë
Bridge
900
800
1000
Stanbury
SCALE:
2½ ins to 1 mile
Lower
Laithe
Reservoir
INN
Moor Side Lane
HAWORTH
Penistone
Hill
Country Park

Charlotte's *Jane Eyre* was the first to know success, while Emily's *Wuthering Heights*, Anne's *The Tenant of Wildfell Hall* and other works were later to be accepted as masterpieces of literature.

Since their early deaths, and then the death of their father in 1861, they were subject to a following that did not cease to grow. Their home, the parsonage at Haworth in Yorkshire – now the Brontë Parsonage Museum – has become a place of pilgrimage for hundreds of thousands of visitors each year. All the family are laid to rest in the Howarth churchyard except Anne who died in Scarborough, North Yorkshire, on 28 May 1849 and is buried there.

St. Michael's Church

One thing you will notice on this walk is that all the footpath signs are written in Japanese as well as English. However when you consider where you are walking then the reason becomes clear. This walk takes you on a literary journey over Haworth Moor to Withens ruins. These insignificant ruins are the supposed site of Wuthering Heights, the home of the Earnshaw Family in the classic novel by Emily Brontë. The ruins are visited by many pilgrims every year including lots of Japanese tourists who seem to love the Brontë sisters, hence the Japanese writing on the signs. This walk is popular. Don't expect to be on your own if the weather is fine. You may get peace and quiet if you walk on a bleak windswept rainy day, and you would then also get the weather moods Miss Cathy endured on her liaisons with Heathcliff on the moor and which was also captured in Kate Bush's 1978 song *Wuthering Heights* where she commences the lyrics with the words, "Out On the wiley, windy moors, we'd roll and fall in green." Perhaps in these conditions 'wiley windy' should be 'wild **and** windy'.

The Walk

From the car park at the Penistone Hill Country Park on Moorside Lane, an unclassified road between Stanbury and Oxenhope, take the main track from the car park and cross the road. There is a sign for Brontë Bridge and Top

Withens. Follow this track across the moor for about ½ mile to pick up a much more distinct track that comes in from the right. Continue following this path as it drops downhill until you reach the falls and Brontë Bridge. A favourite haunt of the sisters, the waterfalls are only impressive after heavy rain. Cross the bridge (a replacement for the one the Brontë's knew, swept away by heavy rain) and start climbing up the hill on the far side to a three-way sign. Follow the signs all the way to Top Withens. You can't go wrong! Cross the beck and the final steep climb brings you to another waymarker. This shows Top Withens 200 yards (200m) to the left and the Pennine Way to the right – the route we will follow shortly.

Brontë Bridge

Follow the path up the hill to the ruins of Top Withens using the Pennine Way path heading south. A Brontë Society plaque on what is left of the building informs us that Emily would have known of this house but that it bore little resemblance to the Wuthering Heights of the novel. Cold winds blow up here but there is a picnic table and you are unlikely to be alone here whatever the weather!

Retrace your steps to the sign and continue straight forward on the Pennine Way – the sign shows Stanbury 2¼ miles and Howarth 3½ miles. The route has been re-flagged and is good underfoot all the way. Pass Upper Heights Cottage on your left and Lower Heights Farm. At the next signpost the Pennine Way leads off to the left but continue straight forward down towards Stanbury. You will see Lower Laithe Reservoir down to your right at this point. Reach the main road and turn right on the main road. Pass through the village with the lovely St. Gabriel's Church on your left and also the Wuthering Heights pub which serves a good pint and sets you up for the final ½ mile (800m) back to the car park. At the end of the village take the road on the right signed to Oxenhope. Go down over the dam of Lower Laithe Reservoir and then gird up your loins for the final ¼ mile (400m) up the hill back to the car. This is a bit of a sting in the tail after six miles.

It is only ½ mile (800m) back to Howarth down the minor road on the right just after turning right out of the car park and worth rounding off your day with a trip to see the Church and Parsonage in the village which is well signed as you approach from the west.

Lower Laithe Reservoir

Hetton and Winterburn

Beginning and ending in the hamlet of Hetton, this walk is for the most part on bridleways and on private roads belonging to the water company, so the going is fairly easy. The climbs also are steady rather than steep and the first takes you to the edge of moorland, with a wide expanse of open country to the north. As it is outside the main honeypot areas of the Dales, you will find it less frequented than say nearby Malham. A walled stone track leads you up to the edge of moorland, continuing to Winterburn reservoir, before moving on to rolling farmland.

Distance	**7 miles (11.5km)**
Ascent	**800 feet (250m)**
Time	**3 hours**
Grading	**Easy / Moderate**
Suggested Map	**OS Outdoor Leisure 2 – Yorkshire Dales – Southern & Western**
Starting point	**Grid Reference: SD 961 588**
Parking	**By the Angel Inn, Hetton**
How to get there	**Take the B6265 Grassington road out of Skipton which is on the A65 and then turn left onto a minor road at Rylstone**
Terrain	**Rural footpaths and track around the reservoir**

Winterburn Reservoir and the Leeds and Liverpool Canal

The reservoir was constructed between 1885 and 1893 by Leeds civil engineers Henry Rofe and Edward Filliter to help maintain levels on the Leeds and Liverpool Canal. The cost of construction was estimated at £45,000 and the reservoir, which is owned and operated by British Waterways, was built as water storage to maintain navigation on the Leeds and Liverpool Canal. Parliamentary permission for its construction included a requirement to release water – known as 'compensation water' – to keep rivers flowing.

Sections of the Leeds and Liverpool Canal had to be closed to leisure boat users during the summers of 2005 and 2010 because water levels fell so low. It is hoped the trials carried out over the last couple of years will help to establish whether more water can be provided to the canal to help keep it open during very dry periods, while still protecting the ecology in nearby rivers and streams. Studies are underway to look at the impact that changes in flow could have on the fish, crayfish and invertebrates which live in the becks. In addition, the research is investigating the overall quality of the wildlife habitat.

The project also is looking for opportunities to improve the river habitat. In the lower reaches of Eshton Beck a build-up of gravel has been moved to improve the way water flows under the canal aqueduct. This reduces the risk of flooding to nearby land and provides better water levels for fish and other

Winterburn Reservoir outflow

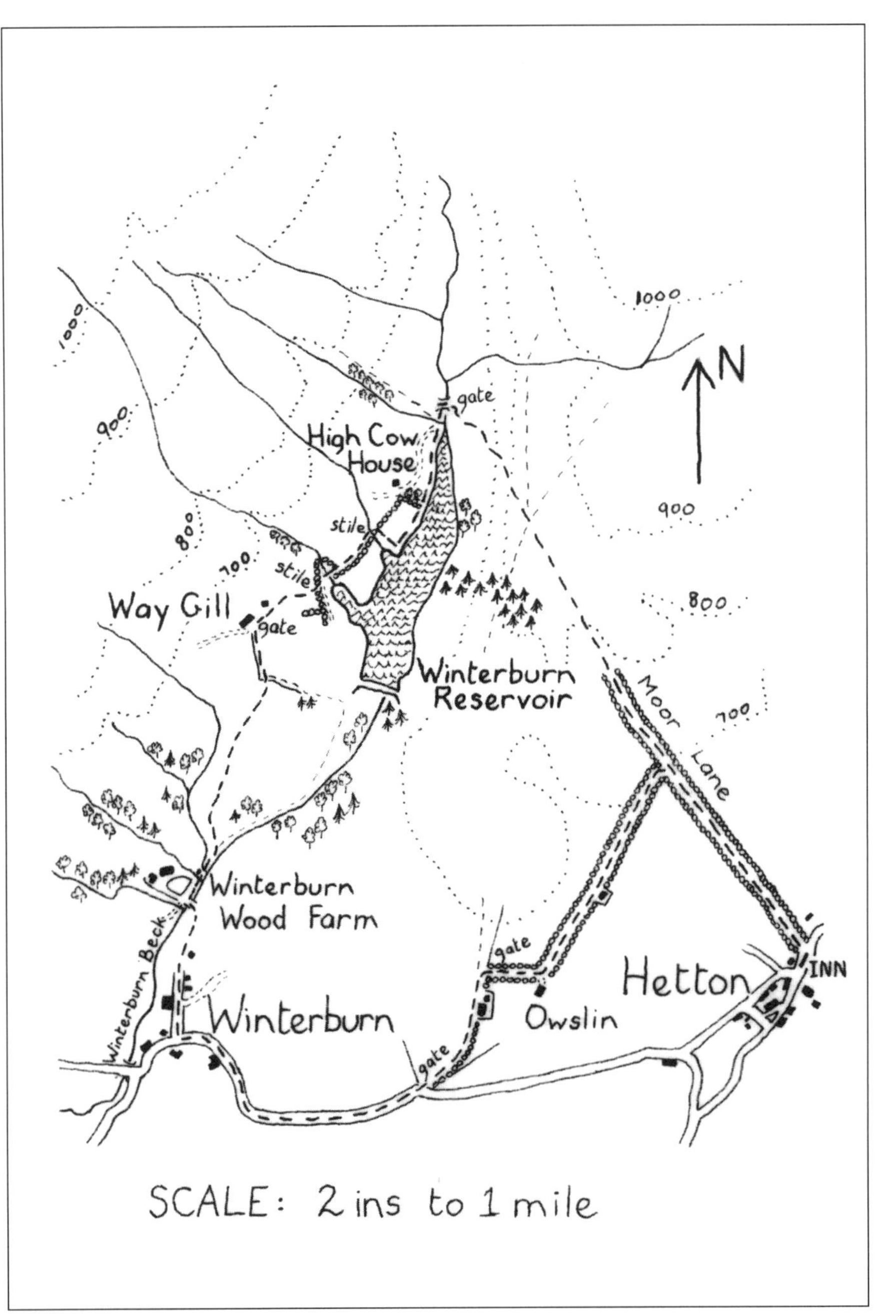

SCALE: 2 ins to 1 mile

river wildlife. The river downstream of the reservoir is a known and valuable spawning ground for species such as brown trout, grayling and bullhead and also the native, but increasingly threatened, white clawed crayfish.

This is a relatively unfrequented part of the Dales so you're likely to have this unspoilt countryside all to yourself. Another of the beauties of this walk is that you can return to the award-winning Angel Inn for refreshment after you have completed the walk. People flock from many miles away for its charming interiors – all oak beams, nooks and crannies – and very fine fare. Its cheeseboard comprises five or six local examples, and the wine list dazzles. The Angel restaurant has a great reputation, which means it gets busy, so book ahead (01756 730263). The Bar Brassiere which is also open at lunchtime is more informal, but the food just as serious.

Angel Inn

The village of Hetton is located on the B6265 from Skipton to Grassington. Turn off this road by the Rylstone duck pond and follow the minor road into Hetton village. It has a small population of 130 at the last census.

The Walk

From the front door of The Angel turn left. Just within sight is Moor Lane, a bridleway on the left – a broad track which leads out of the village and sets a dead straight route for the top end of the reservoir. Whilst uphill all the way it is a gradual rise rather than steep. Turn on to this stone track and as another track sweeps in from the left, continue on the original track. On reaching a junction of five tracks, the way ahead is very clear and the path drops you to the head of the reservoir. Go through the gate and carry on down a bridleway signposted to Malham. Cross the bridge, turn left, following firstly the stream and then the western side of the reservoir. After a footbridge, the path is narrow and sloping; it is easier to climb the bank on the right to more level ground.

At a stream in a deep gorge, a signpost directs you right, uphill, and along the side of the stream to a stone wall with a stile. Cross on to the farm track and turn left. After crossing the stream by a bridge, watch for another stile

Footbridge

on the right. Cross this and go uphill to a gate in the top-left corner of the field. In front you will see a stone step stile over the wall by the farm, **but don't take it.** Our route is through a gate by a signpost. Almost at once, another signpost to the right then guides you on to a farm track. Follow this away from the farm. A road joins from the right and you drop to another junction, signposted for Winterburn.

After walking past some houses, follow a bend to the left across the stream. Just past Winterburn Wood farm you encounter more houses, turn left here and follow the lane. Turn left through the gate where a bridleway is signposted. You will pass a group of barns and an enclosed yard on your right, after which the wall curves toward a gate in the corner. Go through this gate on to an enclosed track (not straight ahead). The track divides by the barn on the right.

Next, turn left by the wall near the conifer trees by the property named 'Owslin'. Carry on up the lane to an open gate. At the cross-wall in front, you meet the track from the first part of the walk. Turn right; and follow this track back to the village. If you have completed this walk during the morning, you will be just in time to sample the lunchtime menu at The Angel in the Bar Brassiere.

WHARFEDALE INTRODUCTION

The third of our rivers is the River Wharfe. It is the river that flows through the town of Otley where I live and is subsequently the area that I have walked the most over the last forty years. For much of its length it is the county boundary between West Yorkshire and North Yorkshire. The name Wharfe is Celtic and means 'twisting, winding'.

The valley of the River Wharfe is known as Wharfedale. Running from north to south, Wharfedale is one of the Yorkshire Dales' longest and most beautiful valleys. Rising on the high moors of Langstrothdale Chase, the infant River Wharfe passes down the remote valley of Langstrothdale and through the hamlets of Yockenthwaite and Hubberholme to the village of Buckden. From here the River Wharfe travels on southwards, through the villages of Starbotton, Kettlewell, Conistone and Kilnsey (famous for Kilnsey Crag, a dramatically overhanging limestone cliff – popular with climbers and tourists alike), and just north of which it is met by the tributary valley of Littondale and the River Skirfare.

Further downstream the River Wharfe passes between the villages of Grassington and Threshfield, then on through Burnsall, The Strid and Bolton Abbey, from where the river passes out of the National Park and on through Ilkley and Otley to meet the River Aire to the east of Leeds en route to its confluence with the River Ouse and final destination of the Humber Estuary and the North Sea.

Wharfedale is often divided into Upper Wharfedale and Lower Wharfedale – lying respectively upstream and downstream of the village of Grassington. Tributary valleys of Upper Wharfedale include Langstrothdale and Littondale, whilst tributary valleys of Lower Wharfedale include Dibblesdale, Skyredale, the Valley of Desolation, Kexdale and the Washburn Valley with its reservoirs that serves the population of Leeds and surrounding areas with its water supply.

Langstrothdale Chase is an area of ancient hunting forest, spanning the valley of Langstrothdale itself. Today much of the area is moorland or open pasture, with the village of Buckden in Upper Wharfedale having been a focal point for huntsmen in days gone by There is a fine Norman church at Hubberholme, perhaps most well known as being the resting place of the ashes of the writer and playwright J.B. Priestley.

Kettlewell is situated at the foot of Great Whernside just north of Kilnsey. This is *Calendar Girls* country – the hit movie having been filmed here and at other locations in the Yorkshire Dales during the summer of 2002. The village is also famous for its annual Scarecrow Festival – which is usually held over a week in August. From Kettlewell a very steep single track road leads up Park Rash and over the moors between Buckden Pike and Great Whernside down in to Coverdale, one of the side valleys of Wensleydale. As we progress down the valley, Kilnsey is famous for its proximity to Kilnsey Crag an impressive overhanging limestone cliff which is very popular with climbers, and also the annual Kilnsey Show during which a fell race to the top of the Crag takes place, while just across the valley is the adjacent village of Conistone.

The village of Grassington is in fact technically a town (hence the suffix 'ton') – albeit a very small one – situated on the edge of Grass Wood. Nearby attractions include Stump Cross Caverns, Linton Falls, and the sinister limestone gorge of Troller's Gill (which is said to be haunted by Scandinavian trolls, evil bloodsucking gnomes, and a huge spectral hound having 'eyes as big as saucers').

Below Burnsall and Appletreewick, and just before Bolton Abbey, we encounter the fascinating phenomenon of 'The Strid' a notorious stretch of water where the River Wharfe is forced into a deep and narrow channel. At its narrowest point the Strid is only about seven feet (two metres) wide and foolhardy visitors have in the past tried to jump across the roaring chasm. Failure is invariably fatal, however, as there is no recorded incidence of anyone having survived a fall into the thundering waters of the Strid – which mercilessly sucks its victims into the underwater caves and eroded tunnels which lie hidden underneath each side of the rocky channel. Needless to say, the Strid is an extremely dangerous place, and visitors should take care to keep a safe distance from the edge, with children and animals being kept firmly under control.

Bolton Abbey is the village adjacent to Bolton Priory, a ruined Augustinian monastery. The monastery was originally founded at Embsay in 1120. Led by a prior, Bolton Abbey was technically a priory, despite its name. It was founded in 1154 by the Augustinian order. The seal of the priory featured the Blessed Virgin Mary and the Child and the phrase 'sigillum sancte Marie de Bolton'. The nave of the abbey church was in use as a parish church from about 1170 onwards, and survived Henry VIII's Dissolution of the Monasteries.

This renowned beauty spot forms part of the Duke of Devonshire's country estate and leads through the so called 'Valley of Desolation' and on up to the rocky crest of Simon's Seat. Much of this area is bracken moorland famed for grouse shooting and hunting. Also close by is the Bolton Abbey terminus of the Embsay and Bolton Abbey Steam Railway from where it is possible to take a ride on a steam train to the village of Embsay, near to the market town of Skipton. In September 1833 the Brontës visited Bolton Abbey on an excursion from their home at Haworth.

Ilkley is a very pleasant spa town made famous through the song *On Ilkla Moor Baht 'at* (On Ilkley Moor without a hat). It is sung in the Yorkshire dialect, and is considered the unofficial anthem of the county of Yorkshire. According to tradition, the words were composed by members of a Halifax Methodist church choir during an outing to Ilkley Moor. Ilkley is surrounded by fine unspoiled scenery, with Ilkley Moor and the famous Cow and Calf rocks positioned just above the town. Also on the moor is the famous whitewashed building known as White Wells which houses a bath at a site which (reputedly) dates from Roman times. (Ilkley was, in fact, an important outpost during the Roman occupation, when it was known as 'Olicana'.)

Other attractions include the Victorian bath house in the town itself, and the recently refurbished Ilkley Pool and Lido, one of the country's last remaining outdoor public swimming pools which is usually open in the summer months only. Regular events in the town include the Ilkley Literature Festival and the Ilkley Music Festival. The town is also home of the Airedale Symphony Orchestra (although Ilkley is, of course, actually in Wharfedale). Charles Darwin stayed in the town during the publication of *The Origin of Species*, a visit which is commemorated by the town's Darwin Gardens and the Millennium Maze.

Famous as the birthplace of Thomas Chippendale (the English cabinet maker), Otley is another pleasant market town dating back to the mid-eighth century, when Otta made his Leah or clearing in the forest. Its parish church houses some of the best examples of Anglo-Danish crosses in the country. Thomas Fairfax, Cromwell's general came from nearby Denton Hall. W H Turner often stayed nearby at Farnley Hall, and used the Chevin (a 1,000 foot hill to the south of the town) as the backdrop for at least one of his famous pictures (Hannibal crossing the Alps).

John Wesley the co-founder of the Methodist Church visited Otley on some twenty occasions and struck up a great friendship with the Ritchie family, who he stayed with on most of his visits at their house on Boroughgate. There is a story that one of Wesley's horses died in Otley and was buried in the parish churchyard. Opposite the north-west corner of the Parish Church can be found a peculiar triangular stone, commonly known as the 'donkey stone', which is where the horse is believed to have been buried. Quoting from Wesley's own journal on Sunday 5th May 1782: "One of my horses having been so thoroughly lamed at Otley that he died in three or four days. They buried him in the churchyard there being no other place. So Robert rests".

The Wharfedale Press, which revolutionised nineteenth century printing, was invented and manufactured in Otley. The Wharfedale has a fascinating history. At the time of its invention engineers throughout the world were seeking ways of modernising the printing press. Little progress had been made since Gutenberg printed his famous Bible on a wooden press in Germany in 1454. The first major improvement came with the introduction of the cylinder which, when used in conjunction with a flat bed offered many advantages over the traditional method of printing from two flat surfaces. However it was the inventive genius of David Payne of Otley that was responsible for the real breakthrough: a stop-cylinder machine with a travelling bed that could deliver print without having to be stopped. Payne had been taken on by another Otley man, William Dawson, in a little back-street joiner's shop in Newmarket, Otley. Soon afterwards, they collaborated in building the new Ulverstonian printing machine for its inventor, Mr Stephen Soulby. There seems little doubt that it was during this project that Payne's fertile brain conceived the stop-cylinder principle that, within the next few years, was to have such a shattering impact on the industry. Indeed there is evidence to suggest that the machine may have been invented as early as 1851. The story that, when the Payne family were moving house in that year, one of the Payne's sons was shown a drawing of what turned out to be the first Wharfedale. The drawing was done on the headboard of a bed which his father kept covered for fear that someone might discover his secret.

For a time Dawson and Payne simply called their revolutionary new machine 'Our Own Kind' and made no effort to take out patents. Inevitably, this led to it being widely copied by other firms both in England and overseas. Not content with copying the machine, a good many firms even went to the lengths of recruiting Dawson men to show them how to build it. At one time, it was estimated that half the firms making the Wharfedale employed men who, at some time or other, had worked for Dawson in Otley. For half a century, the Wharfedale dominated world markets and it continued to be manufactured right up to modern times. As recently as 1965, an order was placed with Dawson, Payne and Elliott for 28 of the machines to print the Holy Koran in Pakistan.

The town of Otley also hosts the country's oldest agricultural show each May. Downstream from Otley, the magnificent stately home of Harewood House is nearby, as is the prominent landmark of Almscliffe Crag, another favourite with rock climbers.

As well as three fabulous walks upstream from Addingham in the upper part of Wharfedale, I have also included two equally impressive walks in Lower Wharfedale; one over the famous Ilkley Moor and one on Otley Chevin.

WHARFEDALE WALK 1
Ilkley Moor

This walk climbs from the spa town of Ilkley over the famous Ilkley Moor passing the Cow and Calf rocks and out to the twelve apostles stone circle before returning over the moor to White Wells. From here a small extension to the walk can be added to visit the famous Swastika Stone.

Distance	**4.5 miles (7km)**
Ascent	**450 feet (130m)**
Time	**2.5 hours**
Grading	**Moderate**
Suggested Map	**OS Explorer 297 – Lower Wharfedale & The Washburn Valley**
Starting point	**Grid Reference:117477**
Parking	**Wells Road, Ilkley**
How to get there	**Ilkley is 14 miles north-west of Leeds on the A660 road to Skipton which joins the A65 at Burley in Wharfedale. It is also 10 miles north of Bradford and is reached by taking the A650 to Shipley and then the A6038 and left onto the B6151 over Baildon Moor**
Terrain	**Good moorland tracks throughout**

Ilkley

Ilkley is one of the oldest towns in Wharfedale and dates back to Roman times when a legion was based here in their garrison at Olicana. Many items dating back two millennia have been found in various locations around the town and they are now housed in the museum adjacent to the parish church.

Ilkley's spa town heritage and surrounding countryside make tourism an important local industry. The town centre is characterised by Victorian architecture, wide streets and floral displays. It is well served by both road and rail. The main A65 road from Leeds to the Lake District runs through the town and Ilkley is the terminus on the Wharfedale Line out of both Leeds and Bradford, a mere 30 minutes journey from either of those two cities. Bus services from both cities also serve the town but the journeys on these are over an hour from both Leeds and Bradford.

Ilkley Moor is a long ridge of millstone grit, immediately to the south of Ilkley. Synonymous with the famous 'Yorkshire Anthem', with or without a hat, Ilkley Moor is a special place, not just for walkers, but for lovers of archaeological relics too. These extensive heather moors are identified on maps as Rombalds Moor, named after a legendary giant who roamed the area. But, thanks to the famous song – Yorkshire's unofficial anthem – Ilkley Moor is how it's now always known. Our walk will take us from the centre of Ilkley out over the moor to a number of these archaeological stones.

To the north end of the moor, where the moor drops steeply down towards the village of Ben Rhydding are two millstone grit rock climbing areas: Rocky Valley and Ilkley Quarry. Ilkley Quarry is the site of the famous 'Cow and Calf', a large rock formation consisting of an outcrop and boulder, also known as Hangingstone Rocks. The rocks are made of millstone grit, a variety of sandstone, and are so named because one is large, with the smaller one sitting close to it, like a cow and calf. Legend has it that there was once also a 'bull', but that was quarried for stone during the spa town boom Ilkley was part of in the 19th century. However, none of the local historians has provided any evidence of the Bull's existence.

According to local legend, the Calf was split from the Cow when the giant Rombald was fleeing an enemy, and stamped on the rock as he leapt across the valley. The enemy, it is said, was his angry wife. She dropped the stones held in her skirt to form the local rock formation The Skirtful of Stones.

July 2006 saw a major fire on the moor which left between a quarter and half of it destroyed. Located on the Woodhouse Crag, on the Northern edge of Ilkley Moor there is a swastika-shaped pattern engraved

The Swastika Stone

in a stone, known as the Swastika Stone This stone is, however, just one of a great abundance of carved rocks on the moor, well known others include the 'Badger Stone' and 'St. Margaret's Stones'. These are earthfast boulders, large flat slabs or prominent rocks that have cups, rings and grooves cut into them and thought to date from either the late Neolithic or the Bronze Age. While some carvings consist of simple cups, others such as the Badger Stone, Hanging Stones and the Panorama Rocks have complex series of patterns. Indeed Rombalds Moor can boast the second highest concentration of ancient carved stones in Europe, with carving as far away as Skipton Moor. There is also a small stone circle known as 'The Twelve Apostles' which we will visit on the walk.

The local millstone grit not only gives character to the town of Ilkley but gives the area its acid soils, heather moors, soft water and rocky scars, like the Cow and Calf rocks. Ilkley Moor, in the Carboniferous period 325 million years ago, was in a swampy area at around sea level with meandering river channels coming from the north. The layers in the eroded bank faces of stream gullies in the area represent sea levels with various tides depositing different sorts of sediment. Over a long period of time the loose sediments were cemented and compacted into hard rock layers. Geological forces lifted and tilted the strata a little towards the south-east and produced many small fractures, or faults.

Since the end of the Carboniferous time there has been a tremendous amount of erosion and more than a thousand metres of the coal-bearing rocks have been completely removed from the area. More recently, during the last million years or so, Ice Age glaciers modified the shape of the Wharfe valley, deepening it, smoothing it and leaving behind glacial debris.

The Walk

And so onto the walk itself. Either cross the road from the Railway/Bus Station or if using your own transport park on Wells Road and walk up here for approximately ¼ mile (400m) passing College Drive on your right and Crossbeck Road on your left. Cross a small footbridge on the left and climb up a small incline to the tarn on top of the embankment. At the far end take a path, uphill at first, then down to cross Backstone Beck again on a little footbridge, then a fair haul uphill to reach the Cow and Calf rocks. It's worth taking a few minutes to investigate the rocks and watch climbers practising their belays and traverses. From here a paved path leads across to a car park where there is a refreshment hut if you are in need of this after the uphill climb. This new café, opened on 31st March 2012. At the end of 2011, Toni Falconi closed his old snack kiosk and turned a nearby former Yorkshire Water building into the new café, which also provides toilets for visitors to

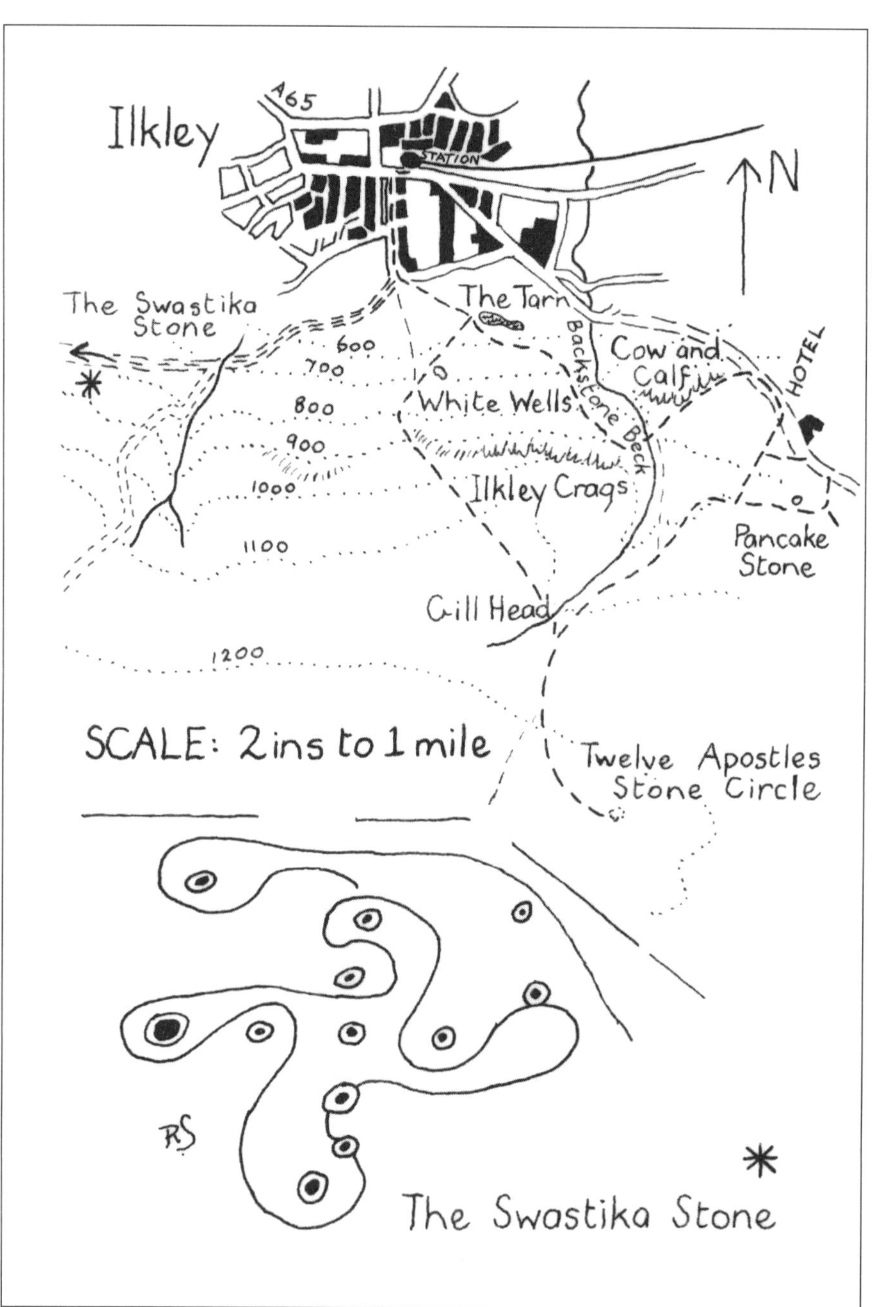

Ilkley
A65
STATION
N
The Swastika Stone
The Tarn
Cow and Calf
HOTEL
600
700
Backstone Beck
White Wells
800
900
1000
Ilkley Crags
1100
Pancake Stone
Gill Head
1200
SCALE: 2 ins to 1 mile
Twelve Apostles Stone Circle
RS
The Swastika Stone

Cow and Calf Rocks

the moor for the first time. Part of the cost for this was provided by DEFRA (The Department for Environment, Food and Rural Affairs).

The steepest of the climbing is now behind us. Walk up the road; and in 150 yards (138m) beyond the Cow and Calf Hotel, where the road bears left, fork right up a grassy path. Head up to the ridge and to the Pancake Stone. Turn right following a path along the edge of the ridge, then cross another track and continue until you reach the Haystack Rock. From here there are extensive views back over Ilkley and Wharfedale. At this point the track bears left, and runs parallel to Backstone Beck. Continue climbing uphill onto the open moorland.

At the very top of the climb you will join the Bradford to Ilkley Dales Way link path. Go left here and onto the stone slabs. At the top of the next rise, pass a boundary stone and continue until you come across the ring of stones known as the Twelve Apostles. This is a delightful circle set in a spectacular location – although it seems to have been restored in recent years as old guide books refer to it as being badly damaged. It now has the twelve stones that its name suggests but the archaeologist Arthur Raistrick suggested that there were originally around twenty in the circle with a diameter of just under 16 metres, set within a rubble bank. None of these stones are particularly tall,

the largest is less than a metre and a half in height and the whole aspect of
the circle is similar to some of those found in Derbyshire.

There have been theories that suggest the stones were used for observation
of the movement of the moon or celestial bodies – indeed it was once known
as a 'druidical dial circle', however the fact that the site has been altered in
the past would make this very difficult to prove. It is also said that from the
circle the rising summer solstice sun appears exactly above the White Horse
at Kilburn.

Retrace your steps from the Twelve Apostles, and instead of turning right
down to the Cow and Calf where you came up from, continue along the Dales
Way link path. Once you have crossed Backstone Beck the open moorland is
replaced by a stony ridge. Again from here, if the weather is good, there are
extensive views across Ilkley and Wharfedale. The path now heads steeply
downhill, part of which has been restored with steps. Beneath the clump of
trees in front of you, you will spot White Wells.

There has been bathing at White Wells since 1703 when there was a bath to
the rear of the premises. This was replaced in 1791 by two baths, one of which
is on display today. Although the water has no significant mineral content it
is the coldness of the water which stimulates the circulation.

White Wells

White Wells was instrumental in establishing Ilkley as a spa town. A number of large hydros were built in the Ilkley area during the 19th century where people could come to 'take the waters', believing all manner of aliments could be cured. Charles Darwin visited Ilkley in 1859 and is believed to have 'taken the waters' at White Wells.

Modern day visitors can still use the plunge bath. New Year's Day is the most popular day for this activity, with usually over a hundred plungers throughout the day. However, providing it is quiet enough in the café the bath gate can usually be opened should visitors wish to plunge at other times of the year too. Plungers must supply their own bathing costumes and towels and the activity is undertaken at the plunger's own risk! There is no charge for plunging, but bathers can buy a certificate to mark the occasion, throw some loose change into the bath and of course support the café by buying hot drinks and snacks afterwards.

From White Wells it is quite a steep descent back down to Wells Road. Bear right, passing to the left of the ponds, and then descend downhill, heading for a pyramid-shaped rock. Here you will reach a track which takes you back down to the tarn and then subsequently back onto the road and down into the town of Ilkley.

Although not visited on this walk, if you wished to extend the walk by a further mile, you could turn left at this point and follow the road until it turns into a track, pass a small reservoir on your right and then up a track on your left, above Woodhouse Crag, you will come across another of the famous Ilkley Moors stones – The Swastika Stone (look out for the railings round it to locate it). The design of this has a double outline with five curved arms enclosing several so-called 'cup' marks, the like of which can be found on other stones nearby.

The design is unique in the British Isles, so its close similarity to Camunian Rose designs in Italy have led some to theorize that the two are connected. In fact, the troops stationed in Ilkley during Roman occupation were recruited from the Celtic Lingones. This tribe was native to Gaul, but in around 400 BC, some migrated across the Alps to the Adriatic coast. Some believe the Ilkley Lingones were recruited from here rather than from Gaul. It is possible that the Italian Lingones passed through the Valcamonica region at some point, took on the swastika designs they found as part of their tribal symbolism, and carved it on the nearby moor when stationed in Ilkley.

Head back into Ilkley with its many pubs, restaurants and tea rooms, particularly the famous 'Betty's' tea room on The Grove which you will pass on the way back to the Station and Wells Road.

Simon's Seat

This is a circular walk from Barden Bridge along part of the Dales Way, climbing to the summit of Simon's Seat and then returning again on the Dales Way to the starting point.

Distance	**9 miles (14.5 km)**
Ascent	**1,000 feet (300m)**
Time	**4 hours**
Grading	**Strenuous**
Suggested Map	**Outdoor Leisure OL2 Yorkshire Dales Southern & Western**
Starting point	**Grid Reference: 052574**
Parking	**Barden Bridge**
How to get there	**Barden Bridge is located a quarter of a mile east of the B6160 running between Bolton Abbey and the village of Burnsall. The B6160 is accessed from the A65 between Ilkley and Skipton**
Terrain	**Riverside path followed by good moorland tracks and riverside path to finish**

The start at Barden Bridge is located a quarter of a mile east of the B6160 running between Bolton Abbey and the village of Burnsall. The walk follows part of the Dales Way downstream from Barden passing 'The Strid' and continuing by the river as far as Cavendish Pavilion. The route then doubles back on itself for about ½ mile on the eastern side of the river to go up the Valley of Desolation to the summit of Simon's Seat. It then drops back down again to the River Wharfe at Howgill and finally heads downstream from here back to Barden Bridge. Please note that dogs are not allowed on the moorland sector of this walk as this is a grouse breeding area. The views of Wharfedale from the summits of Simon's Seat and Earl's Seat are very good and it is therefore worth picking a good day to undertake this walk to make the most of these fine panoramas.

The so-called 'Barden Triangle' is defined as an area around the head of Lower Wharfedale which includes weird places having supposedly supernatural associations such as the reputedly haunted limestone gorge of Troller's Gill, the strange conical knoll of Elbolton Hill (said to be the 'Hill of the Fairies') and the Dibble's Bridge (which – along with several similar other old bridges in England – was allegedly built by the Devil). The area of Barden (including Barden Tower and Barden Bridge) forms the southern apex of the triangle, with Cracoe and the Cracoe Reef Knolls and the top end of Troller's Gill roughly defining the northern-most edges.

This walk is in a popular part of Wharfedale, especially the area upstream from Bolton Abbey as far as the Strid but apart from the half mile section from the Strid to Cavendish Pavilion it is unlikely that there will be crowds of people on the remainder of the walk. If the walk is done midweek rather than at a weekend it is more than likely that you will only encounter a handful of people throughout the day.

The Walk

From the roadside parking by the side of the river at the eastern side of Barden Bridge **do not** cross the bridge itself over the river. Instead follow the Dales Way along the path which stays on the east bank as far as a substantial stone bridge where it then crosses over to the western bank of the river. The path then continues through beautiful woodland to the Strid where the River Wharfe squeezes through rocks before continuing at a gentler pace a few hundred metres downstream.

The spectacular Strid was formed by the wearing away of softer rock by the circular motion of small stones in hollows, forming a series of potholes which in time linked together to form a deep, water filled chasm. The Strid gets its name from the fact that it is said to be a Stride wide, but there is danger here. It is wider than it looks and the rocks are usually very slippery. A number of people have attempted to jump across the river at this point with the majority having lost their lives as a result having drowned in the swirling whirlpools of the rushing river.

The next section from the Strid to the Cavendish Pavilion follows the gentler running river passing through woodland maintained by the Duke of Devonshire's Estate. This ancient woodland is a Site of Special Scientific

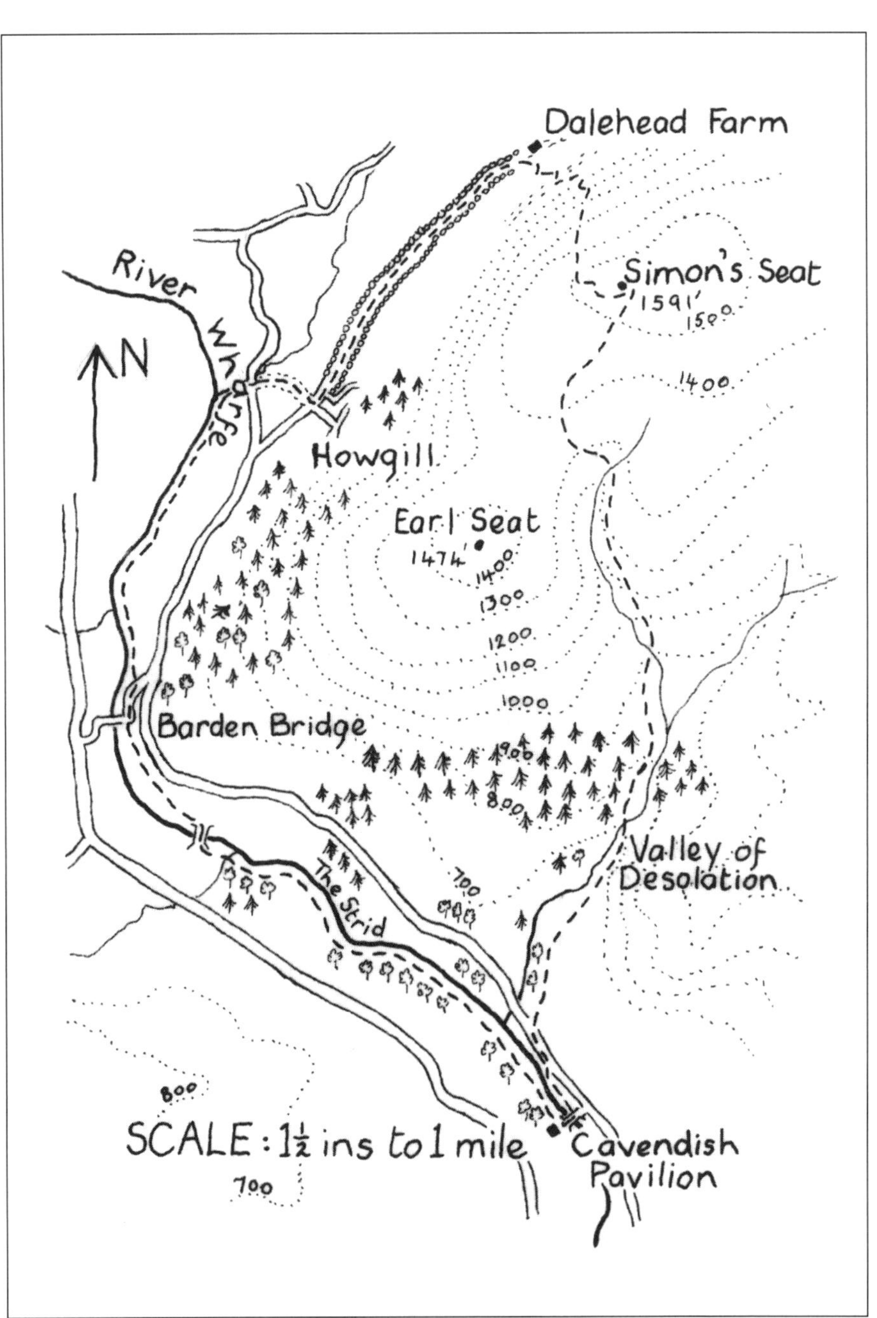

Dalehead Farm
River Wharfe
N
Simon's Seat
1591'
1500
1400
Howgill
Earl Seat
1474'
1400
1300
1200
1100
1000
900
800
Barden Bridge
Valley of Desolation
The Strid
700
800
SCALE: 1½ ins to 1 mile
700
Cavendish Pavilion

Interest and one of the largest areas of acidic oak woodland in the Yorkshire Dales. It is renowned for the flora and fauna, particularly the carpets of bluebells in spring. Cavendish Pavilion was opened in 1890, and it still very much resembles a Victorian style station building. At the pavilion there is a tea room and ice creams are also available here if you wish to partake in some refreshment before the two mile (3km) climb up to the summit of Simon's Seat.

Cross the foot bridge at Cavendish Pavilion and turn left to follow the River Wharfe upstream across a field. At the end of the field turn right. Cross over a stile and follow the tarmac road until you reach Waterfall Cottage. Here turn right and go through the gate and over the fields following a well marked path that leads you to the Valley of Desolation. Adjacent to this is a waymarked path signed for 'Simon's Seat'. Take this path passing through pastures at first but soon entering a valley. You will notice a footbridge down on your left (Grid ref. 078566). Cross this and follow the narrow path upstream to pass Posforth Gill waterfall.

Above the waterfall you enter the 'Valley of Desolation' and soon the path enters a conifer plantation. Immediately after passing through the trees you exit onto open moorland. This section is along a well walked bridleway and the onward path is obvious. As you climb gently on this path the gritstone rocks that mark the summit of Simon's Seat soon come into view. The bird's eye perspective of Wharfedale is particularly fine and it is a perfect place for a break. A short optional visit may be made to Lord's Seat, which lies about 500 metres east. This sees fewer visitors but offers good views across towards Nidderdale. If you visit here then retrace your steps back to Simon's Seat. Rock climbing is a popular pastime in and around the summit rocks area. There are some good routes on the main crag, but most of the bouldering is concentrated on the walls around the summit area. 'Naked Edge' rock is a big detached boulder at the bottom of the crag with an impressive arête, and smooth walls on either side whilst 'The Trunk' is a small boulder just up the hill from 'Naked Edge' and has an unusual elephant's trunk feature.

Summit

After a break at the top to refresh yourself and take in the views, head to

Trig point

the south-western corner of the summit rocks. Here you will find a paved path descending steeply north into the valley. The grade soon eases and you continue to descend through a series of zig-zags down the track that cuts through the gorse to reach a walled track at Dalehead Farm (Grid ref. 075604). Turn left (west) along this pleasant lane to reach a junction of tracks at Howgill (Grid ref. 063591). At Howgill Farm, where there is a camping and caravan site, there is a shop and refreshment area which serves an excellent pot of tea and cakes. This is a perfect resting point and just right before the final mile by the river back to your car. Turn right down the narrow track after 200 yards (190 metres) to reach the road and cross this to join the Dales Way heading south along the east bank of the River Wharfe. This leads pleasantly back to Barden Bridge in approximately one mile (1.6km).

At the end of the walk it is worth walking the extra ¼ mile over the bridge and up the hill to visit the nearby Barden Tower. This was built by the Clifford family of Skipton Castle in the fifteenth century and was the principal hunting lodge of the ancient Forest of Barden and home of the 10th Lord of Skipton, more commonly known as the Shepherd Lord. In 1658 Lady Anne Clifford restored and extended Barden from a Pele tower into a manor house.

The now-ruined tower overlooks the Priest's House, built in the early 16th century which the Shepherd Lord built for his private Chaplain. Barden means 'valley where the barley grew' and the tower was originally one of six hunting lodges within the Forest of Barden. The building has undergone several alterations and served many purposes including being a farm house at one point. Today visitors are welcome to wander round the ruined Barden Tower and enjoy a meal at The Priest House which is now a very popular restaurant. This is open (at the time of writing) on Thursdays, Fridays and Saturdays for morning coffee from 10.30am to noon, the restaurant from noon to 2.30pm, afternoon teas from 2pm to 5pm and the restaurant again from 7pm to 9pm. It is also open for Sunday lunch from 12pm to 3pm.

Other nearby places for refreshment after the walk include the tea rooms in neighbouring Burnsall (3 miles away) plus The Tea Cottage, the Abbey Tearooms and the Cavendish Pavilion on the Bolton Abbey estate and Dusty Bluebells in the car park above Strid Wood.

River Wharfe near Barden

Linton from Burnsall

This walk, whilst low level in the main, is, in my opinion, one of the finest walks in the Dales. It commences from the beautiful village of Burnsall, follows the Dales Way along the side of the River Wharfe, crossing this twice, firstly by a suspension footbridge and secondly by a lovely set of stepping stones (although if the river is high these can be bypassed by a small amount of road walking into the village of Litton). The route then climbs out of the valley and visits the 'hidden' village of Thorpe before crossing a number of field paths back to Burnsall.

Distance	**6 miles (9km)**
Ascent	**500 feet (150m)**
Time	**3 hours**
Grading	**Easy**
Suggested Map	**Outdoor Leisure OL2 Yorkshire Dales Southern & Western**
Starting point	**Grid Reference: SE032611**
Parking	**Burnsall Bridge**
How to get there	**Burnsall is on the B6160 approximately 11 miles from Ilkley. Take the A65 towards Skipton and at Addingham turn onto the B6160**
Terrain	**Good riverside paths to Linton. Some ascent to Thorpe over fields and then field paths back to Burnsall**

Burnsall

Burnsall's five-arched bridge, the starting point for the walk, spans the River Wharfe and the river path dates back to Viking times. Although the 2001 census gave it the village a population of only 112, the village has a parish church, a former chapel (now a day nursery), a primary school (housed in the

Burnsall Bridge

original grammar school building of 1602, which is a grade II listed building), two hotels with restaurants, and a pub. These are supported by the vast amount of tourists visiting this village at all times of the year. Because of its charm and location, Burnsall, with a large, grassy parking area, is a favoured site for walkers, trout fishers, picnics, weddings and other ceremonies. The school building, like the much-photographed bridge (also grade II listed), is an early 17th century legacy of William Craven of nearby Appletreewick, who became mayor of London (and may have been the inspiration for 'Dick Whittington'), and has always been used as a school.

On the early part of the walk we will see on the left St. Wilfrid's Church (a grade I listed building) which is almost entirely Perpendicular. Amongst its well-known internal features are an 11th century font carved with bird and beasts, twelve Anglo-Saxon sculpture fragments and a 14th century alabaster panel depicting the Adoration of the Magi. The churchyard, which has a number of interesting grave stones, is entered from the main road by a large and well-kept Lych-gate, but can also be reached from the riverside path that we follow for the first part of the walk.

St. Wilfrid's history goes right back to its foundation by St. Wilfrid of Ripon before 700AD. Although most of the building has been rebuilt over the years, there are parts that go back many centuries. The font dates from an original Norman church, and the current Lady Chapel in the south chantry was built in the twelfth century. The tower and western portion of the church were built during the reign of Henry VIII (1509-1547). During a refurbishment in the mid 19th Century, a number of Viking stones and artefacts were discovered. Some of these have been retained in the church, and form a

St. Wilfred's Church

fascinating exhibition at the back of the building. The welcoming lych gate was moved to its current position in 1858 when the churchyard was extended. The gate turns on a central spindle, with weights controlling its operation. This gate is believed to be just one of four in the country which operate on this principle. Lych gates were sometimes called 'corpse gates' as a reminder that it was at one time customary for the bier (a stand on which a corpse, or coffin or casket containing a corpse, is placed to lie in state) to rest beneath the lych-gate during the initial part of the funeral service.

The other church in the village, which can also be seen during the first ¼ mile of the walk, is the Methodist Church. This was built in 1840 but has now ceased as a place of worship and is used instead as a nursery for the village and surrounding area.

The Walk

The walk starts by the bridge in Burnsall outside The Red Lion, originally a 16th century ferryman's inn, at a time before the bridge was built, when it was necessary to ferry residents from one side of the Wharfe to the other. The main bar incorporates the original 16th Century structure of the ferryman's inn, which is traditionally panelled and floored in oak.

With the Red Lion pub on your left, go between it and the bridge down to the riverside, then turning left as we start our journey upstream towards Linton. We pass Burnsall church, and the old grammar school and a tea garden on your left. Keep on this path and you will come to the gorge where the current rage of 'tombstoning' takes place. This is where young people jump 20 to 30 feet down into the river from neighbouring rocks of Loup Scar. It seems a very scary and dangerous sport to me.

After a further half mile along this beautiful stretch of river, the path takes

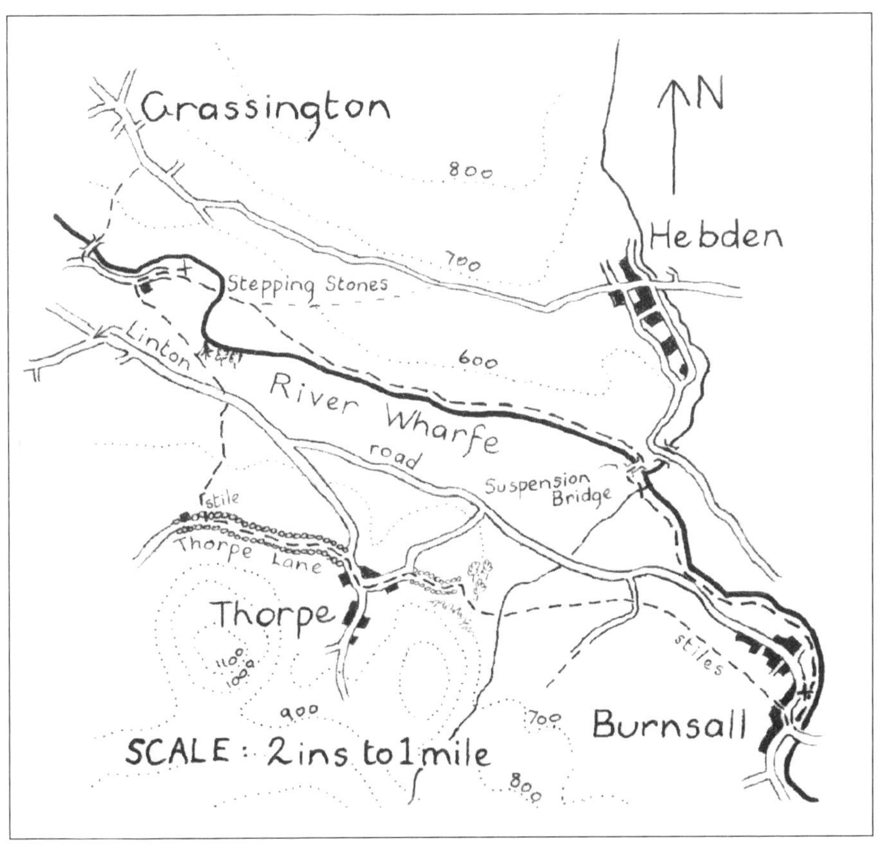

you to the wooden suspension bridge over the Wharfe, which we need to cross. After crossing turn left through the gate, head up stream. This section for the next mile is a very pleasing walk all the way along the side of the river as far as Linton stepping stones. If the river is not too high it is possible to cross these to the church. Otherwise, follow the track off to the right. At Brow Well Fish Farm keep your eyes open for goldcrests and dippers near the stream opposite. After the fish farm, turn left over a stone stile with a gate to continue alongside the river across two more stone stiles to Linton Falls.

Assuming though that you have crossed the stepping stones, go through the next field to Linton church of Saint Michael and All Saints. Dating from the 12th Century, the church is a beautiful building, and an ideal place to stop for a break and to take on refreshment.

Loup Scar

After leaving the churchyard, follow the minor road and although the route to Thorpe turns off at this point, you cannot leave Linton without visiting the falls and the village. If you did not cross the stepping stones, you will have entered the village from the south-east whereas we are now going to enter it from the west over the bridge where there are fine views of the falls. Linton-in-Craven with its sloping green, bridges, beck and trees is often described as the prettiest village in Yorkshire. Dominating one end of the Green is the imposing Georgian facade of Fountaine Hospital which was designed by Sir John Vanbrugh who was responsible for the design of Castle Howard between York and Malton. The hospital was founded and gifted to the village as an almshouse 'for six poor men or women' by Richard Fountaine in 1721. The benefactor was a native of the village who amassed a fortune as a timber merchant in the City of London. The village also boasts, as well as this fine Vanbrugh almshouse, a pub and three stone bridges over its beck. Situated amidst the group of cottages close by the falls, is a charming 14th Century packhorse bridge, called locally 'Little Emily's Bridge', although who Emily was I have failed to find out.

Re-cross the clapper bridge spanning the river again and turn left heading back towards the church. Go for about 150 yards with the river on your left and at the farm on the right is a signpost for Thorpe Lane. Passing the new fencing on your right and the farm, go uphill through three gates. After the third gate turn slightly left, heading for the little stone wall to the left of the woods. Head for the top corner of the field. Follow the path all the way to the stone stile in the wall by the ruined barn on the right, which brings you into Thorpe lane. This is a lovely quiet walled lane with fine views that takes you into the little village of Thorpe. Keep on until the T-junction then turn right which will take you into Thorpe, bearing left and uphill through the village. On your left is the very impressive manor house

At the top of the hill where the road bends to the left you will see a sign for Burnsall – 1½ miles. Going down a walled lane with fine views all around including Simon's Seat straight in front of you. Keeping on this path passing the woods on your left and then cross over a number of fields using the various stiles all the way to Burnsall (about a dozen stiles in all). Believe me you will not get lost. When you come to the last stone stile and the houses in front of you, head for the little electric sub-station, here to the left is a tiny little path (known in Yorkshire as a 'ginnel') that takes you out onto the main road to Burnsall.

As well as the hostelry of the Red Lion there are also a number of tea rooms in the village including the Wharfe View Tea Rooms opposite the village green where there is a fine view of the bridge and river from the tables outside. A good place to rest and be refreshed at the end of this delightful walk.

Grassington to Mosedale Caverns

This is a fine middle distance walk starting off following the Dales Way, then following part of the Six Dales Hike to the Mosedale Caverns before finally returning via some of the old lead mining areas around Yarnbury and back to the village of Grassington. It follows well established paths throughout and there are no real route finding difficulties throughout the walk. I have graded it as strenuous mainly due to the distance, but there are no steep ascents and the paths are good throughout.

Distance	12 miles (19 km)
Ascent	1,000 feet (300m)
Time	5 hours
Grading	Strenuous
Suggested Map	Outdoor Leisure OL2 Yorkshire Dales Southern & Western
Starting point	Grid Reference: 002640
Parking	Grassington Square or Dales National Park car park
How to get there	Grassington is 15 miles north-west of Ilkley on the B6160. Take the A65 towards Skipton and at Addingham turn onto the B6160
Terrain	Good path (The Dales Way) out of Grassington to above Conistone and then moorland track to Mosedale and Yarnbury. Field paths back to Grassington

Grassington

Grassington, although often described by local people as a village, was granted a Royal Charter for a market and fair in 1282 giving it market town status. The market was held regularly until about 1860.

A change in land use from the early 17th century, when lead mining began to assume more importance, brought some prosperity, but Grassington's heyday arrived during the late 18th and early 19th centuries. The opening of the Yorkshire Dales Railway to Threshfield in 1901 also brought new visitors, many of whom settled. In its heyday it boasted a population of over 3,000 – today it is only a third of that.

Today Grassington's main industry is tourism. It boasts a small cobbled square around which is a selection of food, clothing and gift shops, alongside a number of small cafés, restaurants and hotels. It is the quintessential Dales small market town and attracts many thousands of visitors throughout the year, both in summer and winter.

In the summer Grassington holds its two-week long annual arts festival encompassing music, performance and visual arts, held in a variety of venues around the town and neighbouring villages. It attracts many top class performers and over the years these have included stars such as Lesley Garrett, the Ukulele Orchestra of Great Britain, Jules Holland and his Rhythm and Blues Orchestra, Black Dyke Mills Band, Lee Evans, Gerry and the Pacemakers, Boney M, The Real Thing and The Searchers.

At the end of the year the town holds a series of Dickensian Christmas Festivals, on the first three Saturday's in December. During these three Saturdays, Grassington is transported back to the time of Charles Dickens with Christmas lights, the village square and the streets transformed into a traditional market with shopkeepers, villagers and visitors dressed in Victorian costume. It culminates with the torchlight procession around the village with Mary and Joseph leading a donkey, ending with a short carol service in the square. After this, there's evening entertainment in the Town Hall, courtesy of the local Players and Singers.

Grassington also is rich in history. This is one of the richest archaeological sites in the north of England, thanks to the gradual migration of the settlement towards its present location some half-mile east of the river, leaving the older sites still exposed. Here you can see Bronze Age burial mounds, Celtic villages and fields, Romano-British settlements, and medieval farmsteads in close proximity. Research has suggested that these settlements date back to around 2,000BC. There is also evidence of two Celtic villages located between Grassington and Bastow Wood.

The Romans arrived in Upper Wharfedale around 50AD, departing in the 5th century, during which time they quickly developed the area around Grassington as an important grain growing area comprising hundreds of acres of Romano-British development building on the earlier Celtic agricultural site.

The current town of Grassington goes back a very long way, probably to the

7th century, since the Domesday Book in the year 1087 recorded that at this time there was already 300 acres of arable and meadow land in its vicinity, upon which tax was paid to the King. This site would have been chosen on account of it being located on a fairly level shelf above the more densely wooded slope leading down to the river.

Lead mining in the vicinity of Grassington has been carried out since the 15th century when George Clifford, Earl of Cumberland, became Lord of the Manor. He brought skilled men from his Derbyshire mines to work in the mines on Grassington Moor and miners from Swaledale and Cornwall also settled here bringing with them valuable expertise relating to mining techniques. A century or so later, in 1750, the Duke of Devonshire married one of the Clifford heiresses and came to be the Lord of the Manor of Grassington. He developed Grassington with the construction of a water system, the erection of a large new smelt mill and the tall chimney that is still an important feature today. He then greatly improved the road between Grassington and Gargrave, where he owned a wharf on the Leeds to Liverpool canal.

As a result of this great influx of new people into the area, many new properties were built in Grassington from the latter part of the 17th century up to the early part of the 19th century. Also a number of the existing larger properties were each split into two or three smaller dwelling units and thus the unique and quaint character of Grassington came into being. In 1855, the Duke of Devonshire built the Mechanics Institute, with a library for the education and welfare of the miners. This was enlarged in 1895, and in 1896, and the Duke handed over the Institute to the village who added a large hall, stage and dressing rooms in 1923, and the building underwent a further expansion with the addition of a studio theatre and nursery school in 1998.

The lead mining industry declined in the late 1870s and many miners

Mine entrance

Mine workings

and their families gradually left the area. Shortly afterwards, Grassington House changed its use from a private house into a boarding house, thus heralding the birth of the tourist industry which is still so important to Grassington today. With the coming of the railway in 1902, many new people, mainly Bradford commuters, moved into the area. The town has gradually expanded over the last century, from a low point in 1903, when the population was little more than 300, to around 1,100 today. Agriculture, quarrying, and tourism are the mainstays of employment in Grassington today supplemented by many professional commuters, artists and retired people, making a lively mix of locals and 'offcumd'uns' (a Yorkshire term for anyone coming to a town or village from further afield).

The Walk

The walk starts from the centre of Grassington and follows the Dales Way out of the town heading north towards Kettlewell. Go up Chapel Street and before reaching Town Head Farm, turn right up the existing right of way up Bank Lane. This is followed round to the left and on until the right of way makes a sharp right turn. A new path has been constructed from here across fields in a westerly direction to rejoin the previous route of the Dales Way well to the north of the farm. After climbing through the next few fields you will gain tremendous views of the surrounding dales landscape. Continue above the Old Pasture above Conistone village until you reach the junction with Scot Gate Lane coming up from the village.

Here the Dales Way continues straight forward but we now turn right onto the track heading north-east for about ½ mile (700m) before turning initially south-east and then again north-east on a track towards Kelber Gate and Mossdale Scar. This is followed for nearly a mile (1500m) where you will see a track off to the right. We are going to take this shortly but it is worth making the small diversion up to Mossedale Scar and caverns. These are easily spotted on the far side of Mossdale Beck and attached to the rockface at the caverns is a plaque which reads: "in everlasting memory from the families of David Adamson aged 26, Geoffrey Warren Boireau aged 24, William Frakes aged 19, John Ogden aged 20, Michael John Ryan aged 17, Colin Richard Vickers aged 23, who rest here in Mossdale Caverns where they died 24th June 1967. I will lift up mine eyes unto the hills from whence cometh my strength." These young cavers were sought for extensively by the Cave Rescue Organisation at the time but were never found. Because of the dangerous water levels in the caverns it was decided to close these by blocking off the entrances and the bodies were left in the caverns as a permanent resting place.

Retrace your steps to the track which is now on your left and this is followed

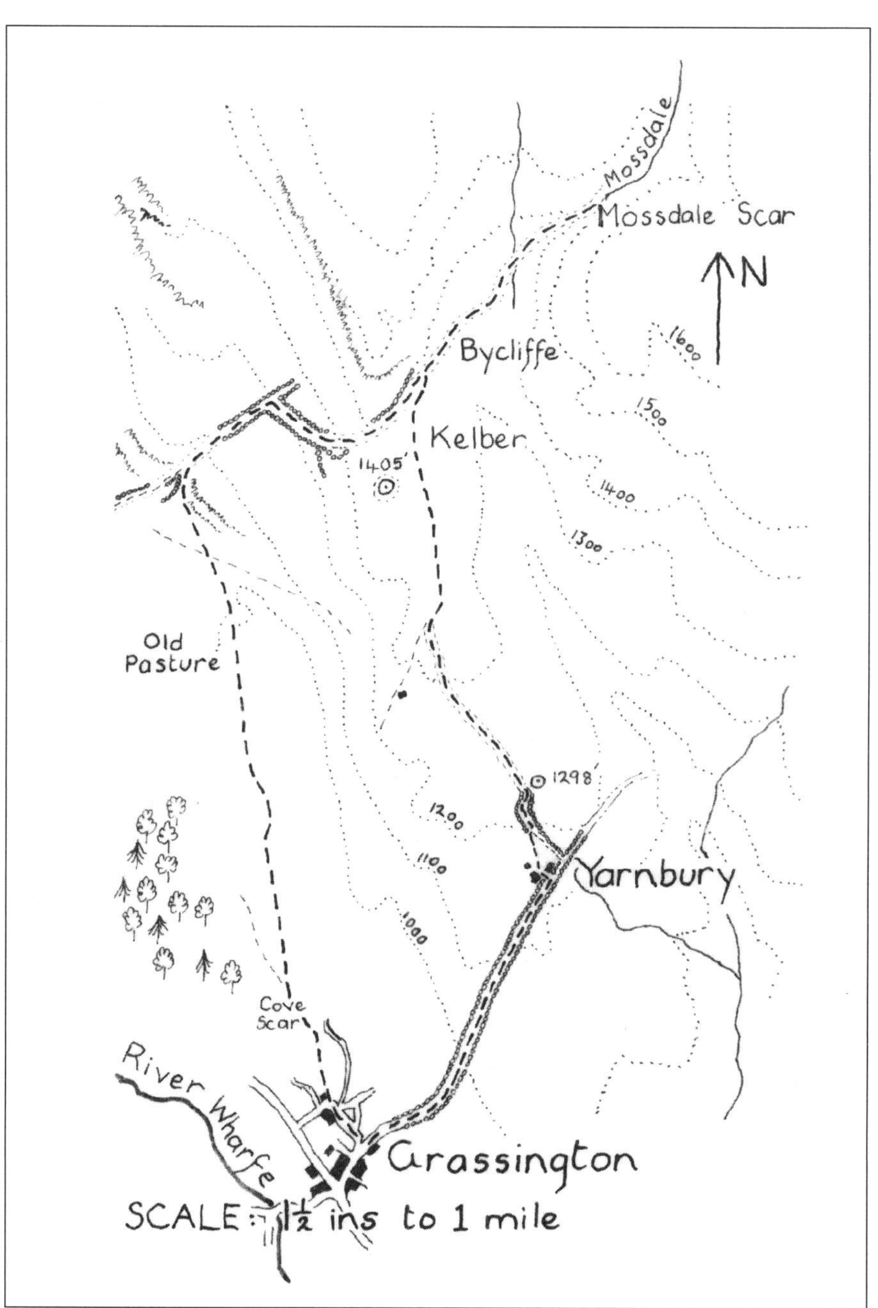

Mossdale
Mossdale Scar
N
Bycliffe
1600
1500
Kelber
1400
1405'
1300
Old
Pasture
1298'
1200
1100
Yarnbury
1000
Cove
Scar
River Wharfe
Grassington
SCALE : 1½ ins to 1 mile

in a south-easterly direction down to Bycliffe Hill a distance of 1¼ miles (2km) and then southwards for just over ½ mile (1km) to a crossroads where five tracks converge. Take the track to the right (heading west) which you follow for a further 1¼ miles (2km) down to the hamlet of Yarnbury. This is a scene of industrial desolation set among the beauty of the dales and well worth exploring for a short while before the return to Grassington. You're now in an area of some of the finest lead mining remains in England. There are various highlights, but the great centrepiece is the chimney (built in 1849) and the system of flues running up to it. The flues run from 'cupola corner' where the lead was smelted up the side of the hill and finish at the chimney.

From here a minor road heading south-west takes you the remaining 1½ miles (2½ km) back into Grassington where there are plenty of pubs and tea rooms to choose from at the end of a most enjoyable walk amidst some great Dales scenery.

Kilnsey Crag

WHARFEDALE WALK 5
Otley Chevin

Climbing from the market town of Otley this walk reaches the summit of Otley Chevin, the 925 foot high hill to the south of the town, before heading east through Danefield Forest Park. It then descends to Old Pool Bank and returns via the old disused railway track.

Distance	**5 miles (8 km)**
Ascent	**1,000 feet (300m)**
Time	**2.5 hours**
Grading	**Moderate**
Suggested Map	**OS Explorer 297 Lower Wharfedale & The Washburn Valley**
Starting point	**Grid Reference: SE 203454**
Parking	**Station Road, Otley**
How to get there	**Otley is 10 miles north-west of Leeds on the main A660 signed for Skipton**
Terrain	**Good track from the town with steep ascent to Surprise View, woodland paths and tracks to Old Pool Bank and field paths and old railway track back to Otley**

The Chevin

The name 'Chevin' is said to derive from the Celtic 'Cefyn' or 'Cefu' meaning a ridge: which is exactly what it is. The story of the Chevin begins some 350 million years ago when, early in the Earth's history, land masses looked very different from those we see today. At this time, 100 million years before the dinosaurs, and with land masses forming a single continent called Pangaea, sea levels rose and fell periodically. These rises and falls created thin mud layers populated by marine life which left evidence of their presence in the form of fossils, some of which are to be found in the rocks of the Chevin today.

Later, but still over 300 million years ago, rivers flowing out of mountainous lands to the north of where Britain is now, deposited layers of mud and sand over a wide and shallow delta within whose area Leeds and the Chevin are situated. These successive layers of sediment were, in turn, eroded and re-deposited before being eventually buried and subjected to the great pressures which eventually hardened them into Millstone Grit.

It was at around this time that Almscliff Crag was formed, as a consequence of an underwater landslip. Eventually, as continents moved and collided, the layers of rock were deformed and the Chevin, part of the long ridge from Addingham to Harewood, was created.

With the Chevin now formed, the story does not end there. During the Ice Age the area, including the Chevin, was clothed in thick ice and the Wharfedale

Summit Rocks

glacier reshaped the land over which it ground relentlessly. Evidence of these remain today in the form of limestone blocks which were transported from the Dales in the north by the glacier which moved through the 'Guiseley Gap' and deposited them near to Reva, four miles to the south-west. Even more recently, just some 20,000 years ago, with annual temperatures hovering around a chilly -6°C to -9°C, this area saw the last great advance of the Ice Age and it is possible that, once again, the Chevin was covered.

The Chevin is largely covered in attractive old woodland and heathland. A Roman road ran along the top of the Chevin, part of the road that linked Eboracum (York), Calcaria (Tadcaster) and Olicana (Ilkley), possibly on the same route as the modern road, Yorkgate, or perhaps about 800m to the south. This route along the top of the Chevin is also now part of 'The Ebor Way' a modern long-distance walk from York to Ilkley.

The highest point of the Chevin is Surprise View, 925 ft (282 metres) above sea level at grid reference SE204442. This point offers extensive views of Otley and Wharfedale, and has an adjacent car park. It has been the site of a beacon where beacons were lit to celebrate both the Queen's Golden and Diamond Jubilees and also the start of the Millennium, and each Easter a cross is erected at the summit of the Chevin. The cross, the brainchild of the Otley Council of Christian Churches, has become a source of comfort and inspiration to many people over the last forty years since it was first erected in 1969.

The first cross, which was 36ft high, was blown down in high winds on the first night it was put up. The badly damaged cross was worked on overnight and put up once again the next day – six feet shorter. It has been erected every Easter since. A new cross was built for Easter 2000; the wood used in the new cross was from timbers salvaged from the bombed Arndale Centre in Manchester. The new cross was built by Brent Thompson of Ilkley. At least 40 people are needed to pull the cross into place at Surprise View where it remains for four weeks throughout the Easter celebrations.

Chevin Cross

Otley

Our walk starts from the centre of Otley, an ancient market town, located 12 miles north-west of Leeds. Otley's name is derived from Othe, Otho or Otta, a Saxon personal name and 'leah', a woodland clearing in Old English. It was recorded as Ottanlege in 972 and Otelai or Othelia in the Domesday Book of 1086. Otley is just off the main A660 from Leeds to Skipton (a bypass was built about 25 years ago) and is served by public transport from both of these places. It is also possible to come by train from Leeds and Bradford to Menston station using the Wharfedale line and then catch the connecting bus service into Otley.

The town dates from Saxon times and was part of an extensive manor granted by Athelstan to the See of York. The Archbishops of York had a residence and were lords of the manor, their palace was located on the site now occupied by the Manor House. Otley is relatively close to Leeds and may have formed part of the kingdom of Elmet. Remains of the Archbishop's Palace were found during the construction of St. Joseph's Junior School. The town grew in the first half of the 13th century when the archbishops laid out burgage plots to attract merchants and tradespeople. The burgage plots were on Boroughgate, Walkergate and Kirkgate. Bondgate was for tenants who did not have 'burgage' privileges. A leper hospital was founded on the road to Harewood beyond Cross Green.

Documented history for the market begins in 1222 when King Henry III granted the first Royal Charter. The town had two cattle markets, Wharfedale Farmers' Auction Mart on East Chevin Road and the Bridge End Auction Mart which has closed. Market days are Tuesday, Friday and Saturday, and there is a Farmers' Market on the last Sunday of every month.

Thomas Chippendale, the cabinetmaker, was born in a cottage at the junction of Boroughgate and Wesley Street and his statue stands next to the old Grammar School that he attended in Manor Square. J.M.W. Turner, the painter, visited Otley in 1797, aged 22, when commissioned to paint watercolours of the area. He was so attracted to Otley and the surrounding area that he returned time and time again. His friendship with Walter Ramsden-Fawkes made him a regular visitor to Farnley Hall, two miles from Otley. The stormy backdrop of *Hannibal Crossing The Alps* is reputed to have been inspired by a storm over Otley's Chevin while Turner was staying at Farnley Hall.

The town was also regularly visited by John Wesley, the founder of the Methodist Church. He visited Otley on some twenty occasions and struck up a great friendship with the Ritchie family, who he stayed with on most of his visits at their house on Boroughgate.

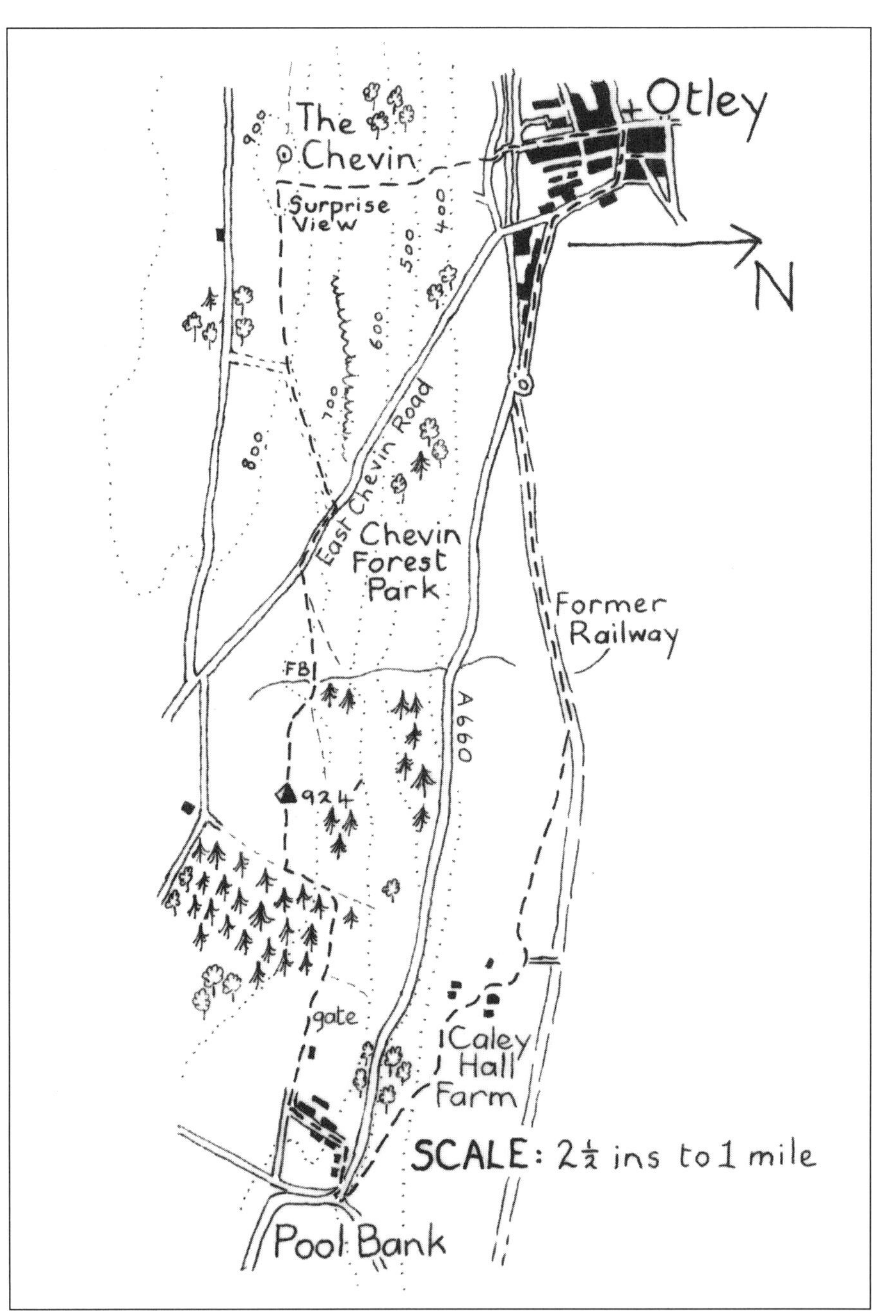

The
Chevin
Otley
Surprise
View
900
400
500
600
700
800
East Chevin Road
Chevin
Forest
Park
Former
Railway
FB
A660
924
gate
Caley
Hall
Farm
SCALE: 2½ ins to 1 mile
Pool Bank
N

The Wharfedale Press, which revolutionised nineteenth century printing, was invented and manufactured in Otley. The town also hosts the country's oldest annual agricultural show, each May. The Grammar School in the town was founded in 1607 by Thomas Cave who named it 'The Grammar School of Prince Henry.' It is built in the Elizabethan style and was also used as a court-house. A new school, entitled Prince Henry's Grammar School, was built in Farnley Lane and was erected in 1923 to accommodate the increasing number of pupils . The gradual move to the new premises took place over the next few years with the official opening taking place on 25th July 1927 by Sir James Hinchliffe, Chairman of the West Riding County Council.

The Walk

Our walk starts at the bottom of Station Road by the parish church at the end of Kirkgate (the road to the church). If you stand by Blue Octopus Recruitment Agency facing south you will see The Chevin in front of you rising nearly 1,000 feet above the town. Go up Station Road and go across the Otley by-pass using the footbridge. Cross the minor road on the far side, Birdcage Walk, and take the narrow passageway (known as a 'ginnel' in the Yorkshire area) in front of you. Follow this uphill until you reach the end of Johnny Lane at which point the route then heads up into the wood. This is a stepped path and rises steeply.

At the end of the wood it levels out for a few yards and this is a good point to stop and regain your breath before the final pull up to the summit at Surprise View. The path makes a beeline up to the summit, which should be reached in between 5 and 10 minutes from this point depending upon your level of fitness. Incidentally, in the annual fell race up the Chevin from the centre of Otley the runners get to the top **and back** in around 16 minutes. I have run back down the Chevin into Otley in around this time but most people will take between 40 minutes and an hour just to climb to the summit.

As mentioned earlier the view from the summit is outstanding with views all across Lower Wharfedale and on a clear day as far as Whernside to the west and York Minster to the east. There is a direction finder near to the summit and this gives distances of some of the main places it is possible to see from the summit.

From the top of the Chevin we are now heading in an easterly direction along a good path, flagged in parts. This drops down to cross the East Chevin Road and once crossed turn right and follow the path up to the car park and entrance to the Danefield Estate. This estate, formerly owned by Lord Horton-Fawkes from Farnley Hall, was given to the people of Otley at the end of the Second World War for public enjoyment and is now managed by Leeds City Council by their Parks Department.

From the car park follow the path straight ahead, noticing the tree donated by Queen Elizabeth II at the start of the main path. Follow this down over a footbridge across a stream and continue straight ahead on this path, which rises slightly. After about ½ mile, close to the wood at the end of the track, the path goes down to the left with the wood on your right. A new pond area at the bottom of the hill is crossed using the wooden footbridge and then you need to turn right going under the electric pylons to a gate at the end. Go through the gate and follow the tack for a further ¼ mile until you reach Park Road on the left. Go down here to the end and down a set of steps to reach the main A660 Leeds to Otley road. Cross this with care and at the top of Old Pool Bank you will see a footbath sign down to the left.

The path descends fairly steeply with fine views across to your right of the Arthington Viaduct and Almscliffe Crag in the distance. Drop down until you reach the old railway line that used to run from Otley to Leeds. Turn left on this and follow it for about a mile until you reach the main road again at the roundabout by the Otley bypass. Turn right here down Leeds Road and follow this for a further ½ mile into the centre of town.

Otley has a large number of eating establishments and pubs in the town centre where you can find refreshment at the end of the walk. The town centre also has a wide variety of shops to suit all tastes – as well as a market on a Tuesday, Friday and Saturday – and it is worth spending a short time here before either returning to your car or heading for the bus station for your transport home.

NIDDERDALE INTRODUCTION

Although technically outside of the Yorkshire Dales National Park boundary, Nidderdale has been designated as an Area of Outstanding Natural Beauty and has every right to be included in any definition of the Yorkshire Dales.

The Nidd rises on the wild moors on the eastern flanks of Great Whernside and Little Whernside flowing out from the moorland reservoirs of Scar House and Angram.

Further down the valley the river feeds another large reservoir, Gouthwaite, just above Pateley Bridge. Below Pateley Bridge the dale becomes much gentler in character as the River Nidd flows onwards to Knaresborough and out of the dale to eventually join with the River Ouse near the historic English Civil War battlefield at Marston Moor in the Vale of York.

Attractions and places in and near Nidderdale include: How Stean Gorge near Lofthouse and Middlesmoor towards the head of the dale, Stump Cross Caverns near Pateley Bridge, Brimham Rocks near Summerbridge, Mother Shipton's Cave at Knaresborough and Ripley Castle near Harrogate.

Nidderdale is often divided into 'Upper Nidderdale' and 'Lower Nidderdale' – lying upstream and downstream of Pateley Bridge, respectively.

Dominating the source of the Nidd is the bulky form of Great Whernside which separates Wharfedale from Nidderdale. At 2310 feet (704 metres) high it is 105 feet (32 metres) lower than Whernside in Ribblesdale but because of its rise from both Kettlewell, on its western slopes, and Angram Reservoir, on the eastern slopes, it was originally perceived as being higher and that is why it received the 'Great' prefix.

Scar House and Angram Reservoirs are two of the reservoirs in Upper Nidderdale, the other being Gouthwaite Reservoir further downstream. Angram and Scar House were built to supply water to the Bradford area of West Yorkshire. Water from here is transferred to Chellow Heights via the Nidd Aqueduct, which is a major engineering achievement as no pumping is involved. The dam at Scar House was completed in 1936 and contains over one million tonnes of masonry. It rises to 180 feet (55 metres) above the river and is almost 2,000 feet (600 metres) long. The dam height is 233 feet (71 metres) and the reservoir is fed almost exclusively from the Angram dam.

One of the notable attractions in the area is How Stean Gorge, a deep wooded limestone ravine near the villages of Middlesmoor and Lofthouse. A stream called How Stean Beck flows along the bottom of How Stean Gorge, and there are also two caves (How Stean Tunnel and Tom Taylor's Cave) which lead out from the sides of the gorge. The gorge is one of the most beautiful and interesting places not only in the region, but in the whole world.

Middlesmoor is at the head of Nidderdale, an unspoilt village with cobbled streets leading to the church. From here you can see down the valley with breathtaking views along the Nidderdale Way. Lofthouse, a mile further down the valley is a typical farming village and is the mid-point on the 42-mile Six Dales Hike which starts in Settle and finishes at the River Swale near Pickhill. The moorland road out of Lofhouse leads over Masham Moor and connects Nidderdale with lower Wensleydale.

The major village in the dale is Pateley Bridge which is more like a small market town. Originally settled as a lead mining village, it takes its name from 'Pate' – an old Yorkshire dialect word for 'Badger'. Until 1964 Pateley was the terminus of the railway line running up Nidderdale from Nidd Valley Junction, near Harrogate. Between 1907 and 1937 the Nidd Valley Light Railway ran further up the dale serving the reservoirs. It was owned by Bradford Corporation Waterworks Department and the Corporation also operated its public passenger services. As far as the Waterworks Department was concerned, the railway's primary purpose was to carry goods, materials and labour to construction sites high in the Nidd valley. Passenger stations were provided at Pateley Bridge, Wath, Ramsgill, and Lofthouse, which was the public passenger terminus of the line.

The moors above Pateley Bridge are home to Brimham Rocks, which are balancing rock formations located on Brimham Moor. The rocks stand in an area owned by the National Trust. There are many variations of rock formations, caused by the Millstone Grit being eroded by water, glaciation and wind, most of which have achieved amazing shapes. Many of the formations have been named, though some imagination is required, and the correct viewing angle is helpful. Examples are The Sphinx, The Watchdog, The Camel, The Turtle and The Dancing Bear. The children's television show *Roger and the Rottentrolls* was filmed in Brimham Rocks and Brimham Rocks features in the Bee Gees' video *You Win Again*.

The River Nidd continues from Pateley Bridge passing through Summerbridge and in a further few miles it reaches Ripley Castle. The castle dates from the 15th century and has been the home of the Ingilby family for 700 years. The present owner is Sir Thomas Ingilby, 6th Baronet, the 28th generation. The castle, which has a priest hole, is open for public tours. The landscaped castle grounds and ornamental lakes are also open to the public.

Five miles (8km) further downstream is the ancient market town of Knaresborough. The town is situated around a magnesian limestone gorge where the famous Mother Shipton's Cave and the adjacent Petrifying Well (where running water gradually coats suspended objects in a limestone deposit – thus turning them to stone) is located. Knaresborough also boasts a fine castle and several other attractions – including a house and chapel (St. Michael's Cave) hewn out of a rock face at the side of the gorge. Knaresborough castle was first built by a Norman baron in c.1100 on the cliff above the River Nidd. There is documentary evidence dating from 1130 referring to works carried out at the castle by Henry I. In the 1170s Hugh de Moreville and his followers took refuge there after assassinating Thomas Becket. King John regarded Knaresborough as an important northern fortress and spent £1,290 on improvements to the castle. The castle was later rebuilt between 1301 and 1307 by Edward I and later completed by Edward II, including the great keep. John of Gaunt acquired the castle in 1372, adding it to the vast holdings of the Duchy of Lancaster. The castle was taken by Parliamentarian troops in 1644 during the Civil War, and largely destroyed in 1648 not as the result of warfare, but because of an order from Parliament to dismantle all Royalist castles. Indeed, many town centre buildings are built of 'castle stone'.

After leaving Knaresborough, the Nidd flows below the 'Great North Road' (the A1) before joining the River Ouse one miles (2km) east of Moor Monkton.

NIDDERDALE WALK 1
Brimham Rocks

Brimham Rocks is a fascinating place to spend some time and is the mid-point of the walk that follows. Rather than just a wander round the rocks from the National Trust car park, I have started this route down in the valley of the Nidd at Summerbridge. Following an initial climb up to Brimham Moor, and after visiting the rocks, the route then crosses the road and uses tracks over the moor to return downhill back to Summerbridge.

Distance	8 miles (13km)
Ascent	950 feet (290m)
Time	4 hours
Grading	Moderate
Suggested Map	OS Explorer 298 – Nidderdale
Starting point	Grid Reference: *???*
Parking	Summerbridge village
How to get there	Summerbridge is located on the B6165 which links Ripley on the A61 between Harrogate and Ripon with Pateley Bridge
Terrain	Mostly good tracks and footpaths throughout with some minor road walking

Brimham Rocks

Brimham Rocks are a set of balanced rock formations located on Brimham Moor some 10 miles west of Harrogate and four miles east of Pateley Bridge. The rocks stand up to 100 feet (30 metres) high in an area owned by the National Trust which is part of the Nidderdale Area of Outstanding Natural Beauty.

Rock formations

There are many variations of rock formations, caused by the millstone grit being eroded by water, glaciation and wind, most of which have achieved amazing shapes. Many of the formations have been named, though some imagination is required and the correct viewing angle is helpful for these. Examples are The Sphinx, The Watchdog, The Camel, The Turtle and The Dancing Bear.

320 million years ago, a huge river washed down grit and sand from granite mountains in northern Scotland and Norway. A delta formed, covering half of Yorkshire. Increasing layers of grit and sand, along with rock crystals of feldspar and quartz, built up to form the tough sandstone known as millstone grit, the exposed sections of which can be seen today at Brimham Rocks. A feature of the rocks is their cross-bedding. As the water from the river flowed, it created bedforms such as ripples or dunes on the floor of the channel. Sediment was deposited on the downcurrent side of these bedforms at an angle – not horizontally. The layering is inclined and dips in the direction the water was moving.

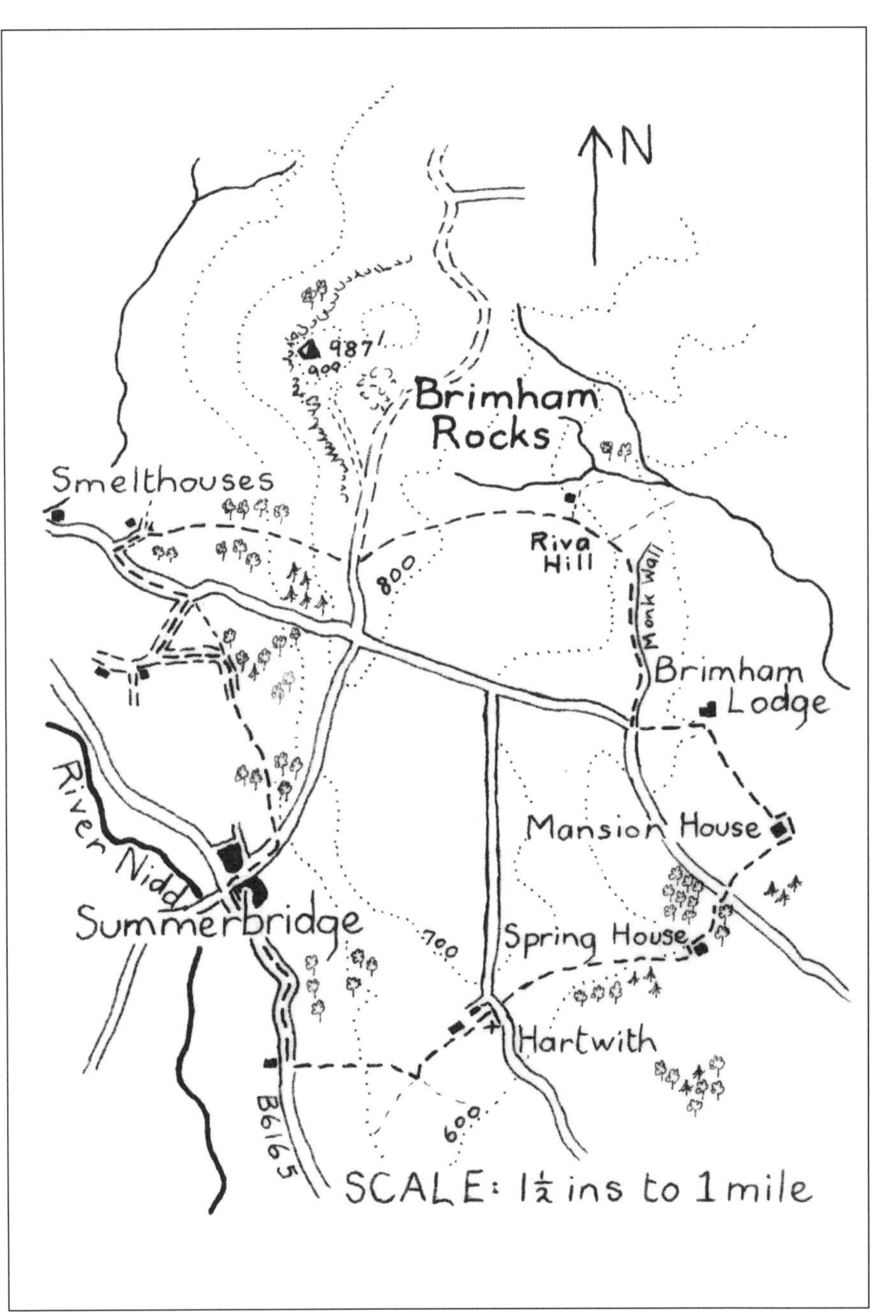

N
Brimham Rocks
987
900
Smelthouses
Riva Hill
800
Monk Wall
Brimham Lodge
Mansion House
River Nidd
Summerbridge
700
Spring House
B6165
Hartwith
600
SCALE: 1½ ins to 1 mile

Most of the rocks here owe their bizarre shapes to erosion during and after the Devensian glaciation. For example, Idol Rock was most likely formed just after the last glaciation when the land lacked any plant cover. Here, sand-blasting at ground level wore away the softer layers of the rock producing a tiny plinth with a massive top. Freeze-thaw action on the joints and bedding planes has shaped many of the tors such as the Dancing Bear.

The Walk

The route of the walk starts in Summerbridge, 2½ miles east of Pateley Bridge. Immediately after leaving the village there is a steep ascent of Hartwith Bank before leaving the road to enter Old Spring Wood. In the wood you will encounter a lovely man-made pond where ducks, moorhens and geese can usually be found. This particular wood dates back as far as the Iron Age. In those ancient days the wood was used for grazing stock. Later on in medieval times it became a hunting ground, part of the 'Chase of Nidderdale' but now it is quiet and serene. After Old Spring Wood you need to follow the track north-north-east though the smaller Braisty Woods before heading down the quiet road towards Smelthouses.

Just before reaching Smelthouses it is necessary to turn right along a bridleway to Low Wood House which leads to one of the toughest parts of the walk. This is a 500 foot (150m) ascent along Monk's Route, one of many in the area which was used by monks to access their estates. After Monk's Route you emerge on the road just south of Brimham Rocks car park.

It is now time to explore some of the rocks around this part of the National Trust owned estate before returning back to the car park for the second half of the walk. At the far end of rocks is the National Trust information centre where refreshments can be obtained if you wish to partake.

After leaving the National Trust car park at Brimham Rocks head east across the open moorland towards Riva Hill. This section of the walk can be boggy after a period of rain but the track is fairly good and it is easy to divert onto the heather over any boggy sections. Riva Hill is a Bronze Age site with carved rocks.

After Riva Hill you need to turn from an easterly direction to a southerly one and follow a bridleway with the Monk's Wall on your left. The wall has a particular characteristic of large boulders, or orthostats providing it with a solid base. After Monk's Wall you head towards a set of telecommunications masts in the field close to Brimham Lodge. You now head south-eastwards to Mansion House Farm, turning right here towards Spring House Farm. After passing the farm the track continues to Spring Wood and then over open fields to the small hamlet of Hartwith. Hartwith consists of a chapel, a school house (more like the cottage it is now) and a church. A few distant farms complete the makeup of this quiet part of rural Nidderdale. After Hartwith you continue walking south-west and then west past Prospect Farm to an old disused quarry. From the quarry you descend slightly to the Ripley to Summerbridge Road at Dougill Hall.

Originally you could descend from here down to the river and follow this into Summerbridge but in 2009 the local council stopped maintaining this path and the route is now no longer possible. Instead, therefore, you have to end the walk with the final half mile on the road back to the village.

Rock formations

Lofthouse to Scar House

This is a walk I know well from my days both walking and marshalling on the Six Dales Hike in the 1970s and early '80s. In fact the checkpoint on the moors above Scar House was the first one that I helped on back in September 1975. Both Lofthouse and Middlesmoor (which we will visit on the return leg of the walk) have been checkpoints on the walking completion over the years.

Distance	7.5 miles (12 km)
Ascent	900 feet (275m)
Time	4 hours
Grading	Moderate
Suggested Map	OS Explorer 298 – Nidderdale
Starting point	Grid Reference: 101734
Parking	Lofthouse Village car park
How to get there	To reach Lofthouse take the minor road out of Pateley Bridge which is located at the junction of the B6165 and B6265. Lofthouse is 6 miles up this road
Terrain	Moorland tracks with some small sections on minor roads

Lofthouse

The monks of Fountains Abbey had a grange at Lofthouse and also built the first house here, which still stands today. Up until 1936 a railway ran up the valley from Pateley Bridge to carry workers involved in constructing the Scar House Reservoir. Work commenced on this before the First World War and continued after the war for a number of years. The Nidd Valley Light Railway was owned by Bradford Corporation Waterworks Department and the Corporation also operated its public passenger services. As far as the Waterworks Department was concerned, the railway's primary purpose was to carry goods, materials and labour to construction sites high in the Nidd valley, where two large reservoirs were built at Angram (1904-1919) and Scar House (1921-1936). However, the 6-mile stretch of line between Pateley Bridge and Lofthouse was constructed under the terms of a pre-existing Light Railway Order of 1901, taken over by Bradford Corporation in 1904, which obliged the Corporation to operate a public passenger service between those two places. Thus, Lofthouse was the public passenger terminus of the line. The station also possessed a modest yard where wagons were assembled for the steep climb to the reservoir sites, a further six miles up the valley. The industrial 0-6-0T locomotives used by the Corporation and the contractor, John Best & Sons of Edinburgh, could take only three or four loaded wagons each up the grades to the reservoirs, so even quite short trains had to be banked. The NVLR was opened in 1907, closed to passengers on the last day of 1929, and was closed completely in 1937.

Buildings in the village of Lofthouse cover many periods – older houses alongside the twisting main street and some newer properties further down the village and stretching down the dale to Ramsgill. The famous Lofthouse Brass Band practises on a Monday evening and other evening entertainment can be found in the Village Hall and Institute where a snooker table is installed.

Scar House

Opened in 1936, Scar House is one of a string of reservoirs in Nidderdale that serve the city of Bradford, 30 miles (48km) to the south – the others include Angram, to the west, and Gouthwaite, down the valley towards Pateley Bridge. It is still possible to see evidence around the dam of the remains of the village in which the navvies who built it lived and of the ancillary buildings where they stored machinery and dressed the stone. There were some protests before the dams were built about the drowning of parts of the valley, and there were rumours that Nidderdale was left out of the Yorkshire Dales National Park when it was designated in 1954 because the reservoirs had blighted the landscape. Redress was made in 1994 when 603 square miles (1562 sq km) of Nidderdale became an Area of Outstanding Natural Beauty.

The Walk

To commence the walk, head north out of Lofthouse village and climb the hill on the road that is signed towards Masham. After a ¼ mile (400m) as the road

Scar House Reservoir

bends right, go left down a grassy track to a gate. Continue along the lower track through four gates, and then follow the waymark signs to the river bank. Cross the river to reach another gate, and then continue along the bank, over two stiles to a gate. At this point you need to turn right towards Thrope farm.

Just after the first buildings on your left, go through a gateway, then through another gate and on to a riverside path. Follow the path over the next two stiles to a footbridge with a stile at its end near to Limley Farm. Cross over the stile and turn left to continue along the riverside, going through a gate and over a stile to reach a gate on to a track. Turn left over the cattle grid, then right just before a bridge. Where the track bends right, go straight ahead through four stiles to a gate.

Cross a stream to another gate and follow the fence down to a field. Go through a waymarked gate to pass between the buildings at Low Wooldale until you reach another gate. The track now climbs right and goes through five gates, turning towards the dam and descending to a track. Turn right and go through a gate where the track becomes metalled. You have now reached Scar House so cross the dam and head for the car park on the far side.

Continue along the left side of the reservoir to a Nidderdale Way signpost, just before a gate. Follow the track left uphill. The track levels and goes through a gate. A few paces beyond, go right through a gate in the wall. Go diagonally towards the wall on your right, and then follow a faint path as it bends left. When you reach a more defined track turn left and go over two cattle grids. While it is possible here to turn right and drop directly down to Howstean Gorge this misses out visiting the beautiful village of Middlesmoor with its fantastic view down the valley. Continue along the track after the

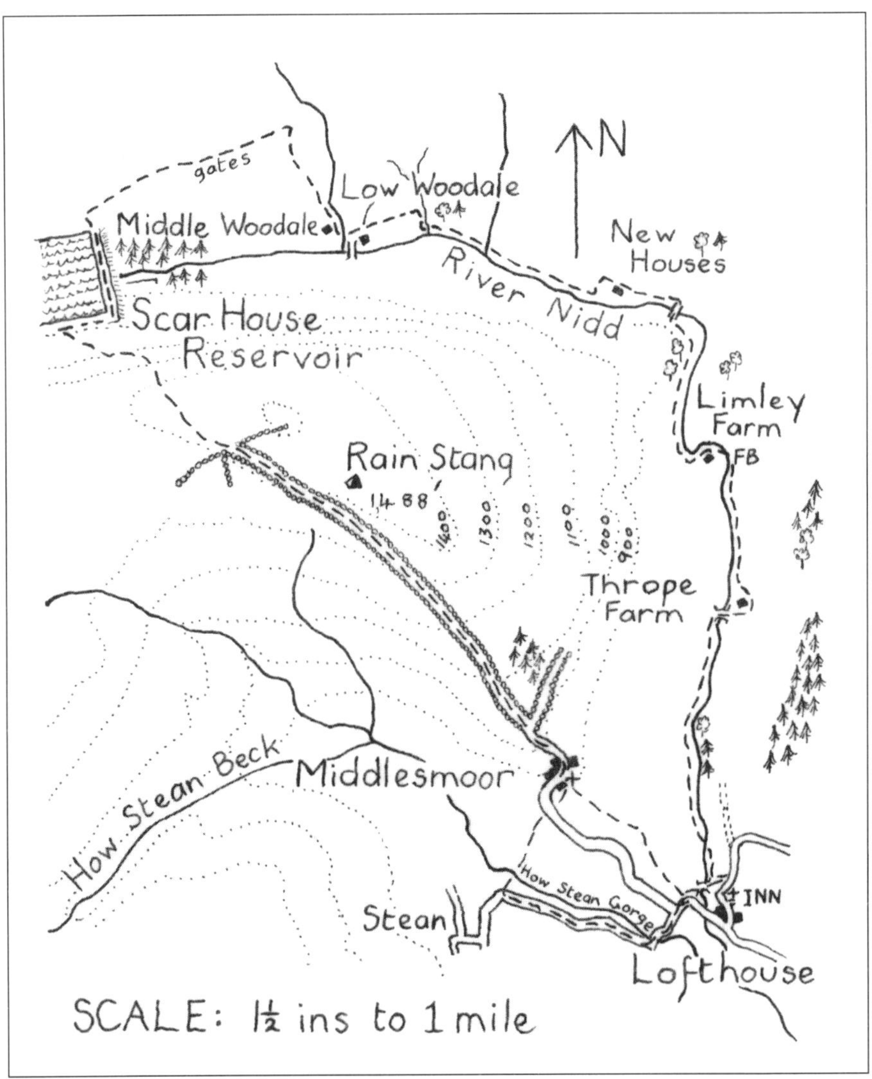

cattle grid until you reach Moor Lane coming in from your left. Follow this for the remaining ¼ mile (400m) into the centre of the village.

Middlesmoor is the northernmost village in Nidderdale and has a good pub (The Crown) and St. Chad's Church where from the churchyard there is a most spectacular panorama down the Nidd valley to Gowthwaite Reservoir and beyond. St. Chad's commands a superb position on a spur of land looking down the length of Nidderdale. There can hardly be a better view from a churchyard anywhere in the British Isles! If you wish to head straight back to Lofthouse from this point you can go out of the end of the churchyard and straight down the hill passing Halfway House and Park House and then turning left to cross the bridge over the stream back into the village. However, by doing so you will miss out on one of the most spectacular parts of the walk, a visit to Howstean Gorge.

Opposite the church and before the minor road drops down to Lofthouse take a small track on the right heading west and follow this for 100 yards (90m) until it forks. Take the left hand fork and go through four fields using

Middlesmoor Church view

the stiles. Descend the bank until you reach a footbridge over the river and climb up the opposite bank to Well House. Turn left and join a good pebbled track, past a converted barn and then a short uphill climb leads past a white-doored cottage on the right and a lean-to shed. Go over the cattle grid onto a tarmac lane and turn left into Stean village.

Go downhill past Wayside Cottage and Beckside Cottage to leave Stean village. On the left-hand side down the single track road is Howstean Gorge. This is a spectacular limestone gorge, with its caves and waterfalls, and was described by a professor of geology at Oxford University as being "unequalled anywhere in England". The beck plunges through a canyon of jagged rocks, which rise up to 70 feet on either side. There are two bridges over the gorge and spectacular views can be obtained from these. Of the caves alongside the gorge the most famous is Tom Taylor's cave near the first footbridge. It is 530 feet long, with steps at each end, and is a safe walk-through cave with little water. In 1868, two young boys discovered 32 Roman coins in this cave. Howstean Tunnel is 170 feet in length and goes under the road and also can be explored.

At the end of the gorge is Howstean Café which if open serves delicious teas and cream cakes and is well worth a visit. A further half mile down the road a small hump-backed bridge crosses the stream; cross this to the road junction. Turn right and walk along the roadside for a couple of hundred yards until a track on the left leads through Studfold Farm Caravan Park. Cross the River Nidd, a small stream at this point, by the bridge, climb up the wooden steps and enter Lofthouse village where you can find refreshment and a welcoming pint at The Crown.

NIDDERDALE WALK 3
Knaresborough

This is an easy walk visiting some of the major attractions of this lovely market town of Knaresborough. From the town centre the walk visits St John's Church, passes beneath the House in the Rock, visits St Robert's Cave and includes the option to visit Mother Shipton's Petrifying Cave towards the end of the walk, finally concluding at Knaresborough Castle.

Distance	**4 miles (6km)**
Ascent	**500 feet (160m)**
Time	**1½ to 2 hours**
Grading	**Easy**
Suggested Map	**OS Explorer 298 – Nidderdale**
Starting point	**Grid Reference: ???**
Parking	**Knaresborough market place**
How to get there	**Knaresborough is located on the A59 between Harrogate and Junction 47 of the A1(M)**
Terrain	**Good footpaths on the northern side of the river, tracks for the final mile on the southern side**

Knaresborough

Knaresborough was once described a century ago by Yorkshire historian Harry Speight as "the Coblenz of the Nidd". Its remarkable position above the Nidd gorge also inspired W.H. Turner the famous artist to perfectly capture the town's Rhine-like qualities in one of his 19th century paintings. Knaresborough has a long history and, as well as being an old and historic market town, it is also a spa town. It is located four miles east of Harrogate.

Knaresborough is mentioned in the Domesday Book as Chednaresburg or

Chenaresburg and Knaresborough Castle dates from Norman times. Around 1100AD, the town began to grow and provide a market and attract traders to service the castle. The present parish church, St. John's, was established around this time. The earliest name for a Lord of Knaresborough is from around 1115 when Serlo de Burgh held the 'Honour of Knaresborough' from the King.

Hugh de Morville was granted the 'Honour of Knaresborough' (in effect the ownership of the town) in 1158. He was constable of Knaresborough and leader of the group of four knights who murdered Archbishop Thomas Beckett at Canterbury Cathedral on 29th December 1170. The four knights fled to Knaresborough and hid at the castle. Hugh de Morville forfeited the lands in 1173, not for his implication in the murder of Thomas Becket, but for "complicity in the rebellion of young Henry", according to the Early Yorkshire Charters.

The Honour of Knaresborough then passed to the Stuteville family. When the Stuteville line was broken with the death of Robert de Stuteville the 4th in 1205, King John effectively took the Honour of Knaresborough for himself. The first Maundy Money was given out in Knaresborough by King John on 15th April 1210. Knaresborough Forest, which extended far south, is reputed to have been one of King John's favourite hunting grounds.

Although a market was first mentioned in 1206, the town was not granted a Royal Charter to hold a market until 1310, by Edward II. A market is still held every Wednesday in the market square. During Edward II's reign, the castle was occupied by rebels and the curtain walls were breached by a siege engine. Later, Scots invaders burned much of the town and the parish church. In 1328, as part of the marriage settlement, Queen Philippa was granted "the

Knaresborough Castle

Castle, Town, Forest and Honour of Knaresborough" by Edward III and the parish church was restored. After her death in 1369, the Honour was granted by Edward to their younger son, John of Gaunt.

During the Civil War, following the Battle of Marston Moor in 1644, the castle was besieged by Parliamentary forces. The castle eventually fell and in 1646 an order was made by Parliament for its destruction (but not carried out until 1648). The destruction was mainly done by citizens looting the stone and it will be noticed on the walk that many of the town centre buildings have been built of 'castle stone'.

Our walk round Knaresborough and along part of the river starts and finishes in the market place where there are a number of fine shops including Ye Oldest Chymist Shoppe, reputedly the oldest in the country dating back nearly 400 years to 1720. The shop still produces its own lavender water on its premises.

The Walk

Head north out of the market place and then turn left along past the library and right into Kirkgate. This is one of Knaresborough's oldest streets and opposite the Station Hotel you will see Ye Olde Cottage, one of the oldest buildings in the town. Using the subway to go under the railway line this will bring you down the lane to the parish church on your right. The church is open from early morning until late afternoon every day and many people visit it for prayer or just out of interest. St. John's dates from 1114 when King Henry I gave the church to the Augustinian Priory at Nostell. Evidence of the early church can be seen in the string course and in the blocked up windows in the chancel, which is flanked on either side by 13th century chapels.

Of special interest in the church is the Slingsby Chapel which contains the tombs and memorials for this notable Yorkshire family. The largest tomb is that of Francis and Mary Slingsby and in front of this is a large black marble slab which it is said came from the chapel of Robert of Knaresborough, a hermit whose cave in the hillside we will pass later in the walk. Under this slab is the headless body of Sir Henry Slingsby who was a staunch Royalist and was beheaded by Cromwell in 1658 on Tower Hill in London. There is also a single lone tomb and effigy to Sir Charles Slingsby who drowned when thrown from his horse into the river during a fox hunt in 1869.

Upon leaving the church turn right and follow the steps down to Waterside. Turn left along the side of the river and head towards the viaduct. This was built 160 years ago in 1851 when the line from York to Harrogate was being constructed. Go underneath the viaduct and continue along by the river passing various tea shops and restaurants until you reach Low Bridge at the bottom of Briggate. Cross the B6163 and continue along Abbey Road until in about ¼ mile (400m) on the left you will see the aforementioned House in the Rock above you and just below it the Chapel of our Lady of the Crag which is a tiny shrine carved out of the cliff by a gentleman called John the Mason in 1408. The House in the Rock was built in the 18th century by Thomas Hill to

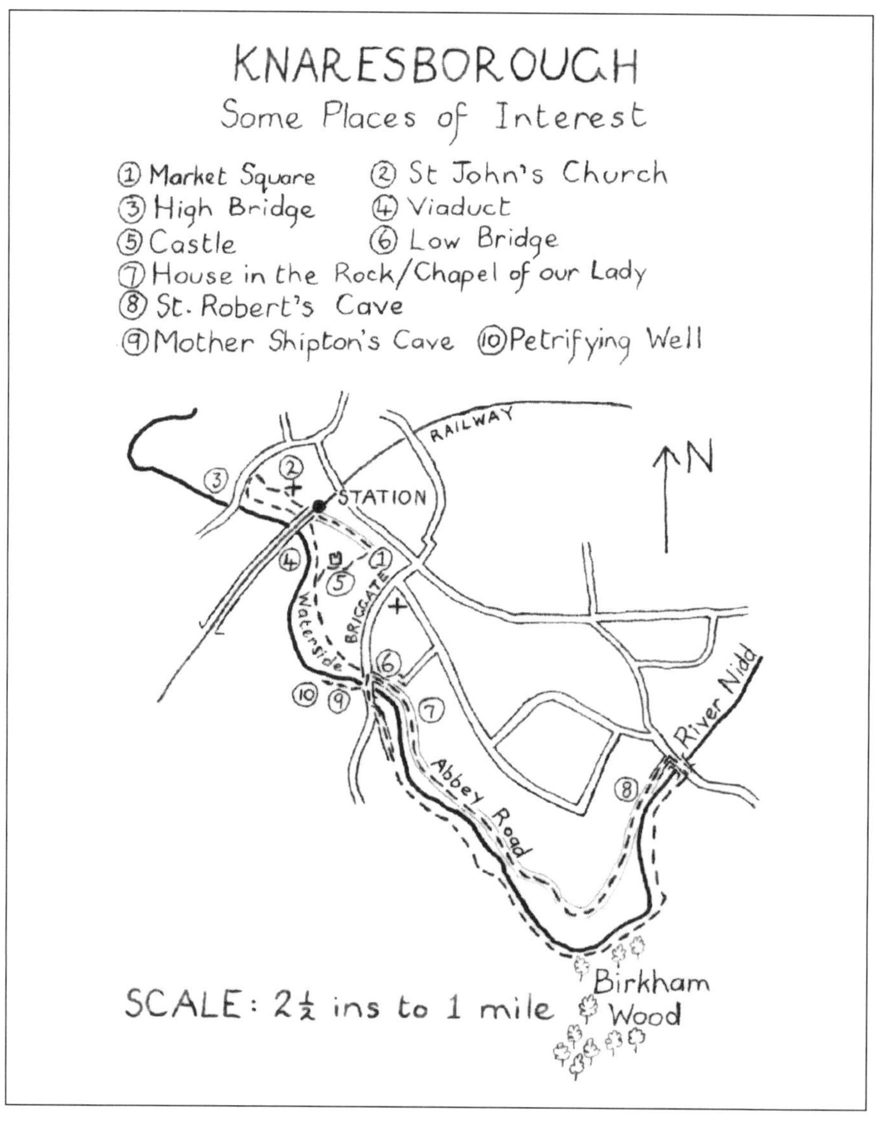

accommodate his family of sixteen children. Previously to this he had lived in a whitewashed cottage at the foot of the cliff.

In 1770, armed with pick, chisel and hammer, and with the goodwill of Sir Charles Slingsby Bart and his wife Margaret, Duchess of Buccleugh, he commenced his assault on the rock face. Over a period of sixteen years he hollowed out an elongated deep cleft in the rock; this extended from the foot of the cliff at the Abbey Road area to the top of the cliff at the Crag Top area thus facilitating a split level system of dwelling. The resulting mass of rocks and rubble caused by the excavation was recycled.

The House in the Rock

The rocks were fashioned into building blocks to build up the front wall so that the completed dwelling consisted of three walls of solid rock and a front wall of dressed, excavated stone. Excesses of rubble were burned in kilns on site to obtain lime to be used in the building process. Eventually the house was to have four rooms leading up from one another, lighthouse fashion. The top room protruded from the cliff face reversing the lower construction in having a rear wall of rock and three built walls.

At a later date castellations were added to both upper and lower levels by Thomas Hill and his elder son, also named Thomas, giving the appearance of a fort. The house then became known as Fort Montague at the request of Margaret duchess of Buccleugh – the principal subscriber to it. The views from all windows were, and indeed are to this day, breathtaking. The house, although a dwelling place, was a viable tourist attraction from its completion in 1786. The second Thomas Hill, who helped his father finish the house and complete the gardens, produced mock white five pound notes which were sold as souvenirs at the house. The five pound notes were withdrawn when the Bank of Newcastle was duped by them! (Shades of a much earlier Northern Rock scandal.) In the early 19th century a rather strange child appeared in the family, although not in the direct line. This child had abnormal very blonde woolly hair resembling the fleece of a sheep and was known as the Woolly-Headed Boy of Fort Montague. He conducted visitors around the house and must have been a great curiosity himself. There are steps leading up to the house if you wish to climb these.

The walk now continues along Abbey Road which is named after the small Trinitarian Priory built here in the 13th century. You will see on your left a cluster of houses relating to this – Priory Cottage, The Old Priory and Priory Farmhouse. On the right is a gate and a noticeboard marking a path to Saint Robert's Cave which is well worth a visit. In the late 12th century Robert Flower, son of a Mayor of York, renounced the world and began his monastic career in the Cistercian Abbey of Newminster in Northumberland. After some months he returned to his father's house and then travelled on to Knaresborough where, it is said, he took up residence in a cave by the River Nidd called St. Giles Chapel which already had one occupant – a knight. Soon after Robert arrived the knight departed to return to his family, and Robert was left on his own.

Robert's brother, Walter the Mayor of York, failing in his attempt to persuade Robert to give up such a vulnerable and poor existence and join a monastery, had a small chapel and dwelling place built for him. The Chapel was dedicated to the Holy Cross. Over the next few years Robert gained a great reputation both locally and further afield as a healer. At some point King John is thought to have visited Robert and been so impressed by his piety that he made him a gift of land. Robert died on 24th September 1218. The monks of Fountains Abbey wanted to bury him in their ground, no doubt for the visitors – and hence donations – that such a burial would bring. But Robert had prophesied that this would happen and impressed upon his followers his desire that he be buried in the Chapel of the Holy Cross. The Chapel became a place of pilgrimage and also a source of medicinal or healing oil. In 1252 Pope Innocent IV granted an indulgence to those who "helped in completing the monastery of Saint Robert of Knaresborough where that saint's body is buried".

Continue on Abbey Road until its finish at the Knaresborough to Wetherby road and here cross the bridge. Turn back on yourself where it is signed to Calcutt and pass through the caravan park. You now enter the lower edges of Birkham Wood and follow the footpath along the riverbank until it becomes a small tarmac lane called Spittal Croft. At the end of the lane turn right and drop down to the bridge where you will see Mother Shipton's Cave on the left.

Mother Shipton is England's most famous Prophetess. She was born in 1488 and lived during the reigns of King Henry VIII and Queen Elizabeth I. Her prophetic visions became known and feared throughout England, with many of them still proving uncannily accurate today. The Cave, her legendary birthplace, is near to the famous, unique, geological phenomenon – The Petrifying Well whose magical cascading waters turn items into stone! The Petrifying Well is England's oldest visitor attraction, first opening its gates in 1630! Since 1641 there have been more than 50 different editions of books about Mother Shipton and her prophecies, some purporting to tell her life story in considerable detail. One of the earliest such accounts was said to have recorded the sayings of Mother Shipton as told to one Joanne Waller, who died soon afterwards at the great age of 94. That would mean Joanne, as a young girl, had listened to the old lady not long before her death in 1561.

To complete the walk, cross the bridge and turn left again into Waterside. Soon on the right is a flight of steps which leads up to the Bebra gardens and behind these is Knaresborough Castle, well worth a visit and a fitting end to the walk. Turn right at the castle to return to the market place where there are plenty of tea rooms, restaurants and pubs to visit, whichever takes your fancy.

River Nidd and Viaduct

Yorke's Folly

From Pateley Bridge this walk initially follows the river downstream to Glasshouses before climbing through Guisecliffe Wood to the 18th Century Yorke's Folly. The return to Pateley passes the beautiful Bewerley Grange Chapel.

Distance	**4 miles (6.5 km)**
Ascent	**350 feet (110m)**
Time	**2½ hours**
Grading	**Easy**
Suggested Map	**OS Explorer 298 – Nidderdale**
Starting point	**Grid Reference: ??**
Parking	**Pateley Bridge town centre or by the bridge**
How to get there	**Pateley Bridge is located at the junction of the B6165 and B6265**
Terrain	**Good tracks throughout with some minor road walking back through Bewerley for the last mile**

Pateley Bridge

The attractive market town of Pateley Bridge is the self-styled capital of Nidderdale. Set against a steep hillside, the town offers a wide variety of speciality shops, cosy tearooms and welcoming public houses. Pateley Bridge takes its name from Patleia – 'The Path through the glade' – and was first mentioned in the12th century. It is an important river crossing and centre for farming and countryside industries.

In 1320, after the town had been ravaged and plundered by the marauding Scots, a market and fair were granted to the town. Pateley's prosperity,

Pateley Bridge

however, came with the opening of the nearby quarries in the 19th century and much of the stone from here has been used for slabs on the country's railway stations.

Whilst in the town it is worth visiting the award-winning Nidderdale Museum, housed in the former workhouse and situated opposite St. Cuthbert's Parish Church. Its eleven rooms illustrate the rural life of Nidderdale in both the recent and more distant past. Nidderdale Museum shows how ordinary people lived, in imaginative and realistic settings. There are sections devoted to agriculture, industries, religion, transport and costume. The corridors are lined with photographs of local interest. Included in the museum are the cobbler's workshop, schoolroom, Victorian parlour, general store, costumes of the 19th and 20th century and history of transport in the Dales.

Also worth a visit are the Pateley Playhouse, known as the 'Little Theatre of the Dales'. You should also call and look at the creative talents of a potter, jeweller and glassblower hard at work in their craft workshops just off the

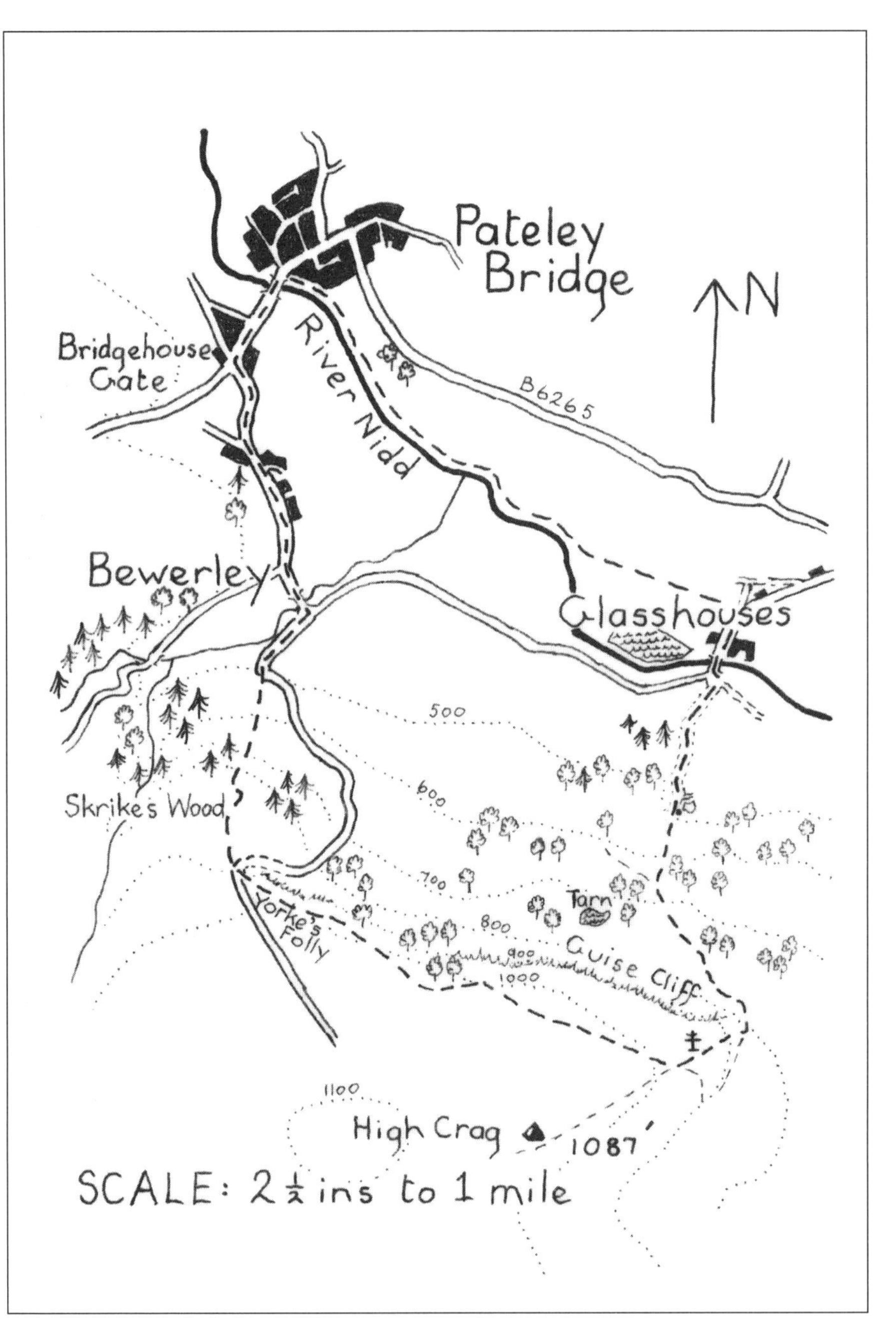

Pateley Bridge
N
Bridgehouse Gate
River Nidd
B6265
Bewerley
Glasshouses
500
600
Skrikes Wood
700
Yorke's Folly
Tarn
800
900
Guise Cliff
1000
1100
High Crag
1087
SCALE: 2½ ins to 1 mile

main street. Farming traditions are also preserved in Pateley with annual events such as the Nidderdale Festival and the Agricultural Show, one of the country's finest.

The Walk

We start the walk down by the River Nidd and with the river on your right walk away from the bridge, on the paved riverside pathway signposted to Glasshouses. For about a mile keep walking with the river to your right, passing a private bridge leading to Castlestead built by the flax mill owner George Metcalfe. In addition to this palatial home, he built his own weir for the mill, which you will pass on the side of the path and later, a man-made lake on your right, also built for the flax mill.

At Glasshouses before continuing further on the walk it is worth visiting Yorkshire Country Wines, housed in the old flax mill in the village. The Mill's impressive water turbine is housed in the flagged floor of the wine tasting room. Here throughout the day, visitors can sample the different varieties of wines, including blackberry and gooseberry, along with the ever popular elderflower and elderberry. On Fridays and Saturdays at 11.45 am, there are winery tours, providing visitors with an opportunity to see for themselves how the Country Wines are produced. Also the former Steam engine room has been converted into a tearoom in a truly idyllic setting.

On reaching the minor road, turn right, going over a metal bridge. Take the left hand fork of this road signed for Heyshaw and Guisecliffe and turn right up the track, towards Low Fold Cottages. At this point continue along the well used lane. The track rises towards Guisecliffe and as you ascend fine views can be seen across the valley. Cross at a small wooden stile, and follow the path to its end. Go over the stone steps, and turn right, then follow the path through the woods.

It is important to keep to the main path now. Stay with the widest path and always head uphill. You will come upon a track, half way up the hill at right angles and here take the left path always ascending up the hill. Not long after, the path swerves off to the right, **do not take the left path** but continue uphill. Eventually, after about ¼ mile (400m), you find the pathway levelling out. The crags of Guisecliffe are soon seen ahead. The crags have been the haunt of rock climbers for over a hundred years but have always played second fiddle to the more popular nearby Brimham Rocks.

Ahead on your right you will soon notice a telecommunications mast up on the top of the rise. This is the direction in which you need to be heading. Follow the path rising all the time and pass an open metal bar gate over on the left. Finally reaching the top, cross over the seven stepped wood stile to the left of the mast. However, please be aware of slippery stones at this point.

Ignore the path to the left and go straight on for a few yards and then turn right to go behind the mast. From here follow the path that keeps close to the drystone wall, always keeping the wall on your right.

The next section of the walk is relatively straightforward. Keep to the path and after about ¼ mile (400m) cross over a four stepped wooden stile. Follow the pathway keeping close to the wall over on your right which avoids any muddy areas which are usually prevalent after rain. Go over the next stile and after a short while you will eventually see Yorke's Folly ahead. Head down to the wall, and cross at a five stepped wood stile, turning left and going down to the folly on your left.

The Yorke family arrived in Nidderdale in 1547 where they became both lead mine operators and also major landowners. In 1674 they bought nearby Bewerley Hall, the site of which we will pass later, and this stayed in the family until the 1920s. They built this folly at the end of the 18th century, not purely as a symbol of their wealth and power, but more to provide work for the local people of the area at a time of hardship and unemployment. The building is reputedly modelled on properties in the German Rhineland. Two towers can be seen these days, but originally there were three, the third one being destroyed in a great gale in November 1893 when it came crashing down and was never replaced.

After taking the obligatory photographs at the folly, follow the obvious path away from it downhill. Keep to the path heading for the road ahead and cross the road. Go

Yorke's Folly

through the metal kissing gate and head down in the direction of the Public Footpath sign. At this point if you go sharp right just inside the kissing gate you can visit the crocodile stone from here. The path now winds left dropping down to a wall and at the end of this wall turn right over the stile. Go down the hill and enter Strikes Wood nature reserve.

Leave the wood by the stile at the bottom. Cross and follow the pathway forward and down to the road. Once on the road, turn left and head for Bewerley and Pateley Bridge (signposted), via Turner Bridge. Climb the short hill up to Bewerley. On the right is the Bewerley Grange Chapel. Bewerley is actually older than Pateley and is mentioned in the Domesday Book as Bevrelei, owned by one Gospatric who held land valued at 50 shillings (£2.50). A century later it was owned by one of the great Norman barons, Roger de Mowbray, who gave Bewerley, Brimham, Dacre and other lands in the area to the monks of Fountains Abbey. He died in 1195 and is interred at Byland Abbey which he had founded.

The monks established a grange at Bewerley and also at Brimham, Dacre and Ramsgill. These granges produced meat, wool and dairy goods from the cattle that the monks kept and reared. The monks were also the first to tap into the mineral wealth of the area. In the early 16th century, Marmaduke Huby, the abbot at Fountains from 1494 and 1526, arranged for a grange chapel to be built at Bewerley. His initials, MH, can be seen on the windows of the chapel and also three of the exterior walls. There is also the inscription Soli Deo Honor Et Gloria (To God Alone Honour and Glory) on the chapel, the same inscription that adorns the great tower at Fountains Abbey.

Bewerley Grange remained in the ownership of the monks of Fountains until it was bought by the Yorke family in 1674. It passed down the generations of the Yorke family until the 1920s when they vacated Bewerley Hall which was then pulled down and the estate was sold off. The chapel was bought by a local man, Edward Roberts who, when he died in 1960, willed the chapel to the Society for the Protection of Ancient Buildings and in 1965 they restored it and it became a chapel of ease.

The grounds of Bewerley Hall and Park became an outdoor education centre which is now run by North Yorkshire County Council and the grounds are used annually for the local Nidderdale Show which always takes place each year on the first Monday after 18th September.

After viewing the chapel, continue through the village of Bewerley, past the green and turn the corner. It is now an easy ¼ miles (400m) back down to Pateley where there are plenty of pubs, restaurants and cafés to partake in refreshment after what has hopefully been a good walk.

Greenhow Mines

Step back in time on this walk to visit the lead mining areas around Greenhow. Part of the walk takes in the Niddlerdale Way before returning to Toft Gate via rural farmland.

Distance	6 miles (10km)
Ascent	1200 feet (360m)
Time	3 hours
Grading	Moderate
Suggested Map	OS Explorer 298 – Nidderdale
Starting point	Grid Reference: 128643
Parking	Car park at Toft Gate Lime Kiln
How to get there	Located on the B6265 which runs between Pateley Bridge and Grassington
Terrain	Good tracks, both grassy and stony with some minor road walking

Greenhow and its mining history

Greenhow is one of the highest villages in Yorkshire, located at around 1,300ft (396m) above sea level. Until the early 17th century this was all bleak and barren moorland. When lead mining on a significant scale developed in the area in the 1600s, a settlement was established here, though most of the surviving buildings are late 18th and 19th century. Many of the cottages also have a small piece of attached farmland, for the miners were also farmers, neither occupation alone giving them a stable income or livelihood. In a way typical of such mining villages, the church and the pub - the Miners Arms, of course - were at the very centre. Joseph Kipling, the grandfather of Rudyard Kipling was the minister at the Methodist Chapel at Greenhow and Rudyard himself is known to have visited the village. There is a 'Kipling's Cottage' next door to the former 'Miners Arms', but it is not known whether his grandfather actually lived there. The Miners Arms closed in 2010 and is now a private dwelling.

There is no local accommodation for visitors in Greenhow village but as Greenhow is less than 3 miles and about five minutes drive from Pateley Bridge, you will find plenty of accommodation there.

The village was developed by Stephen Proctor in the early seventeenth century. Scattered amongst the heather and bracken strewn moors are remnants of lost dwellings and hamlets where people once lived in this close knit community. There is little evidence left of the earliest workers, but it may be that that the Brigantes were forced into slave labour by the Romans to mine lead, a useful metal that could be easily moulded into pipes or used to seal roofs. Evidence of Roman mining comes from three ingots of lead found near Greenhow, two at Heyshaw, near Dacre and one at Nussey Knot.

Evidence of Saxons and Vikings in the area lie in the place names they left behind, such as Coldstones, the original name being the Norse, 'Kaldestaines'. This served as a simple reminder of the nature of the place, where the cold, strong winds led to a climate several degrees colder than the nearby market town of Pateley Bridge, only three miles to the east. It was the Cistercian monasteries of Fountains and Byland Abbeys who really exploited the area. These 'millionaire monks' ensured that Roger de Mowbray gave them valuable mineral rights and in return generously allowed him to continue to use the Chase of Nidderdale for hunting forays. Lead was such a valuable asset that the two abbeys frequently disputed their boundaries and their right to mine the various minerals which lay within these.

Some areas were, it seems, worked fairly amicably by the two abbeys as there is evidence of an agreement in 1226 that a groove on Kaldestaines, previously worked in common, should continue to be worked in the same way until exhausted. If any lay brother or monk of either Byland or Fountains Abbey was convicted of breaking the agreement they must go on foot to the other abbey to apologise and then have only bread and water on a Friday for a year. The life of the ordinary people would have been hard in such as isolated place. The Black Death of 1349 probably killed off many of Greenhow's population although documents of the Archbishop of York at the time suggest that there was still a thriving industry as workers paid tithes individually. Lead was used locally as well as being transported to Windsor and abbeys in Northern France. Local stone was also valuable and used for building monastic granges and lodges at Bewerley, Hardcastle, Coldstonesfold, Moorhouses and Kell House.

Fountains Abbey must have made enormous profits from its sale of lead, iron and stone and held power and influence for at least two centuries. In 1502, the York Guild of Merchant Adventurers chastised the then Abbot of Fountains, Marmaduke Huby, (who built the delightful chapel at Bewerley whose windows and walls are adorned by his initials as mentioned in Walk 4 – Yorke's Folly walk): "we understand that you occupy buying and selling lead and other merchandise as a free merchant, contrary to God's laws and man's, you being a spiritual man and of religion, and so your occupying is great damage and hurt to us merchants in these parts."

Even in the 16th century lead mining attracted many workers and Bolton Priory also claimed rights to work the mines in the western area around Mungo Gill. Disputes over ownership attracted much attention and 500 miners are recorded as having assembled in 1530 near Craven Keld accusing the Bolton Priory men of sinking shafts within the Forest of Knaresborough boundaries. It is not known how many of these people actually lived on the hill; it is thought most of the workers walked in from out lying areas. The earliest known settlements belonged to Fountains Abbey. Monastic farms

Mine workings from Green Moor

were recorded at Coldstonesfold and Hardcastle and it is thought two monks lived in a cottage, the original Kell House, thought to have been built around 1526-1530. The ruins of this cottage still stood in the garden of the present day Keld House in the 1920s. The job of the monks who lived here was to guard the mines and look after the monastic sheep. The monastic grange of Bewerley and lodge at Moorhouses lay on slightly more hospitable, lower lying land.

With the dissolution of the monasteries in 1539, the power of the church ended and the ownership passed to the rich mineral lords. Sir Stephen Proctor bought the Manor of Bewerley, including the mineral rights in 1597. He was one of the nouveau riche but also a staunch Protestant, frequently in dispute with his Roman Catholic neighbours. His father, Thomas, had patented a new process of lead smelting, accumulating much wealth into the bargain. Stephen Proctor was also responsible, as part of a settlement with John Armitage over disputed land, in the founding of the actual village of Greenhow as prior to this date the only settlement recorded on the hill itself was the monks at Kell House.

In 1613 an agreement also sought to protect the Greenhow miners' rights: "...there may be cottages erected for the miners and mineral workmen upon the said waste ... and also for the keeping of draught oxen and horses for the maintenance of the mines, always leaving the tenants sufficient common". Most of the monastic smelting was done in bales which were basically wooden bonfires strategically placed on hillsides to catch the wind. There are still several evident in the Greenhow area including the one at nearby Bale Bank. Stephen Proctor built the first recorded smelt mill at Greenhow, probably on Brandstone Beck around 1606 and also installed an 'engen' to drain the mines. Little is known about the mining methods of this time but the next hundred years are thought to have seen extensive exploration in the area.

The Walk

The walk around the lead mines area starts at the car park at Toft Gate Lime Kiln. Cross the road from the car park where you will notice a stile leading into the field. Go over this and head downhill on a faint path until you reach a gate in the wall. Pass through this with a barn on your left. After another stile continue descending until you reach a track where you need to turn left. Ascend the hill and after passing through two gates you reach a minor road at which point turn left and continue ascending up to the main road ahead. Turn right here and follow this past the burial ground and the former Miners Arms. There is still the sign with two railway trolleys situated outside the property. Pass Kiplings Cottage, Bowscale Cottage and one called Blencathra

1100
1000
900
800
700
cattle grids
Ashfold Side Beck
Low Wood
FB
Old Mine Workings
stile 1000
900
N
1100
Brandstone Beck
1000
800
900
Coldstonesfold Farm
ford
Old Mine Workings 1100
1200
Gill Beck
stile
Far Side
B6265
Toft Gate
Greenhow
1300
SCALE: 2 ins to 1 mile

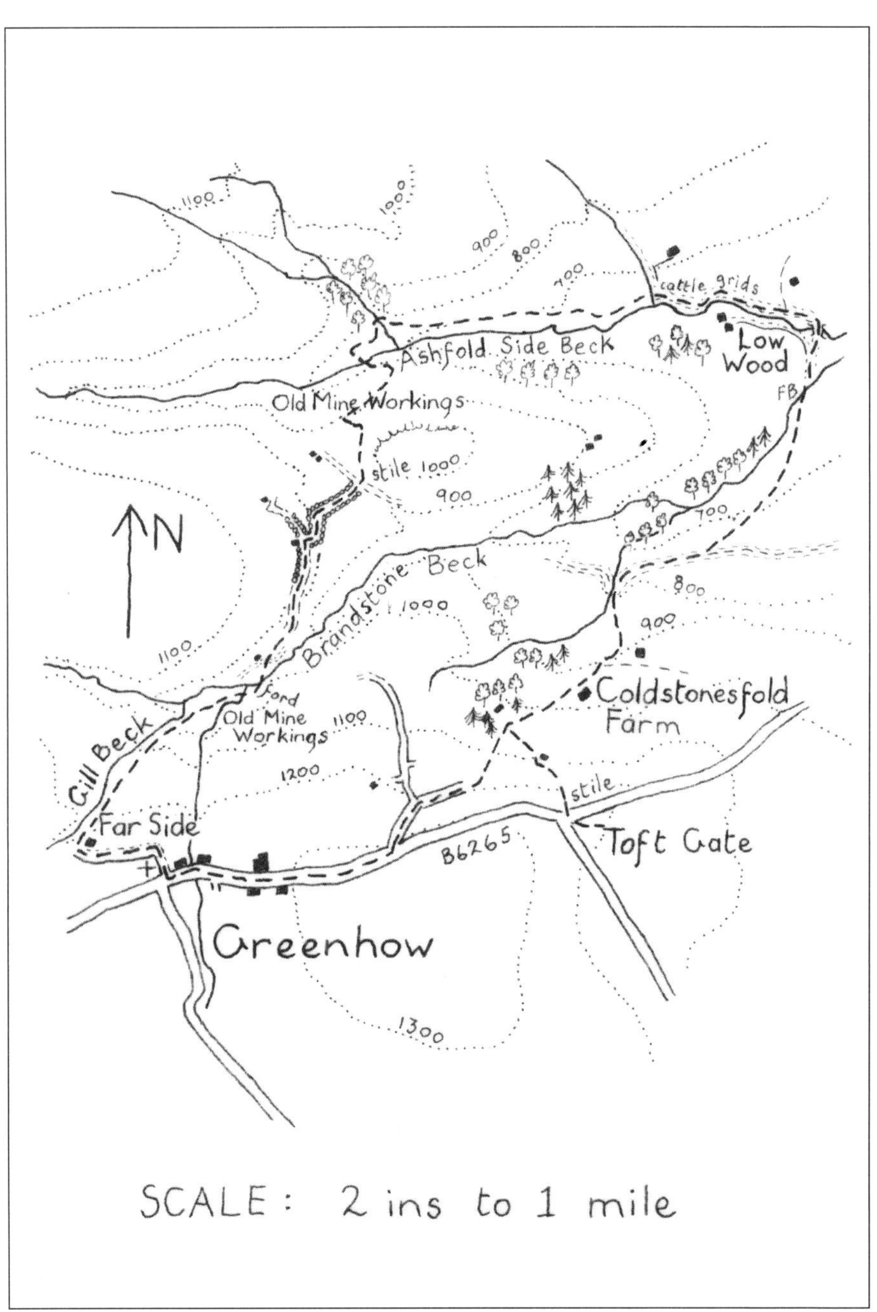

154

(no you are not in the Lake District) on the right and further on just past a converted chapel, take a lane to the right signed Stripe Lane.

When you reach a junction head left and continue on the track until you reach a cattle grid and a gate immediately afterwards. After passing through the gate bear to the right heading towards the farmhouse. Follow the track behind the farmhouse and continue on this track past Low Side Farm where you will be welcomed by the farm dogs. The next ½ mile is all downhill heading into the valleys of Gill Beck and then Brandstone Beck. You now have your first encounter with the extensive remains of lead mining activity.

The track now turns off to the left but continue ahead making for a large concrete building in front until you reach the main track. At the building go to the right of it and continue down the valley until you reach a ford. Cross the ford and ascend the hill ahead until you reach a gate with a stile next to it. Cross over the stile, continue ahead for about 100 yards (90m) and go over the stile on your right. At this point you will see a farm ahead and you follow the track towards this. You should now be between a pair of stone walls and soon you will encounter another stile.

Cross this stile onto a track and turn left, pass through a gateway and look for a spoil heap ahead. At this, turn right along the track now heading downhill. Go past the cogwheel in front and go across Ashfold Side Beck using the concrete causeway to reach a gate opposite.

Here you will see a bridleway sign, turn right and ascend the hill to a sign for the Nidderdale Way. At this sign turn right and follow the path until you reach a gate. The track now goes round the head of the valley; continue on this passing through two gates and over a series of three cattle grids. After you have crossed over the third of these, turn right through the metal gate and go over the bridge ahead. Bear left towards another gate, following the track uphill, bearing slightly left until you reach a wall. At the end of the stone wall turn to the right and head along the track with walls now on both sides. Soon after you will encounter another gate and then a footbridge.

After crossing the bridge, turn right when you reach a gate and continue climbing until you reach another gate. Go through this and when you reach a track ahead turn left heading for the farmhouse in front but before you reach this cross the grass on the right until you reach a metalled lane. At the lane turn right again and continue along the lane until you reach the cattle grid in front.

Once you have passed the farm, after about a further 100 yards (90m) take the path to the left and continue forward to another cattle grid. Here turn right and continue along the track to another gate. By the entrance to Coldstonesfold Farm turn right and ascend the hill to a final gate before going

Farmer and dogs from Coldstonesfold Farm

over a stile on your left to bring you onto the path that leads unerringly back to Toft Gate Lime Kiln car park.

With the closure of The Miner's Arms there is no longer a local establishment for the provision of refreshment at the end of the walk. The two possibilities, therefore, are to either go down Greenhow Hill and into Pateley Bridge where there are a number of pubs and cafés, or alternatively to take the Blubberhouses Road opposite the Church for approximately 4 miles to the Stone House Inn by the turning to Thruscross Reservoir.

WENSLEYDALE INTRODUCTION

Running from West to East, Wensleydale is one of the few valleys in the Yorkshire Dales which takes its name from a village (Wensley), rather than the river (the Ure) which flows along it (although the valley has in past times also been known as 'Uredale', or even by the Norse name of 'Yoredale').

Villages and hamlets in Upper Wensleydale include Hawes (at the head of the valley), Hardraw (famous for what is arguably England's highest unbroken waterfall, Hardraw Force), Bainbridge, Askrigg and Aysgarth (where the River Ure descends a series of limestone steps at the famous beauty spot of Aysgarth Falls). Further down the valley are the villages of West Burton, West Witton, Castle Bolton, Middleham, Coverham and East Witton, the market towns of Leyburn and Masham, the pretty riverside village of West Tanfield and the cathedral city of Ripon on the edge of the Vale of Mowbray.

Tributary valleys of Wensleydale include Widdale, Sleddale, Raydale, Bishopdale, Waldendale and Coverdale, while near the head of the dale the famous Buttertubs Pass leads up over the moors and down into Swaledale. Wensleydale is also famous as the home of Wensleydale cheese and the Cat Pottery at West Burton.

Wensleydale is often divided into 'Upper Wensleydale' and 'Lower Wensleydale' – lying approximately upstream and downstream of Leyburn respectively. The Wensleydale Railway runs along the eastern part of the dale from Redmire (near Castle Bolton) to Leeming Bar (near Northallerton). Towns and villages along the line play host to the Wensleydale 1940s Weekend which is usually held sometime in July.

Sometimes described as the 'capital' of Upper Wensleydale, Hawes lies near the head of the valley, and is most famous for its Wensleydale cheese. The name, Hawes, means a 'pass between mountains', and it stands between Buttertubs and Fleet Moss and the town is also overlooked by Great Shunner Fell. Hawes is Yorkshire's highest market town and was granted a charter to hold its market in 1699. From a walking point of view, Hawes lies on the route of the Pennine Way. Hawes is also the home to the ancient art of rope making, a craft which has been passed down from generation to generation and still draws visitors from all over the world.

A mile north of Hawes is the tiny hamlet of Hardraw and the famous Hardraw Force. Comprising a single drop of 100 feet from a rocky overhang, Hardraw Force is claimed to be England's highest (above ground) unbroken waterfall. Geologically, the bed of the river and the pool into which the fall plunges is slate; on top of that is sandstone and the top layer is carboniferous limestone. Public viewing of Hardraw Force is rather unusual, if not unique, as the visitor has to go through the bar of the *Green Dragon Inn* public house in Hardraw to reach the falls. An entrance fee is payable on the way through the pub, which is currently £2.50 per adult and £1.50 per child.

Three miles south-east of Hawes is Semerwater which is the largest natural lake in North Yorkshire and from which flows the River Bain to join the River Ure at Bainbridge. According to legend, a town once stood where the water now runs deep, but it was doomed to a watery grave after a weary traveller was refused shelter from a raging storm. As he left, he cursed the town, decreeing that it should be drowned under rushing waters. Semerwater is also the 35 mile point of Wainwright's *Pennine Journey.*

Near the village of Aysgarth the River Ure flows over a set of limestone steps which are known as Aysgarth Falls. The waterfalls are one of Wensleydale's most famous beauty spots (having been featured in the Kevin Costner film *Robin Hood – Prince of Thieves*), with a pleasant riverside walk linking the Upper, Middle and Lower Falls.

Eight miles (12km) downstream from Aysgarth is the village of Middleham which is famous for two things, its castle and its horse training. The castle was built by Robert Fitzrandolph, 3rd Lord of Middleham and Spennithorne. Building commenced in 1190 and its location is near the site of an earlier motte and bailey castle. In 1270 it came into the hands of the Neville family, the most notable member of which was Richard Neville, 16th Earl of Warwick, known to history as the 'Kingmaker', a leading figure in the Wars of the Roses.

Today the town is a major centre of horse racing in the UK and is home to the Middleham Trainers' Association. The first racehorse trainer to train at Middleham was Isaac Cape in 1765. Today there are several racehorse trainers based here including Mark Johnston, and Patrick Haslam. Racing is the number one employer in the town closely followed by tourism.

Masham is 10 miles (16km) downstream of Middleham and its name derives from the Anglo-Saxon 'Mæssa's Ham', loosely translated as the homestead belonging to Mæssa. The Romans had a presence here, but the first permanent settlers were the Saxons. Around 900AD the Vikings invaded the region, burning and laying waste to the church and causing great suffering in Masham. They also introduced sheep farming, something that has continued for over 1,000 years.

The other industry Masham is famous for is that of brewing. T&R Theakston Ltd. was founded in 1827 by Robert Theakston and John Wood at The Black Bull pub in Masham. By 1832 Theakston had sole ownership of the brewery and in 1875 he passed control over to his son Thomas who expanded the range of buildings by building the new brewery on the Paradise Fields. In 1919 the company acquired and closed down the Lightfoot Brewery, also in Masham. In the 1980s & 1990s the company was taken over and owned by firstly Matthew Brown Plc and then by Scottish & Newcastle breweries but in 2004 the business returned to family ownership after being purchased back from Scottish & Newcastle by four Theakston brothers – Nick, Simon, Tim and Edward. Major development works at the Masham Brewery enabled the company to announce that in 2009 brewing of Theakston Bitter would return to Masham and is now brewed at the Black Sheep Brewery in the town.

Five miles (8km) further downstream is the delightful village of West Tanfield, another location through which the Six Dales Hike passes. West Tanfield has nearly everything anyone could wish for in an English village; wooded hills, the River Ure flowing below the old bridge and a fine medieval church. The Marmions came to the village in 1215 and their monuments are to be found in the church. The nearby gatehouse was built by Henry Fitzhugh, Elizabeth Marmion's husband, but the Manor House in which the Marmions lived no longer remains. In the church the nave, chancel and low arcade were built about 1350 and the north aisle and its chapel in the mid-15th century. The interior has fine wooden pews and rails, some constructed by Robert Thompson and signed with his little mouse, and there is a lovely oak figure of Saint Michael. There are rich altar rails, a beautiful nativity scene, gold figures of Saint George and Saint Michael and on the reading desks four monks playing the harp, horn, fiddle and flute. The pulpit has a fine linefold and on the stairway is St. Nicholas with three children in a tub – the pickle boys who he saved.

The fine quality alabaster tombs of the Marmions are in the church but the churchyard itself provides some interesting viewing. The tombstone of Francis Maximillian Walbran, for example, has a fishing tackle carved into the stone and the inscription "erected by voluntary subscription – accidentally drowned whilst angling at Tanfield on February 17th, 1909, aged fifty seven". This tombstone is at least as moving as the armoured effigy of the Marmion tomb inside the church especially because the local people decided to pay for it.

The fine city of Ripon is the final place we will look at in Wensleydale. Although no larger than many similar market towns, Ripon is actually defined as a city (the fourth smallest in the country) by virtue of having a magnificent cathedral. The city is just over 1,300 years old and was originally known as Inhrypum being founded by Saint Wilfrid during the time of Angle kingdom Northumbria. The Normans destroyed much of the city in the 11th and 12th centuries but after a period of building projects under the Plantagenets, the city emerged with a prominent wool and cloth industry. Ripon is a delightful city to visit before or after any of the five walks in Wensleydale.

Aysgarth and Bolton Castle

This walk offers good views of the river and falls. The area is abundant with wild flowers in the spring and summer, and wild birds, squirrels and deer may also be seen. The name Aysgarth originates from Old Norse, meaning the open space in the oak trees.

Distance	**7 miles (11km)**
Ascent	**330 feet (100m)**
Time	**3 hours**
Grading	**Moderate**
Suggested Map	**OS Outdoor Leisure 30 – Yorkshire Dales – North & Central**
Starting point	**Grid Reference: 013887**
Parking	**Aysgarth Falls National Park Visitor Centre**
How to get there	**Aysgarth is on the A684 approximately 16 miles West of the A1 passing through Bedale and Leyburn**
Terrain	**Rural footpaths and riverside paths throughout**

Aysgarth

Aysgarth is located about sixteen miles south-west from Richmond. According to the 2001 UK census the parish had a population of 197 people in 88 households, but its numbers are boosted a hundredfold during the summer with visitors to the village and particularly the nearby Aysgarth Falls.

The George and Dragon Inn in Aysgarth dates from the 17th century when it was a coaching inn and is now a Grade II listed building. Local real ale from the Black Sheep Brewery and the Yorkshire Dales Brewing Company is served here, and it makes a delightful finishing point after this delightful walk.

On the way down to the falls from the village is St. Andrew's Church in Aysgarth. It was substantially rebuilt in 1536, restored in 1866 and is also a Grade II listed building. The unusually large churchyard extends to about four acres and is reputed to be the largest in England. The church preserves a number of fittings that were rescued from Jervaulx Abbey at the time of the Dissolution of the Monasteries, including a medieval painted rood screen and the abbot's stall.

Near the village the River Ure flows over a series of limestone steps and are known as Aysgarth Falls. This triple flight of waterfalls is surrounded by both forest and arable land, and has been carved out by the River Ure over a one-mile stretch as it descends through mid-Wensleydale. The falls are particularly spectacular after heavy rain, as thousands of gallons of water cascade over the series of broad limestone steps. The falls have attracted visitors for over 200 years; with notable visitors being Ruskin, Turner and Wordsworth, all enthusing about the falls' outstanding beauty. The upper fall was also featured in the 1991 Kevin Costner film *Robin Hood – Prince of Thieves*. The

Aysgarth Falls

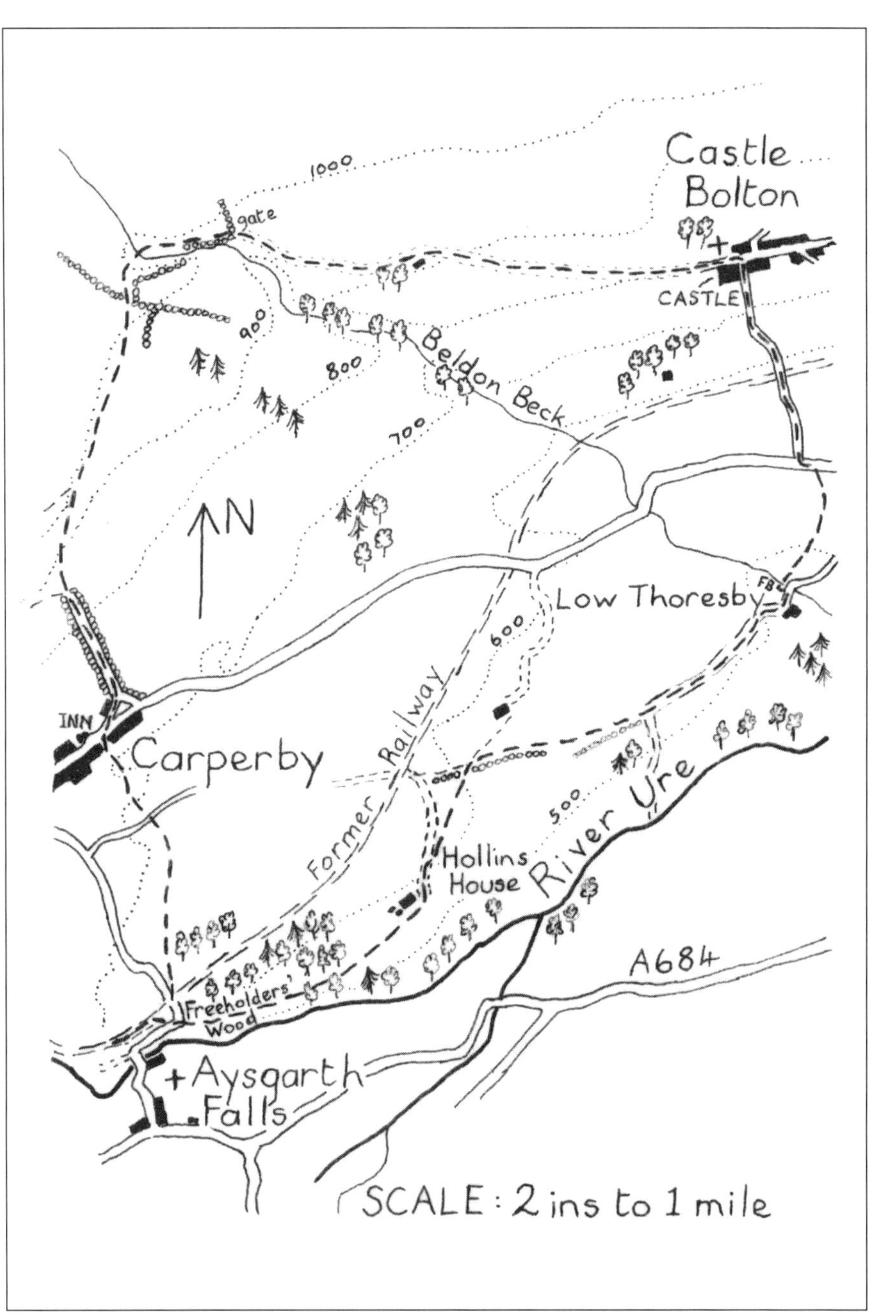

1000
gate
900
800
700
Beldon Beck
Castle Bolton
CASTLE
N
Low Thoresby
FB
600
Former Railway
Carperby
INN
500
River Ure
Hollins House
A684
Freeholders' Wood
Aysgarth Falls
SCALE: 2 ins to 1 mile

falls were also featured on the television programme *Seven Natural Wonders* as one of the wonders of the North.

The Walk

Our walk commences by the Aysgarth Falls National Park Visitor Centre. From the visitor centre, turn right along the path and head up to the Middle and Lower Falls. Cross over the road and go straight ahead to enter Freeholders Wood. Continue straight forward and follow the signs for Bolton Castle. The path now takes you away from the river and alongside a wooden fence. Continue north-east along this path until you reach Hollins House.

After you have passed the house, follow the path to the right and go across the meadow ahead of you. When you reach a wall, don't attempt to cross it but instead go through two gates whilst keeping the wall on your right hand side. Continue straight ahead to eventually reach Thoresby Lane. Continue along this narrow lane, and shortly Bolton Castle comes into view. Keep on this narrow lane until you reach Low Thoresby Farm. After about 50 yards past the farm, turn left via a footbridge and head north. Continue straight ahead passing through two meadows to meet a road. Pass over the road with care and go straight up the opposite road which leads to Bolton Castle. Continue straight ahead on this road to emerge at Bolton Castle.

Bolton is one of the country's best preserved medieval castles, and has stunning views over Wensleydale. Completed in 1399 by Richard le Scrope, Chancellor of England to Richard II, it has over 600 years of fascinating history including involvement in the Pilgrimage of Grace, Mary Queen of Scots imprisonment for six months in 1568 and a Civil War siege. The castle has never been sold and still remains in the private ownership of Lord Bolton, Sir Richard le Scrope's direct descendant. In 1991 a grant from English Heritage enabled the castle to meet safety requirements which meant it could be opened to the general public.

The castle is now preserved in outstanding condition with many interesting rooms and features to discover including the old kitchens, dungeons, nursery, the armoury, great chamber and Mary Queen of Scots bedroom. About one third of the rooms are fully intact and the tour of the castle is brought to life by use of life-sized models giving visitors great insight into its turbulent past.

The route of the walk now goes round the castle and up towards the parish church of St. Oswald. Walk through the gate, turn left and follow the farm track for next 2½ miles (4km). This is easy walking with some outstanding views. At the end of the farm road continue straight forward through a gate. Keep the wall on your left hand side, go across a stream and then turn left heading in a southerly direction and follow this track. Continue along the

Bolton Castle

track for a short while before the path eventually descends to meet a walled lane. Follow this path which leads to a road and into the village of Carperby. The village was originally settled in Viking times as the name with its 'by' ending implies. In the centre of the village is a high-stepped cross dated 1674. Carperby was granted a market in 1305 and in the 17th century the village was an important Wensleydale centre of Quakerism, and its biggest building even today is the classically-styled Friends' Meeting House of 1864, which is now a private residence. The name of the Wheatsheaf Hotel suggests a corn-growing past, and the inn itself was where James Herriot (Alf White) and his bride spent their honeymoon in 1941. Also the breed of Wensleydale sheep originated in Carperby, originally known as 'mugs'.

Turn right onto the road and go as far as the Wheatsheaf In where you should turn right along the path opposite. Continue straight ahead to pass through a couple fields to emerge back at Freeholders' wood. Just inside the wood turn right and then left to emerge once again onto the road. Turn left on this road and pass under the railway bridge to emerge back at the Aysgarth Falls National Park Visitor Centre.

WENSLEYDALE WALK 2
Hawes and Hardraw

From the market town of Hawes this walk visits the famous Hardraw Force which can only be accessed by going through a pub! The walk then returns via the delightful village of Sedbusk.

Distance	**5 miles (8km)**
Ascent	**430 feet (130m)**
Time	**3 hours**
Grading	**Easy**
Suggested Map	**OS Outdoor Leisure 30 – Yorkshire Dales – North & Central**
Starting point	**Grid Reference: 875898**
Parking	**Gayle Lane car park, Hawes**
How to get there	**Hawes is on the A684, 25 miles west of the A1 passing though Bedale, Leyburn and Aysgarth and 13 miles east of Sedbergh passing Garsdale Head**
Terrain	**Rural footpaths and riverside tracks throughout. Can be wet and slippery near Hardraw Force – care needed!**

Hawes

Hawes is often referred to as the 'capital' of Upper Wensleydale and lies near the head of the valley. It is probably most famous as the modern day home of Wensleydale cheese. The name, Hawes, means a 'pass between mountains', and it stands between Buttertubs and Fleet Moss. The town is also overlooked by Great Shunner Fell. Hawes is Yorkshire's highest market town, was granted its market charter in 1699 and lies on the route of the Pennine Way. The River Ure runs through the town and has now become one of the honeypot tourist attractions of the Yorkshire Dales National Park. The Anglican parish of Hawes also includes the neighbouring hamlet of Gayle.

Wensleydale cheese has been made in Wensleydale since 1150, when Cistercian monks settled in the dale and established a monastery at Fors, just 4 miles from Hawes. The art of cheese making, perfected by the monks back in 1150, was passed down to local farmers' wives who continued to produce the cheese in their own farmhouses. In 1897 a local corn and provisions merchant of Hawes began to purchase milk from surrounding farms to use it for the manufacture of Wensleydale cheese on a large scale.

Back in the 1930s the industrial depression made trading conditions difficult, leaving the creamery in significant debt to farmers and the dairy faced closure. In 1935 local businessman Kit Calvert rallied support from local farmers, raising enough capital to rescue the only dairy producing cheese in the heart of Wensleydale. In 1966 Kit Calvert sold his now well established cheese business to the Milk Marketing Board. In 1979 the creamery title passed to Dairy Crest but in May 1992 after a number of years of losses by the company the creamery closed with the loss of 59 jobs.

Six months later, however, following many offers to rescue the creamery, four ex-managers together with a local businessman completed a management buy-out. It was then, with the skilled help of eleven members of the former workforce, that cheese making recommenced and Real Yorkshire Wensleydale was produced in time for Christmas. Over the following years increasing demand for Wensleydale, added-value and speciality cheeses with an extensive marketing campaign featuring the cartoon characters Wallace and Gromit, saw a major upturn in the business. This eventually led to the acquisition of another creamery at Kirkby Malzeard, near Ripon. Now employing over 200 people, The Wensleydale Creamery continues to enjoy global acclaim for its award-winning cheeses. Today the Wensleydale Creamery supplies a vast range of customers including major multiple retailers, wholesalers, and the food service sector, plus a large number of exports. Wensleydale cheese is still produced to a time-honoured recipe, using milk from local farms, produced by the cows that graze the sweet limestone meadows that are rich in wild flowers, herbs and grasses. It is this herbage that gives the milk, and hence the cheese, its special Dales flavour.

It was announced in December 2013 that Wensleydale cheese had been awarded official protection by the European Union. The newly conferred status means no other cheese-maker outside the designated area can produce a cheese and call it Yorkshire Wensleydale. The Wensleydale Creamery has finally won its long campaign for Protected Geographical Indication (PGI) status for its product. The creamery will now add the PGI symbol to its packaging, reaffirming its true Yorkshire credentials.

Other local tourist attractions include the Dales Countryside Museum, based in the old Hawes railway station of the Wensleydale Railway; nearby Hardraw Force waterfall; and the Buttertubs Pass, which links Wensleydale to Swaledale. Hawes itself has a regular weekly market, as well as many shops, pubs and tearooms.

The Walk

The walk commences from the Gayle Lane car park which is on the western side of the town. From the car park turn left, then just after the Wensleydale Creamery go right over a stile signed to the Youth Hostel. Follow this track, heading uphill to a stile. Pass a barn, cross the fields using a further six stiles to reach firstly a lane then a road. Turn left, then right through a gate signed to Thorney Mire House. Continue along this path for ½ mile (800m) to a gate leading onto a lane. Turn right at this point and follow the lane for ¾ mile (1.2km), passing under the viaduct to the road at Appersett.

Turn left across the bridge. Follow the road and cross the next bridge, then bear left at the junction. Go through a stile, signed to Bluebell Hill. Cross the field, go through a gate and over a bridge, then bear slightly left and head uphill. Go through a gate and continue along the track until you reach a crossroads signpost. Here turn right and follow the valley to a stile known as Bob's Stile. Cross the field beyond, go over a stile then turn left to a ladder stile over a wall. Cross the field towards Hardraw, going over wooden stile, then over another ladder stile into a lane.

Turn right then left at the main road and cross the bridge to reach Hardraw Force. Comprising a single

Hardraw Force

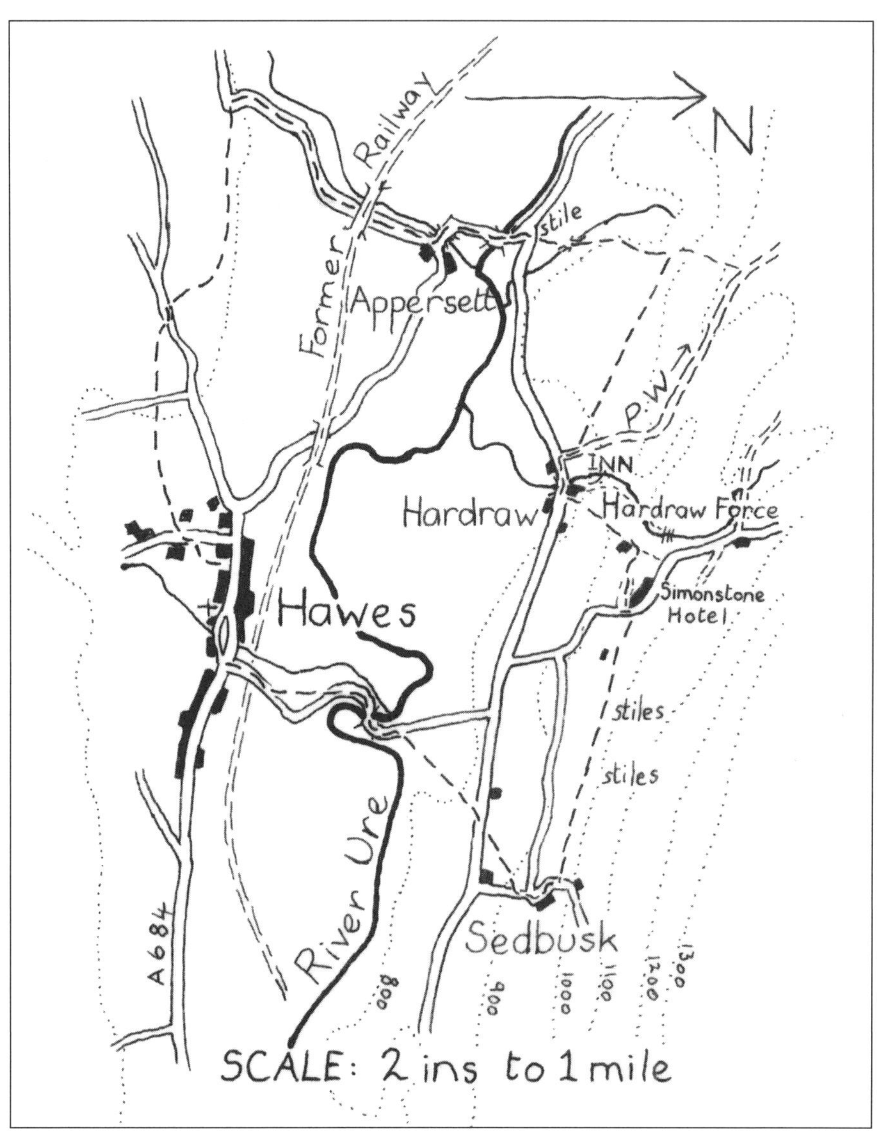

drop of 100 feet from a rocky overhang, Hardraw Force is claimed to be England's highest unbroken waterfall – at least discounting underground falls. Geologically, the bed of the river and plunge pool is slate; on top of that is sandstone and the top layer is carboniferous limestone. Public viewing of

Hardraw Force is rather unusual, as the visitor has to go through the bar of the Green Dragon Inn public house in Hardraw to reach the falls; an entrance fee is payable on the way through the pub. It is currently £2.50 per adult. Access behind the falls is now prohibited.

On the way to and from Hardraw Force you will pass the circular bandstand for the annual Hardraw Scar Brass Band Contest, usually held in September. It was founded in 1881, and is reputed to be the second oldest brass band competition in the world. Bands from throughout the North of England – and beyond – compete in the championship, cheered on by supporters who crowd the valley floor and hillsides of this natural amphitheatre.

To continue with the walk itself, immediately beyond the pub, turn left and go right through a signed gap in the wall, through a courtyard and over a stile. Follow the path over another stile, steeply uphill, over a stile and up steps. By the house, go through a stile and right of the stables, then through two more stiles on to a lane by the Simonstone Hall Hotel.

Turn right then left along the road. Almost immediately turn right though a stile signed for Sedbusk. Follow the track through a metal gate and over two

Hardraw Scar Bandstand

ladder stiles and another gateway then through a total of fourteen stiles into Sedbusk itself. From this village came the area's first-known rope maker, John Brenkley, who died in 1725. The rope making tradition is continued today in Hawes by W. R. Outhwaite and Son in their Hawes Ropeworks. Visitors can see work in progress on ropes of all types, including ropes for bells, barriers and banisters, as well as dog leads and braids.

Turn right along the road, bear left near the post-box and go downhill. Go right, over a stile signed to Haylands Bridge. Cross the field, bend right to a stile in a crossing wall, then down to a stile on to a road. Cross to another stile and follow the path, cross a stream, go over a stile then bear right over a humpback bridge. Go through a gated stile on to a road.

Turn left. Cross Haylands Bridge and beyond go right through a kissing gate signed for Hawes. Follow the path, go over a stile, turn left, then right on to the main road. At the junction go across and turn right at the post office. Follow the main road through Hawes, turning left after the school to bring you back to the car park.

In Hawes at the end of the walk there is an excellent selection of places to eat and drink, from quaint little tea rooms to pubs, restaurants and take away establishments. For more formal dining there is everything from a reservation only bistro style restaurant with contemporary menus and a list of fine wines, to a 17th Century Inn serving traditionally cooked local produce and real cask ales. Other restaurants include French, Italian, Indian and Thai, so there is sure to be something to please everyone. Around the town there are the usual take away outlets with fish and chips, pizza and Chinese options. Several sandwich bars, coffee houses and cafés offer light snacks to take away and will even prepare picnic food on request.

WENSLEYDALE WALK 3
Semerwater

- This walk takes us round Yorkshire's only natural lake, with an option at the end of the walk to visit Stalling Busk with its early 17th century Church and the award winning Raydale Preserves shop.

Distance	5 miles (8km)
Ascent	850 feet (260m)
Time	2 hours
Grading	Moderate
Suggested Map	OS Outdoor Leisure 30 – Yorkshire Dales – North & Central
Starting point	Grid Reference: 921875
Parking	Car park by the lake (small fee payable)
How to get there	Bainbridge is 4 miles east of Hawes on the A684 and from here take a minor road for 2½ miles though Countersett to Semerwater
Terrain	Moorland footpaths throughout

Semerwater

Two and a half miles south of Bainbridge lies Semerwater, which is Yorkshire's only natural lake. It is approximately half a mile (800m) long, covers and 100 acres (0.40 km2) of the valley. It is at the end of the River Bain which is legally designated as a Main River, so at around two and a half miles long is reputed to be the shortest river in England.

Semerwater was formed at the end of the last Ice Age when glacial meltwater attempted to drain away down the valley the glacier had gouged out of the underlying limestone. However, it was prevented from doing so by a wall of boulder clay, which was dumped by the glacier across the valley's end. So the water built up, eventually forming a lake which once stretched 3 miles (4.8km) up Raydale. Over the last few milleania, however, natural silting has gradually filled the upper part of the lake bed and reduced the size of the lake to its current level.

According to legend long ago the spot was occupied by a prosperous city. One night an old man (or in some versions, an angel in disguise) came down to the city, in search of food and drink. He went from door to door, and at each house he was turned away. Finally, he came to the hovel of a poor couple just outside the town; the couple took him in and treated him with great kindness.

When the stranger was about to leave, he turned to face the town and uttered the curse: "Semerwater rise, and Semerwater sink, And swallow the town all save this house, where they gave me food and drink." And as soon as this was said, the waters of the lake rose up and flooded the city, drowning the proud inhabitants and leaving only the hovel of the poor couple on the hillside unscathed.

Semerwater

Every August Bank Holiday Sunday a special lakeside service is held on the shores of Semerwater. The vicar of Askrigg takes the service from a small boat on the lake and the hymns are accompanied by the local band. All other activity on the lake is suspended while the event takes place so quiet descends on the beautiful dale. It's a tradition dating back to the mid-20th century.

Accommodation for visiting Semerwater needs to be sourced at Hawes, Bainbridge or Askrigg as there is only one small B&B at High Blean at Raydaleside on the road to Stalling Busk that is within walking distance of Semerwater.

The Walk

The walk starts at the car park by the lake, there being a small charge for parking here. Leaving the car park head up the road in an easterly direction climbing over the ladder stile just opposite some farm buildings which is signed to Stalling Busk. Ahead you will see a barn, go through a stile and head for this crossing two stone stiles, after which you will spot a Wldlife Trust sign. Another two stiles in front lead you to a gate where there is a sign to Marsett. Go across the field heading for the corner where you reach another stone stile. The route now follows the river, heading for a barn in front. Cross the stile above the barn and go over the field to another stile and a second barn after which in another ¼ mile (400 metres) you go across the stream.

Here you will encounter a good footpath and ahead is a barn with its roof missing. Continue, crossing three more stiles after which you turn right. In front is a copse of trees which you need to head towards, keeping the wall on your right hand side. After the copse, go through two more stiles to reach a footbridge. Cross this and head along the track, turning right to drop down to the ford. Do not cross this if in flood but instead turn to the left and go over the footbridge and back to the track which heads unerringly up to the hamlet of Marsett.

Marsett is one of three settlements based around the hills surrounding Semerwater. Just before reaching the village turn right following the stream and head for the road in front by the phone box. Cross the bridge and after a further 100yds (90m) turn aside from the riverside path and follow the track by the signpost to Burtersett and Hawes. Head uphill to a gate by the stone wall, cross the stile continuing uphill over the next three stiles until the track levels out. You will now encounter another path joining yours by the gap in the wall. Turn right here and pass through the gate in the wall. You will soon come across a fork in the path and here you need to take the right hand fork, heading downhill from here onwards until you reach another stile, after which there is a much steeper descent. Pass through two gates until you reach a crossroads. Take the track straight ahead, which then curves to the left until you reach a gate which leads onto the road.

Turn right on the road and head downhill to the crossroads at which you should turn right and then immediately left by the sign to Stalling Busk. You are now on the last ¼ mile (400 metres) and it is merely a question of following the road downhill, cross the bridge and arrive back at the car park.

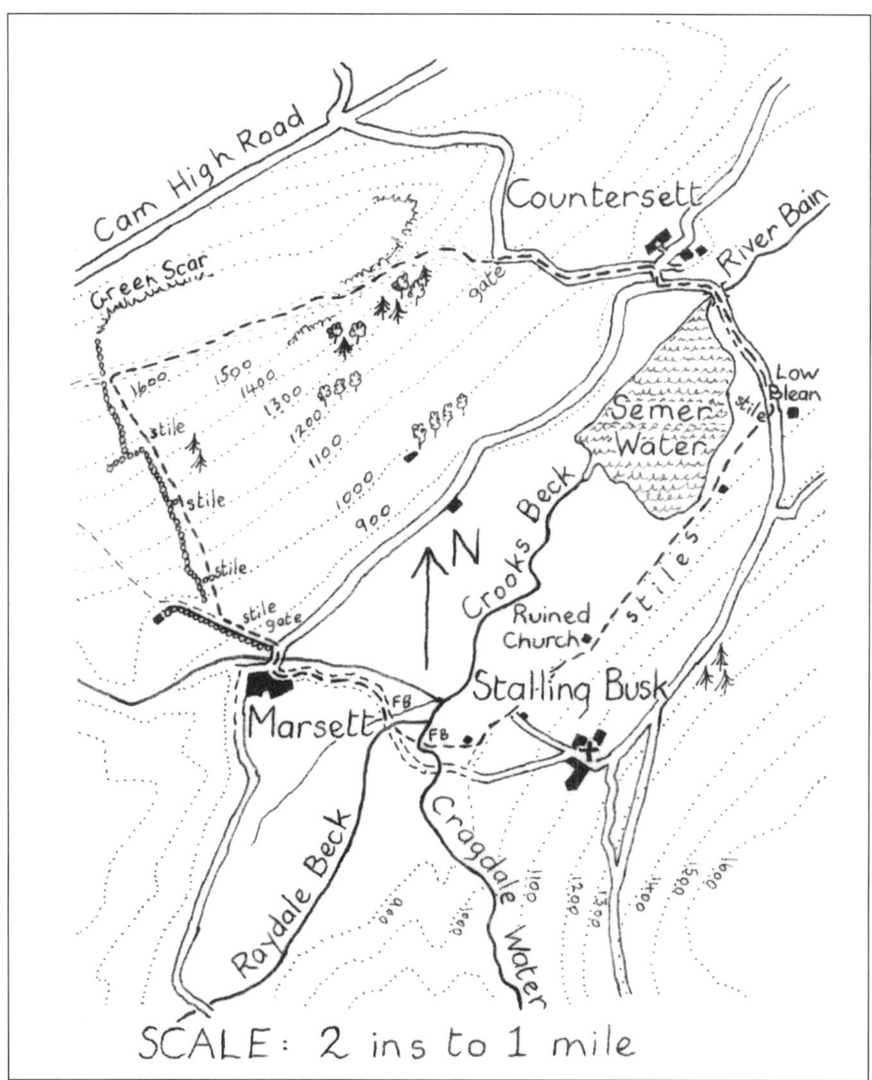

It is worthwhile, after reaching the end of the walk, driving up to the nearby village of Stalling Busk as the award winning Raydale Preserves is made here, and in the shop you can sample some of the wonderful preserves on offer. There is also St. Matthew's Church in the village that was built in the early 20th century and this is also well worth a visit, along with Stalling Busk Old Church.

The very first church at Stalling Busk dates back to the early 1600s and was built on common land. During the civil war the church fell into ruin. Stalling Busk inhabitants bought the land and rebuilt the church in around 1722. The first curate was Anthony Clapham whose stipend was twenty-seven pounds and five shillings per annum. The interior of the church is divided by two arcades which run north-south rather than follow the usual plan of east-west alignment. These arcades probably date from the early 19th century.

The church was still in use in the early twentieth century, but it was in a poor state of repair. When the new church of St. Mathews was built in the village of Stalling Busk in 1908-09, the Old Church fell into disuse and was soon stripped of its roof and furnishings. Some consolidation work was carried out in 1981, when the altar was also rebuilt in its present position against the north wall rather than in its original position in the east aisle. Further restoration was then undertaken in 2000. In its early years this building was a chapel of ease. Stalling Busk became a perpetual curacy in the 1750s and a fully independent ecclesiastical parish in the 1860s.

Stalling Busk Old Church

For refreshments at the end of the walk, there is sometimes an ice cream van parked in the car park at the northern end of Semerwater. If not, the nearby village of Bainbridge has a number of facilities or for more establishments venture into Hawes, a three mile drive down the main road (see Walk 2 in this section for full details).

Middleham

An easy walk initially following the River Cover and heading into Coverdale before crossing Coverham Bridge and returning to Middleham over Middleham Moor.

Distance	**7 miles (11.5km)**
Ascent	**500 feet (150m)**
Time	**2.5 hours**
Grading	**Easy**
Suggested Map	**OS Outdoor Leisure 30 – Yorkshire Dales – North & Central**
Starting point	**Grid Reference: 127878**
Parking	**Middleham market square**
How to get there	**Middleham is on the A6108 approximately 1½ miles south of Leyburn which is 10 miles west of the A1 and 17 miles north-west of Ripon on the A6108**
Terrain	**Field paths and tracks throughout the walk**

Middleham

Middleham is a small market town on the north-facing side of the Ure valley just above the junction of the River Ure and River Cover. There has been a settlement there since Roman Britain and the town was recorded in the Domesday Book as 'Medelai'. Middleham is twinned with the northern French town of Agincourt, and both have fine historical connections.

The first known settlement at Middleham was during the Roman Era. The IXth Legion of the Roman Army conquered York in 69AD and moved north quickly. Their road heading north from London passed through Middleham en-route to Bainbridge. Near Middleham, the Romans built a guard station to control traffic on the River Ure. Before the Norman Conquest the lands in this area were controlled by Gilpatrick but after 1069, the land in the area of Middleham was given to William the Conqueror's nephew, Alan Rufus. Rufus built a wooden motte-and-bailey castle above the town, whose earthworks are still visible today and called 'William's Hill'. Rufus also built the nearby castle at Richmond.

The present castle which dominates the town, Middleham Castle, was started in 1190. It was called the 'Windsor of the North'. The castle was in the possession of Richard Neville, 16th Earl of Warwick when his young cousin Richard, Duke of Gloucester (the future Richard III) came here to learn the skills of knighthood in 1462. During the Wars of the Roses, both Edward IV and Henry VI were held prisoner here. Richard, Duke of Gloucester became master of the castle in 1471 after Warwick died at the Battle of Barnet. Richard used the castle as his political base whilst he was administrator for the North for his brother Edward IV. Richard married Warwick's daughter, Anne Neville,

Middleham Castle

in 1472. Middleham Castle is where their son Edward was born in 1473 and where he died in April 1484. When Richard III died at the Battle of Bosworth Field in 1485, Middleham lost one of its favourite residents. Locals don't believe the propagandist version of Richard, promoted by Shakespeare's play, that he was a murderer – the Lord Mayor of York reported to his council after Bosworth that "King Richard, late lawfully reigning over us, was through great treason piteously slain and murdered".

Middleham Castle today is well worth visiting whilst in the town. It is a splendid ruin, with one of the biggest keeps in England, impressive curtain walls and a deep moat and is now maintained by English Heritage.

At the time of King Richard III, Middleham was a bustling market town and in 1389 the lord of Middleham Manor received a grant from the crown to hold a weekly market in the town and a yearly fair on the feast of St. Alkelda the Virgin. The town itself is built around two markets; the larger, lower market and the upper, or swine market. At one end of the market cross is a worn effigy of an animal reclining.

Most buildings in the old part of Middleham were built at the end of the Elizabethan era although the old rectory of the church has some mediaeval elements incorporated into it. The Church of Saints Mary and Alkelda was founded in 1291. The only remaining Norman artefact is a section of zig-zag moulding that was once around a door or window, and today is high up above the north aisle. Just west of the church is St. Alkelda's well, whose waters are reputed to restore strength to weak eyes. In 1915 the yearly livestock market was still one of the most important in the North, though the weekly market had already fallen into disuse. Today the livestock market has moved to Leyburn.

The town is a modern centre of horse racing in the UK and is home to the Middleham Trainers' Association. The first racehorse trainer to train at Middleham was Isaac Cape in 1765. Today there are several racehorse trainers based here including Mark Johnston, and Patrick Haslam. Racing is the number one employer in the town with tourism the second biggest industry. More than 500 horses train in Middleham, under the watchful eyes of 13 trainers. Both the Low Moor and the High Moor have been used for exercise for more than 300 years; one of the earliest recorded winners was Bay Bolton, born in 1705, which won Queen Anne's Gold Cup at York Races. Among early jockeys was the splendidly-named 'Crying Jackie' Mangle, who won the St. Leger five times in the 1770s and 80s.

The Walk

Our walk commences from the cross in the square. Walk uphill past the Black Swan Hotel and few yards beyond the pub turn left up a narrow passage beside the Castle Tea Rooms, continuing across the road and left of the castle to a gate.

Go half left across the field, following the sign pointing towards the stepping stones. Cross the next three fields, over the various waymarked stiles. After crossing the third field, turn along the side of the field, ignoring a track to the right. Turn right at a waymarked crossing wall down to the bank of the River Cover by the stepping stones.

Turn right (do not cross the stepping stones) and follow the riverside path, going through a gate and up some steps. After returning to the riverbank, go right where the path forks. Go over two more stiles, turning immediately right after the second. Follow the waymark uphill to a marker post. Turn left and follow the line of the wood. At the end of the field go left through a waymarked stile, through the trees to a second stile, then straight down the field back to the river bank. Go over a waymarked stile and onward to the bridge.

Go through the gate over the bridge. Follow the track as it winds right and uphill through two gates on to a road, opposite Braithwaite Hall. Owned by

Middleham Castle from the Downs

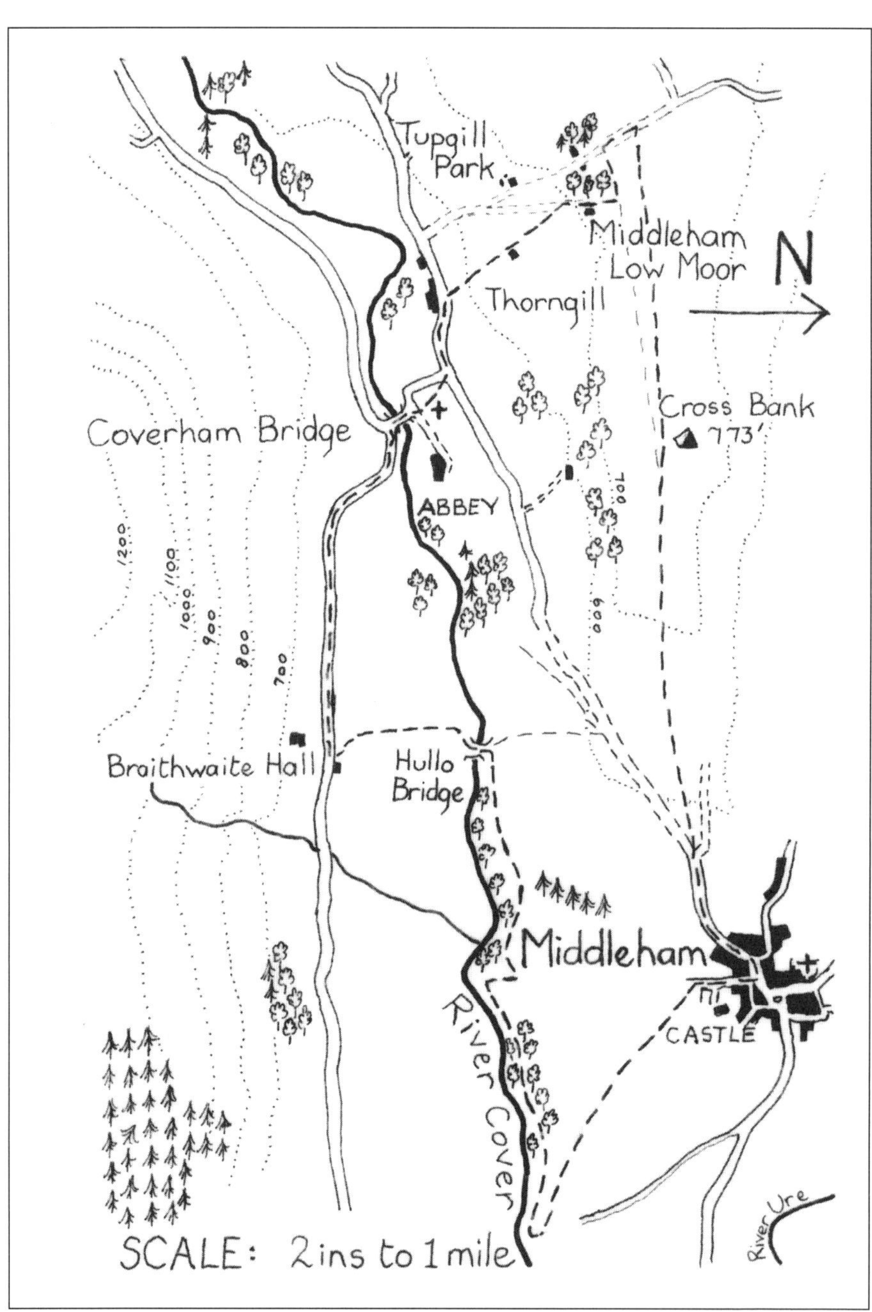

Tupgill Park
Middleham Low Moor
Thorngill
Cross Bank 773'
Coverham Bridge
ABBEY
1200
1100
1000
900
800
700
600
700
Braithwaite Hall
Hullo Bridge
Middleham
River Cover
CASTLE
River Ure
N
SCALE: 2 ins to 1 mile

the National Trust and open by appointment only, this is a modest farmhouse of 1667, with three fine gables and unusual oval windows beneath them. Inside are stone-flagged floors, a fine oak staircase and wood panelling all of the late 17th century. On the hillside behind are the earthworks of a hill fort, thought to be Iron Age. Turn right, and follow the road for one mile (1.6km) to Coverham Bridge, probably built by the monks of nearby Coverham Abbey. There are a few remains of the Abbey, founded in the 12th century, mostly incorporated into later buildings on the site. Miles Coverdale, who was the first man to complete a full English translation of the Bible, came from here. Turn right over the bridge, then right again.

Before the gates, turn left through a small gate, walk beside a waterfall and into the churchyard. Leave by the lychgate and turn left along the road. After ¼ mile (400m) go through a gate on the right opposite a disused factory, bearing slightly left. Go over three stiles. Go through a gate, pass between buildings and go over three stiles through a belt of woodland.

Cross the field to a gateway the right of the wood. After passing the house, bend left to a gate on to a track. Turn right, go through a gate and turn right again. Don't follow the track, but go half left to meet a bridleway across the moor. Middleham, as mentioned earlier, is the home of famous racehorses, and you may be lucky enough to see some in training as you walk over Middleham Low Moor. Follow the bridleway across the moor for 1½ miles (2.4km) to the road.

Here turn left and just before the Middleham sign, take a signposted path on the right. Turn left over the stile and follow the path parallel to the road. Go through two more stiles, and then take another towards the castle, passing through a gate on to the lane. Turn left and return to the square.

There are plenty of facilities in Middleham for refreshment at the end of the walk, including the tea rooms by the castle which is well worth a visit at the end of the walk.

West Burton

Nestling in a hollow of the little-known Walden Valley, West Burton is one of the Yorkshire Dales' jewels not to be overlooked. It has a broad village green and small, but spectacular waterfall, Burton-cum-Walden, to give it its official title, which has delighted visitors to Wensleydale since the days when the great artist, J. M. W. Turner, captured its watery magic.

Distance	**4 miles (6.5 km)**
Ascent	**400 feet (120 m)**
Time	**1.5 hours**
Grading	**Easy**
Suggested Map	**OS Outdoor Leisure 30 – Yorkshire Dales – North & Central**
Starting point	**Grid Reference: 017867**
Parking	**Adjacent to the green in the centre of the village**
How to get there	**West Burton is 1 mile south-east of Aysgarth, just off the A684. Aysgarth is approximately 16 miles west of the A1 passing through Bedale and Leyburn**
Terrain	**Riverside paths and footpaths**

West Burton

Many people regard West Burton as the prettiest of all the villages in the Dales. Its wide, irregular green, with a fat obelisk of 1820, is surrounded by small stone cottages, formerly homes to the quarrymen and miners of the district – but it has no protestant church, villagers instead having to make the trek to Aysgarth for services. West Burton has always been an important centre being

Cottages in West Burton

at the entrance to Bishopdale, with its road link to Wharfedale. South of the village is the road to Walden Head, now a dead end for motorists, but for walkers an attractive high level alternative route to Starbotton and Kettlewell. The name Walden is Norse for wolf's den. Another theory is that the name comes from the Anglo-Saxon words 'wealh' (meaning foreigners and used for Britons – hence 'Welsh') and 'denu' (meaning valley).There is also plenty for the visitor to see and do in the village of West Burton. As well as The Old Smithy Antiques there are the Moorside Designs Cat Pottery and Aardvark picture framers.

West Burton was once a thriving market town, and still boasts its ancient octagonal market cross and the remains of the old wooden stocks. The market has long been obsolete, but fairs are still held in March and May for horses, cattle, and sheep. The Wesleyan Methodists and the Independents have chapels in the village, the former erected about the year 1813, and the latter in 1851, at a cost of £350.

The Walk

Our walk commences by the Green and near the Village Shop. Look out for a property called Meadowcroft where there is a sign for Eshington Bridge. Turn left here, cross over the road and after first a right and then left turn you will reach a gate. Pass through this and go down the stone steps, heading for the barn in front. Go through another gate and across the field in front heading for a gap in the wall after which you will see another stile which leads onto the road. Turn left here, cross the bridge and follow the narrow lane ahead until you reach a sign for Aysgarth by a stile. Cross this to another stile and then proceed to the barn where you will see a gap in a fence by the side of it. Turn left and head for the corner of the field where a gate is located. Cross

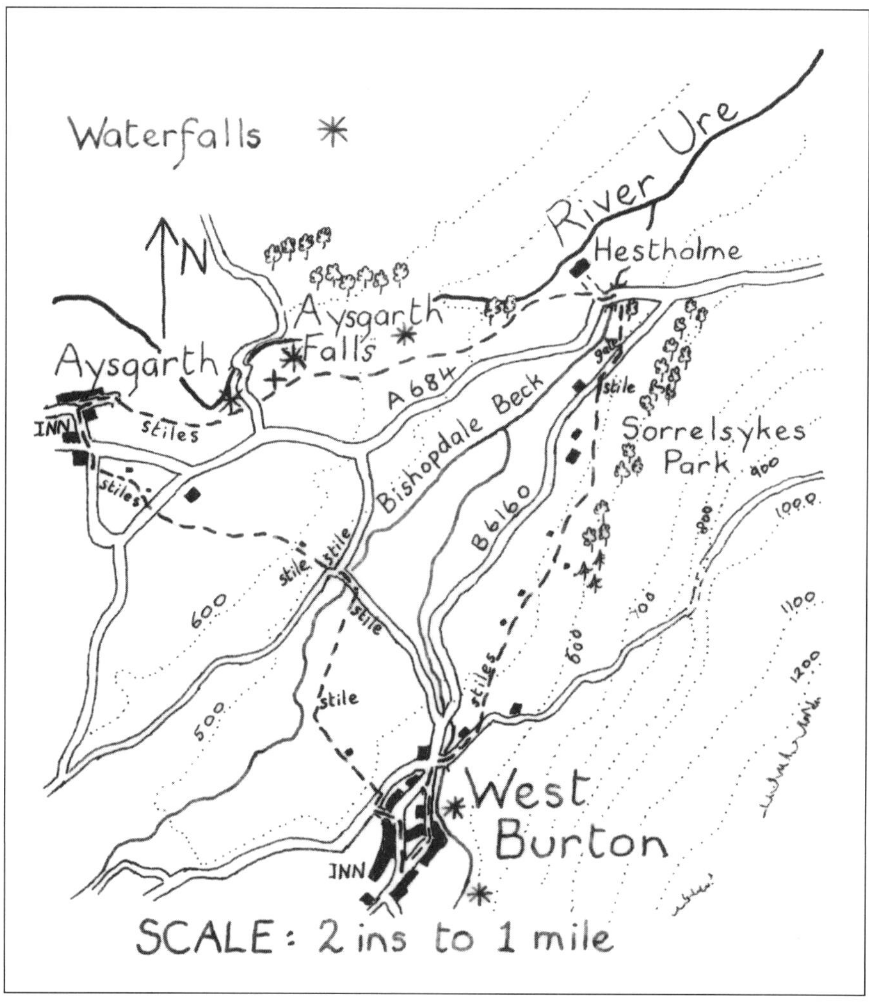

this and turn right with a signpost ahead. Now go uphill to another gate and stile. Cross the field in front, heading off to the left to reach the lane at the end. After a left and then right turn at the stile you will see another sign for Aysgarth. Continue across a further three stiles until you reach the road where you need to turn right to enter the village. Go past the George and Dragon inn and where the road bends to the left proceed forwards until you reach the chapel. Turn right by the green and follow the lane ahead. When you reach a property called Field House pass through the stile, onto the next stile and turn left onto the track. The route is straight ahead and you go through a series of stiles (eight in total) until you reach the road.

Head into the churchyard and keeping to the right of the church go across two more stiles and into the wood. Continue following the track over another stile and then down a series of steps towards the river. Go through firstly a gate and then a stile. Upon reaching the river go over the stile on the right and follow the track over a further two stiles. Here, at the signpost, bear right and across the field to reach another road. Cross the bridge on your left and immediately turn right into the next wood by a sign to Edgley. Go over the stile and across the field to reach a gate leading onto another road.

At the road turn right and after 150yds (135m) go over the stile on your left by the sign to Flanders Hall. At this point you pass two oddities in the parkland behind the house at Sorrellsykes Park. These two follies were built in the 18th century by Mrs Sykes and no one seems to know why. One is a

Follies in Sorrelsykes Park

round tower, with a narrowing waist like a Diablo. The other, sitting like a Saturn space rocket ready for lift-off, is known to local people as the 'Rocket Ship'. It is of no practical use, except for minimal shelter in the square room in its base, but it is just one of many folly cones throughout Britain. None of the others, however, have this elaborate arrangement of fins – presumably added because the builder had doubts about its stability.

Keep below the follies until you reach a footpath sign at the end of the ridge. Cross over the track and head uphill until you reach a series of steps with a stile at the top. Turn right by the barn, pass through another gate and then head downhill going firstly through two gates and then across three stiles until you reach a lane at the end of the path. Turn right to cross the bridge which then leads to the road heading towards the village. A left turn onto the track will lead you back up to the green in the village of West Burton. At the end of the walk refreshments are available at the West Burton Shop and Tea Room.

SWALEDALE INTRODUCTION

Swaledale is one of the more remote dales and runs west to east as far as the town of Richmond where the River Swale turns southwards and flows in to the northern end of the Vale of Mowbray. Swaledale stretches from Hollow Mill Cross on Great Shunner Fell where the River Swale rises, down to Myton-upon-Swale where it joins the River Ure, which in turn becomes the River Ouse. The walks in this book, however, concentrate on the dale west of Richmond, the area best known to walkers. The river's name comes from the Old English meaning 'the whirling, rushing river'. In its upper reaches, the Swale has the steepest gradient of any major English river – about 1 in 160.

There are numerous villages and hamlets in Swaledale including Reeth, Grinton, Low Row, Gunnerside, Muker, Thwaite and Keld. Along the Swale there are a number of spectacular waterfalls including Richmond Falls at Richmond, and Kisdon Force near Thwaite. Tributary valleys include Arkengarthdale – once the centre of a long deserted local lead mining industry.

From Thwaite and near the head of the dale the famous Buttertubs Pass leads up over the moors and down into Wensleydale. Another road from Keld leads north over the moors to Tan Hill – well known as the site of the highest public house in England.

Swaledale is less frequented than the other dales we have looked at and its tributary Arkengarthdale can seem even more remote. One of the walks in this remote side valley is from Langthwaite to the hamlet of Booze and is one of the most spectacular short walks in the book.

The River Swale's unpredictable nature and tendency to flash flood has led to many tragedies over the centuries. Safe crossing points have always been important and there are relatively few in the dale. Grinton was one of the first crossing points to be established and it became the centre of a huge parish from medieval times under the wing of Bridlington Priory.

The dale was very sparsely populated until the 18th century due to its harsh climate and lack of decent land in the valley bottom that was suitable for agriculture. Centuries before, in the Bronze Age, work began clearing fields of stones, leaving stone cairns that can still be seen. The Romans had little influence in this part of Yorkshire and left the native population well alone, but in the years following the withdrawal of the Roman army, Swaledale become a stronghold for native peoples resisting Anglo-Saxon invaders. Medieval monastic houses were not as influential here as they were elsewhere in the Yorkshire Dales, but two small nunneries were established at the east end of the Swaledale where the land and climate was a little easier for farming.

Agriculture, however, took a back seat three hundred years ago when lead mining developed in the dale. Swaledale and lead mining go hand in hand and on the moorland areas above Keld, Muker, Gunnerside and Reeth are the relics of this former industry which employed many thousands of men. The hills of Swaledale and Arkengarthdale have rich veins of lead ore and these were exploited from at least Roman times onward. The 18th and 19th centuries saw a large-scale industry established and the population of the area surged. Medieval wood pastures in Swaledale survived because the lead industry needed wood to burn in its smelt mills. When farms were divided equally amongst sons, this led to the characteristically dense pattern of small fields and field barns that still survives in Swaledale today. Lead mining also directly changed the landscape with its sprawling spoil heaps and remains of smelt mills and ore processing areas. This is even more apparent on the road between Langthwaite in Arkengarthdale and Low Row in Swaledale. Here vast scars caused by washing out lead veins using dammed sources of water (hushing) can be seen.

Reeth at the meeting point of Arkengarthdale with Swaledale, became the economic hub of the lead industry and grew enormously. The wealth from lead mining led to many beautiful new country houses being built in the dale with fashionable gardens and parkland around them. The late 19th century saw another influx of wealthy landowners, this time lured by the attraction of grouse shooting on the heather moorland above the valley. They built well-appointed shooting lodges and travelled up from their estates in the south by train. The train also brought tourists of more modest means, but it was not really until cars became popular from the 1950s onward, that tourists managed to get to Swaledale in any numbers. This led to the provision of tourist accommodation, tea shops, and garages.

Keld is the most westerly of the settlements in Swaledale. Its name derives from the Viking word Kelda meaning a spring, and the village was once called Appletre Kelde – the spring near the apple trees. Keld is the crossing point of Wainwright's Coast to Coast Walk and the Pennine Way long distance footpaths at the head of Swaledale. Unfortunately it does not contain a shop. There used to be a Youth Hostel but this closed in October 2006; the building has since reopened as Keld Lodge, a fine hotel with bar and restaurant. There is a series of four waterfalls close to Keld at a limestone gorge on the River Swale. These are Kisdon Force, East Gill Force, Catrake Force and Wain Wath Force.

The next village down the dale 2 miles (3km) away is Muker. Its name reflects its origin as a Norse settlement, derived from the Norse word 'Mjor-aker' meaning 'the narrow acre'. The earliest recorded evidence for occupation in and around Muker takes the form of a skeleton found, with flints, on Muker Common in the early 20th century. The location at the meeting of the River Swale and the Straw Beck with plenty of good meadow land around is most likely why the Vikings chose to settle here, giving them the opportunity to make a living out of mixed and pastoral farming. Agriculture continued to be the basis of the economy in Muker until lead mining became more important during the late 18th and early 19th century. Muker was also a major centre for hand knitting during this period. The importance of these industries is reflected in the many cottages, workshops and other buildings constructed at the time.

With the decline of the mining industry, farming remained the principal occupation. From the late 19th century Muker began to see an increasing number of visitors and holiday makers and today the village is a popular starting point for walks in the area. The traditional late 18th and early 19th century barns and drystone walls of Swaledale are the most characteristic feature of the landscape. The flower-rich hay meadows around Muker are of international importance and are carefully protected. Farmers receive grants which allow them to farm the land by traditional methods, without using artificial fertilizers.

A further three miles downstream we come to the village of Gunnerside. The village is situated between the River Swale and its tributary, Gunnerside Beck. Gunnerside Ghyll is a smaller valley running northwards, at right angles to Swaledale and was one of the major areas of the lead mining industry in Swaledale until the late 19th century. Gunnerside village contains a traditional Yorkshire Dales public house at the foot of Gunnerside Ghyll, the Kings Head, as well as a Methodist Chapel, a part-time post office (located in the Literary Institute), a primary school and a working smithy/museum.

Seven miles further down The Swale is the important village of Reeth which is situated at the meeting point of Swaledale and Arkengarthdale. In Saxon times, Reeth was only a settlement on the forest edge, but by the time of the Norman Conquest it had grown sufficiently in importance to be noted in the Domesday Book. Later it became a centre for hand-knitting and the local lead industry was controlled from here, but it was always a market centre for the local farming community. Its 18th-century houses and hotels are clustered around a triangular green. The village has three pubs all situated on the green. They are the Black Bull, the King's Arms and the Buck Hotel. The village is overlooked by the fells of Fremington Edge and Calver Hill.

Adjacent to Reeth is the village of Grinton famous for its church. Often called 'The Cathedral of the Dales', Grinton church is dedicated to St. Andrew and was for centuries the main church for the whole of upper Swaledale, with many burials coming from miles away. The bodies were carried as much as 16 miles down the valley along the footpath from Keld, now known as the Corpse Way or corpse road, in wicker coffins. Several long stones, located at intervals along the path, traditionally called 'coffin stones', are said to be where the coffin would have been set down while the pallbearers rested.

Fragments of the old Norman church remain, including the font and the tower arch, which dates from the late 12th century. Other parts of the building date from the late 13th or early 14th century, and the pulpit is Jacobean, but St. Andrew's is now mainly a 15th century rebuild. Grinton's stone bridge across the River Swale was widened in the 18th century. The river is reputedly the fastest-flowing in England, and Grinton was the first point above Richmond where it could normally be forded. Above the village, on the Leyburn road is YHA Grinton Lodge, a former shooting lodge which is now a youth hostel.

Marske is the last village on The Swale before the town of Richmond is reached. It is on Marske Beck just before that river's confluence with the River Swale. Marske was long associated with the Hutton family, landowners and High Sheriffs of Yorkshire and Matthew Hutton, who became an archbishop of Canterbury was born there. He became a royal chaplain to George II in 1736, was the Rector of Trowbridge and of Spofforth, in Yorkshire, and held prebends at York and Westminster. In 1743 he became Bishop of Bangor, and in 1747, Archbishop of York, before finally, in 1757, becoming Archbishop of Canterbury, but died the next year without having ever lived in Lambeth Palace.

Richmond is the main market town of Swaledale and is the administrative centre of the district. It is the most duplicated UK place name, with 57 occurrences worldwide. The *Rough Guide* describes the entire town as 'an absolute gem'. Betty James wrote that "without any doubt Richmond is the most romantic place in the whole of the North East of England", and Joseph E. Morris agreed, although he went even further to comment that "Richmond is, beyond all question, the most romantic town in the North of England".

Richmond was founded in 1071 by the Breton Alan Rufus, on lands granted to him by William the Conqueror. Richmond Castle, completed in 1086, consisted of a keep with walls encompassing the area now known as the Market Place and is now a major tourist attraction. Richmond was eventually willed by Francis II, Duke of Brittany to Henry VII of England, whose grandson Henry FitzRoy, 1st Duke of Richmond and Somerset was independent Richmond's first duke. The town prospered with firstly the Swaledale wool industry and then the lead mining industry in nearby Arkengarthdale. It is from this period that the town's attractive Georgian architecture originates the most notable examples of which are to be found on Newbiggin and in Frenchgate.

The cobbled market place is one of the largest in England and the Green Howards Regimental Museum is based in the old Trinity Church in the centre of the market place; the town is also home to the Richmondshire Museum. The Georgian Theatre Royal, founded in 1788 by the actor Samuel Butler, is just off the market place. A decline in the fortunes of theatres led to its closure in 1848 and it was used as a warehouse for many years. In 1963 the theatre was restored and reopened, with a theatre museum added in 1979. More recently, the theatre has become the Georgian Theatre Royal and was extended in 2003 with the addition of a new block providing services and access next to the original auditorium. It is one of Britain's oldest extant theatres.

Richmond has been used as a filming location for a significant number of TV programmes and films including *The Fast Show*, *Century Falls*, *Earthfasts*, *A Woman of Substance* (1984) and *All Creatures Great and Small* amongst others. Lewis Carroll, author of *Alice in Wonderland* and *Alice through the Looking Glass*, attended Richmond School and lived in nearby Croft on Tees.

One of the local legends is that 200 years ago some soldiers found an entrance to a tunnel near the castle keep. They could not fit into the tunnel so they elected to send a regimental drummer boy into it instead. The boy was asked to walk along the tunnel and beat his drum so that above ground the soldiers could follow the noise. They did this for three miles before the sound stopped unexpectedly. This was never explained and today a stone marks the spot where the noise stopped. More confusingly the entrance can also not be found. Today schools celebrate this local legend with children marching through town annually. Legend claims that on some cold nights you can still hear the faint sound of the drummer boy.

Gunnerside Gill

What is a hush? By the end of this walk you will have seen several so should be able to answer that question.

Distance	**9½ miles (15km)**
Ascent	**1820 feet (560m)**
Time	**4 hours**
Grading	**Strenuous**
Suggested Map	**OS Outdoor Leisure 30 – Yorkshire Dales – North & Central**
Starting point	**Grid Reference: 950982**
Parking	**Gunnerside village**
How to get there	**Gunnerside is on the B6270 14 miles west of Richmond. Take the A6108 out of Richmond and turn right after about 3 miles onto the B6270**
Terrain	**Mining tracks and riverside paths. Boots or strong shoes recommended**

Gunnerside Gill

Gunnerside Gill (or Ghyll) is a small valley which branches off Swaledale into moorland to the north of Gunnerside. The area had intensive lead mining in the 18th and 19th centuries and the valley still contains much evidence of its industrial past. Streams were dammed, and the water released as a torrent to scour soil off the surface and reveal lead ore (galena) seams. The resultant scars are known as hushes (perhaps onomatopoeia of the sound that the water made). Bunton, Friarfold, and Gorton hushes are on the east side of the valley, with the North Hush being on the opposite side. Large areas of the upper valley are covered in spoil heaps from the mining activity, and a number of the mining buildings remain but most are in a derelict state. Care is therefore needed when visiting these. Many of the buildings and mine structures are now scheduled as ancient monuments.

The geologists will be particularly interested in the waterfalls in Botcher Gill, a tributary of Gunnerside Beck, as they contain numerous fossils. The Sir Francis Mine is located in the lower reaches of the gill. This mine was opened further down the valley in 1864 to exploit deeper seams, and was the first to use compressed air drills. It was abandoned in 1882 however after failing to make decent returns. The evidence of centuries of lead mining in this area is clearly visible in spoil heaps, the entrances to disused mines and in the ruins of smelt mills scattered across the region.

Alfred Wainwright's Coast to Coast Walk crosses the upper reaches of the valley before heading over to Surrender Bridge and Cringley Bottom and down into Reeth. As the valley descends southwards the scenery changes from mainly industrial to become a mixture of woodland and sheep pastures, before the beck joins the River Swale in the village of Gunnerside.

The circular walk you are about to undertake takes in firstly the west side of the Gill and then returns down the eastern side. The first mile, however, is on the banks of the Swale to reach the hamlet of Ivelet before heading up the moorland track over Gunnerside Pasture to Botcher Gill Gate. The route then passes the disused Lownathwaite Lead Mines and North Hush before reaching the ruins of the Blakethwaite Smelt Mill. After crossing the river, the walk heads back down Gunnerside Gill on its eastern side, passing Swina Bank Scar, Middlebank and Birkbeck Wood before returning to the village.

The Walk

Leave the village along the B6270 as it turns south after crossing the Gill, and a quarter of a mile after leaving the village, pass through a narrow gate on the right just before the bridge over the Swale. Follow the meadow path with the river on your left for just under a mile (1.5km) before it climbs sharply up to the right, with the river falling away to the left. This first section of the walk is part of the Corpse Way mentioned in the Swaledale introduction. As there was no burial ground in this part of the valley, the dead had to be carried from up the dale to the consecrated ground at Grinton, near Reeth.

Follow the path across half a dozen fields until a footbridge over a small, but deep valley takes you into the hamlet of Ivelet. On the north side of the bridge, set into the verge, is a coffin stone where pall bearers rested with the coffin on their journey from Muker down to the church at Grinton. A hundred yards (90m) further on, near to the phone box, turn right and follow the road

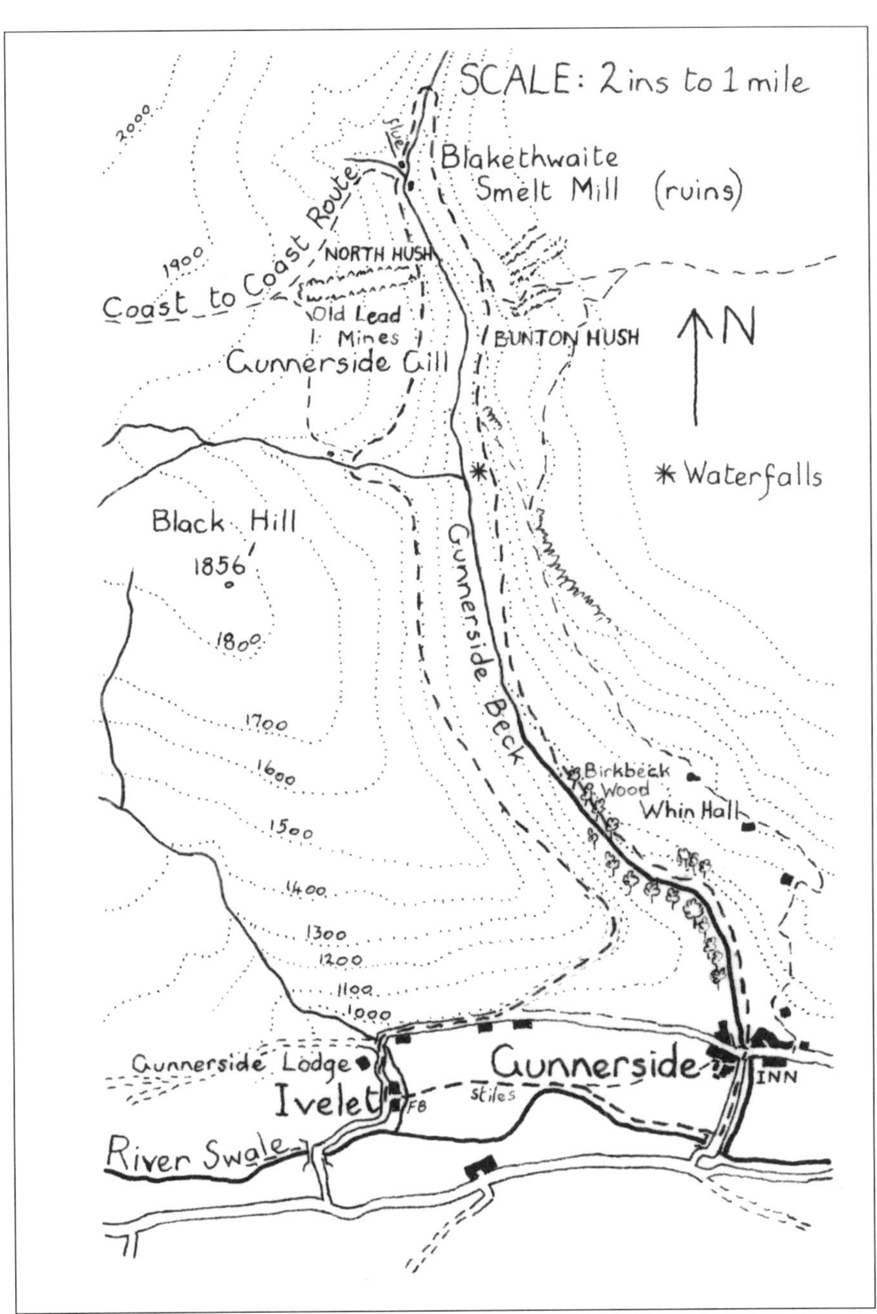

SCALE: 2 ins to 1 mile
Blakethwaite Smelt Mill (ruins)
flue
2000
1900
Coast to Coast Route
NORTH HUSH
Old Lead Mines
Gunnerside Gill
BUNTON HUSH
N
* Waterfalls
Black Hill
1856
1800
1700
1600
1500
1400
1300
1200
1100
1000
Gunnerside Beck
Birkbeck Wood
Whin Hall
Gunnerside Lodge
Gunnerside
INN
Ivelet
FB
stiles
River Swale

uphill towards Gunnerside Lodge. This was owned for many years by the Peel family whose ancestors included Sir Robert Peel, founder of the Police Force. Pass the lodge on the left and follow the minor road as it turns sharply to the right heading back towards Gunnerside. Just after the first farm buildings on your right, a broad track leaves the road on the left.

Follow the track as it climbs steeply uphill initially and then levels out. Continue for approximately one mile (1.5km) curving first to the left and then heading north. At Botcher Gill Gate the side valley forces it to take a sharp left through the gate itself. Cross the stream, and turn right onto a path that heads back towards the Gill and then drops sharply past the old Lownathwaite lead mine. On your left hand side you will notice the steep North Hush heading off to the left. Follow the path with the Gill on your right and eventually you drop down to the waterfall, where you have to cross to the other side. As the valley begins to curve away to your left you will see the old Blakethwaite lead mine in front of you.

I spent a very enjoyable day up in this part of Gunnerside Gill in September 2008 with the team from *Skyworks* when they were filming the *Coast to Coast*

Near the mine workings

Walk for the BBC with Julia Bradbury. With us we had an expert Alan Mills, the author of *Mining and Miners in 19th Century Swaledale & Arkengarthdale* whose expert knowledge of the history of this area is second to none.

After picking your way around the old mine workings (care needed if children are with you), retrace your steps back to the waterfall and continue down the gill with the stream now on your right. After about three-quarters of a mile (1km) a track leads off to the left up to Bunton Hush and over to the Old Gang Mines. If you have time, this is worth exploring and then cut back by turning right across the moor and down to Whin Hall before returning to Gunnerside village. The main route, however, continues down the valley with the stream on your right passing firstly Swina Bank Scar on your left and then a set of delightful waterfalls just opposite the stream joining the gill at Botcher Gill Nook. Keep to the lower path below Middle Bank which takes you then underneath Birbeck Wood and down to the village.

There is an Inn in Gunnerside, The Kings Head, for refreshments at the end of the walk. In the village there is also the Old Working Smithy, dating back to 1795.

Kings Head in Gunnersidei

SWALEDALE WALK 2
Kisdon Force and Keld

Keld is at the western end of Swaledale and the final settlement in the valley and is the mid-point on Wainwright's Coast to Coast walk. The walk initially follows part of another long distance footpath – the Pennine Way – to Muker before returning on the eastern side of the Swale back to Keld.

Distance	7.5 miles (10km)
Ascent	800 feet (240m)
Time	2.5 hours
Grading	Moderate
Suggested Map	OS Outdoor Leisure 30 – Yorkshire Dales – North & Central
Starting point	Grid Reference: 910978
Parking	Muker village
How to get there	Muker is 16 miles west of Richmond on the B6270. Take the A6108 out of Richmond and turn right after about 3 miles onto the B6270
Terrain	Good footpaths throughout although it can be muddy particularly down by Kisdon Force

Keld

The name Keld derives from the Viking word Kelda meaning a spring, and the village was once called Appletre Kelde – the spring near the apple trees. Back in the late 19th century at the height of the lead mining boom in Swaledale the village had a population of around 6,000, but this has diminished now to only a few hundred. Keld is also the crossing point of Wainwright's Coast to

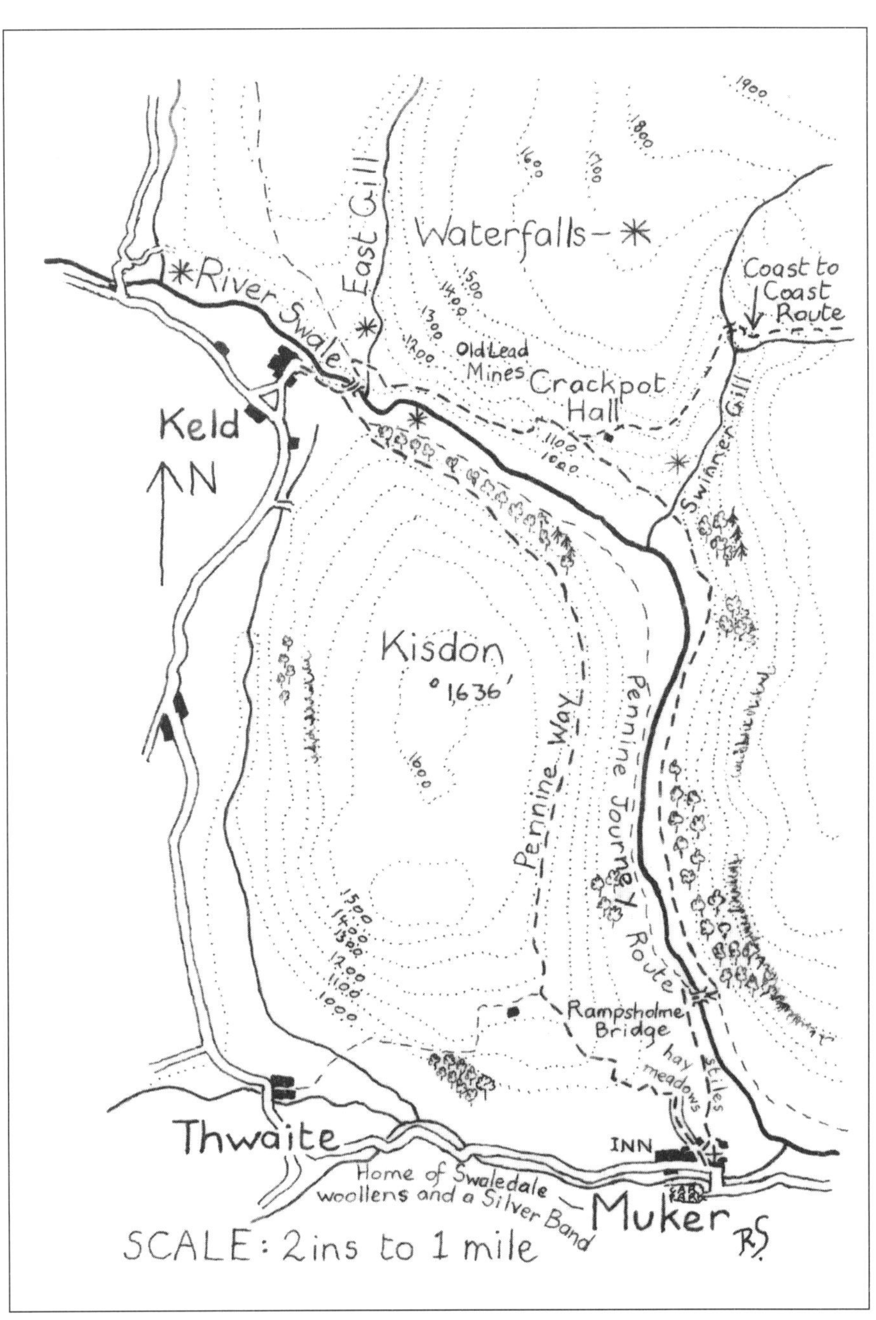

East Gill
Waterfalls —
Coast to Coast Route
River Swale
Old Lead Mines
Crackpot Hall
Swinner Gill
Keld
N
Kisdon
1,636'
Pennine Way
Pennine Journey Route
Rampsholme Bridge
hay meadows
stiles
Thwaite
INN
Muker
Home of Swaledale woollens and a Silver Band
SCALE: 2ins to 1 mile
1900
1800
1600
1700
1500
1400
1300
1200
1100
1000
RS

Coast Walk and the Pennine Way and subsequently results in many visitors walking these two routes, particularly in the summer months. In the 19th century, many buildings were erected in Keld as a result of the local mining industry. Two chapels, the Congregational and Methodist, the Library Institute and the School were all built at this time and many of them are now Grade II listed buildings.

Unfortunately Keld does not have a shop in the village. There was a Youth Hostel there when I walked the Pennine Way in the mid 1970s but this closed in October 2006. The building was subsequently converted and has since reopened as Keld Lodge, a fine hotel with bar and restaurant. There is a series of four waterfalls close to Keld at a limestone gorge on the River Swale. These are Kisdon Force, East Gill Force, Catrake Force and Wain Wath Force which you will see on the walk.

A number of the listed buildings in the village are being restored and brought back into community use by the Keld Resource Centre, a local charity linked to the faith sector. The first of these was the Congregational Church (United Reformed Church) Manse which was completed in 2009 and is now rented out as a holiday cottage, the proceeds from which support the Centre's work.

Also, in 2010, the Centre created the Keld Well-being Garden in the chapel churchyard. This provides a peaceful haven for visitors who can sit, relax and take in the glories of this part of upper Swaledale. The Centre's latest project is the Keld Countryside and Heritage Centre. This was opened on 14 May 2011 and tells of the history of Keld, its social and industrial past, and includes a display on loan from the Swaledale Museum in Reeth. It is open throughout the year. Forthcoming projects by the Resource Centre include restoring three of the buildings mentioned above – the former school, Literary Institute and the Methodist Chapel. These are long term projects as time and finances permit.

The Walk

Our walk follows, for part of its way, the traditional route by which the dead of the upper Dales were taken the long distance for burial in Grinton churchyard. With there being no consecrated ground in the upper part of the Dale, the coffins had to be transported the dozen miles further down the dale. Leaving the village, the walk takes in part of the Pennine Way as it follows the sweep of the Swale on its way down to Muker. This is known as Kisdon Side, on the slopes of the conical hill known as Kisdon. It was formed at the end of the Ice Age; previously to this the Swale used to flow to the west of the hill but glacial debris blocked its course and forced it to the east, in its current form.

As the Pennine Way goes west, eventually to climb the slopes of Great Shunner Fell, the walk joins the Corpse Way and descends down into Muker. This village is well worth exploring during the walk. Like many Swaledale settlements, it expanded considerably in the 18th and 19th centuries because of local lead mining. The prominent Literary Institute was built for the mining community; though in a nice reverse of fortunes, when the new chapel came to be built in the 1930s, dressed stone taken from the ore hearths at the Old Gang Mine down the valley was used. The Anglican Church, which eventually reduced the necessity of taking coffins the remaining eight miles to Grinton, dates from 1580.

Beyond Muker, the walk passes through various hay meadows and along the banks of the Swale. Both sandstone and limestone are found in this section; with sandstone the underlying rock beneath the river. The limestone of the area is part of the thick Ten Fathom bed, one of the Yoredale series of sedimentary rocks. Where the valley of Swinner Gill crosses the path are the remains of a small smelt mill which served the nearby Beldi Hill and Swinner Gill Mines. As you ascend the hill beyond, you will notice the ruins to your right of Crackpot Hall, a former farmhouse but abandoned many years ago because of mining subsidence and changes in farming fortune. Its name means 'Crows Pothole', and nothing to do with the sanity of the previous owners.

As the track descends the valley side, you will encounter below you the waterfall of Kisdon Force near to the Swale, and there are high overhanging crags on the opposite bank. Further along, the route drops downhill to the footbridge over the river, beside East Gill Force. The volume of its water, like all the Dales falls, can vary wildly from a small trickle in the summer months to a raging torrent after storms or heavy snowfall in the winter. Whatever its condition, the rocks around the falls can be very slippery and special care is needed if you decide to leave the path to get a better view.

From the centre of the village walk down the road from the car park entrance and go straight ahead down a gravel track signed to Muker. Continue along the higher of the tracks, ignoring a path that heads downhill to the left. After you have gone through a gate go past the sign to Kisdon Upper Force, and head along the track until you reach another signpost. Here you need to turn right and follow the Pennine Way National Trail. The path goes through a stone stile by a gate, then through a gap in the wall. Continue along the track with the wall being maintained on your left. Go on through another gate and over the next four stiles after which the track descends towards Muker village and reach a signpost at the point where the Pennine Way goes off to the right.

Go straight ahead on the track, descending slightly, still signed for Muker, between a pair of stone walls. Pass through a wooden gate, still following the

Kisdon Force

track towards Muker. The track eventually becomes metalled, as it descends through two more gates and leads via a walled lane to emerge in the village at a T-junction.

Muker's name reflects its origin as a Norse settlement, derived from the Norse word 'Mjor-aker' meaning 'the narrow acre'. The earliest recorded evidence for occupation in and around Muker takes the form of a skeleton found, with flints, on Muker Common in the early 20th century. Details suggest a burial of Bronze Age date. The location at the meeting of the River Swale and the Straw Beck with plenty of good meadow land around is most likely why the Vikings chose to settle here, giving them the opportunity to make a living out of mixed and pastoral farming.

Agriculture continued to be the basis of economy in Muker until lead mining became more important during the late 18th century and the early 19th century. Muker was also a major centre for hand knitting during this period. The importance of these industries is reflected in the many cottages, workshops and other buildings constructed at the time.

The church of St. Mary the Virgin was built during the reign of Elizabeth I. A chapel of ease had stood on this site previously but in 1580 it was substantially rebuilt and a graveyard consecrated so that residents of Upper Swaledale no longer had to transport their dead all the way to the parish church in Grinton. The tower, nave and chancel all date from this period. The church was restored in 1891.

With the decline of the mining industry, farming remained the principal occupation. From the late 19th century Muker began to see an increasing number of visitors and holiday makers. The traditional late 18th and early 19th century barns and drystone walls of Swaledale are the most characteristic feature of the landscape. The flower-rich hay meadows around Muker are of international importance and are carefully protected. Farmers receive grants which allow them to farm the land by traditional methods, without using artificial fertilizers. You are therefore requested, in this area, to keep to single file along the paths to help protect this important and unique landscape.

In the centre of the village turn left and then soon after go left again by a signpost for Gunnerside and Keld. You should now be on a paved path which needs to be followed through the next five stiles to reach the river. Turn right and go over a stile to reach the footbridge. Climb up the steps beyond the footbridge and then turn left at a signpost to Keld. Follow by the side of the river along a good track. This curves to the right around Swinner Gill, where you cross over by a footbridge near to the remains of some lead workings, and pass through a wooden gate.

From here, continue straight ahead up the hill and into a wooded area. The track turns firstly left and then right near a stone barn, and then heads downhill through a wooden gate to reach another gate just above Kisdon Force. At the wooden seat go left following a sign to Keld. Follow the stream down to a footbridge and here go through the gate and turn right climbing uphill to a T-junction. At this point turn right and follow the path back to the centre of the village.

Refreshments are available at the Keld Lodge Hotel where my good friends Nick and Karen will make you more than welcome.

SWALEDALE WALK 3
Booze

Despite the name, the only drinking you will do on this walk is drinking in the magnificent views around Arkengarthdale, a valley that once resounded to the industrial sounds of lead mining in the hills.

Distance	**5 miles (8km)**
Ascent	**650 feet (200m)**
Time	**2 hours**
Grading	**Easy**
Suggested Map	**OS Outdoor Leisure 30 – Yorkshire Dales – North & Central**
Starting point	**Grid Reference: 005024**
Parking	**Car park on the road just before the right hand turn down into Langthwaite Village**
How to get there	**Langthwaite is 10 miles west-north-west of Richmond. Take the A6108 out of Richmond and turn right after about 3 miles onto the B6270. Turn right off this road after 8 miles at Reeth**
Terrain	**Farm and moorland tracks throughout**

Running roughly north-west to south-east, Arkengarthdale contains the Arkle Beck, and is the northernmost of the Yorkshire Dales. It joins the River Swale at Reeth.

On its way up the dale from Reeth the unclassified road crosses many other small streams and their catchments, such as Great Punchard Gill, Roe Beck, Annaside Beck, and William Gill. It also passes through several small villages and hamlets including Raw, Arkle Town, Langthwaite, Booze, Eskeleth and Whaw.

From Eskeleth Bridge it is possible to take the road over the moor to Barnard Castle via Whaw although in winter this is often closed due to snow, but is a delightful drive in the summer. Arkengarthdale itself ends at Tan Hill Inn, the highest Public House in England. After reaching Tan Hill you then have three alternative routes, west to Brough, south to Keld and south-west to Kirkby Stephen.

Langthwaite is one of the few villages in Arkengarthdale, most of the others being merely hamlets. It is usually classed as the main settlement of Arkengarthdale and is one of the most northerly settlements in the whole of Yorkshire Dales National Park. It has a pub, The Red Lion, a small shop and an unusual commissioners' church. This was built in 1817 and was one of many built at the time with money being provided by Parliament in an attempt to counteract atheism and free thinking after the French Revolution. Langthwaite also has an unusual hexagonal powder house. This was built in

Langthwaite Church

1807 and was used to store gunpowder and supplied it for use in the lead mines around this area.

Arkle Town is the neighbouring hamlet and gets its name from the nearby Arkle Beck. At one time it had a parish church, inn and a workhouse but nowadays there are none of these. The nearby hamlet of Booze that you will pass through on the walk is about 1 mile (1.6 km) east of Langthwaite and Arkle Town. In July 2008 the Royal Mail announced it was withdrawing its postal services to the hamlet on health and safety grounds because access to Booze involved an 'excessively steep' rural track. As a consequence, this means that local families have to make a one-hour round-trip into Richmond and back to collect their mail. Totally unacceptable, or what!

Until the beginning of the 20th century the surrounding hills of Arkegarthdale were mined for lead. The metal was first dug here in prehistoric times, but industrial mining began on a major scale in the 17th century. By 1628 there was a smelt mill beside the Slei Gill, which you will pass on the walk, and it is possible to pick out the evidence of some of the early miners' methods.

Booze

Booze, Norse for 'the house on the curved hillside', is now just a cluster of farm buildings, but was once a thriving mining community with more than 40 houses and a chapel in the early 1800s. Between Booze and Slei Gill the walk passes the arched entrance to an old miners' tunnel known as a level, and behind it the remains of Tanner Rake Hush. As mentioned in the Gunnerside Gill walk, hushes were formed by the release of water from a temporary dam to strip the soil and expose the lead beneath the surface. This desolate valley by Tanner Rake Hush is full of tumbled rock, left behind when the dammed stream at the top of the valley was allowed to rush down, thus exposing the lead veins. On the walk you will also pass the spoil heaps of Windegg Mines, before returning to the valley near to Scar House, which is now a shooting lodge owned by the Duke of Norfolk but in the 18th century was used by the manager of the mine.

Near to Eskeleth Bridge is the powder house, a small octagonal building, set safely by itself in a field. Built about 1804, it served the nearby Octagon Smelt Mill, the remains of which can be traced in this area. Just after you turn right along the road are the ruins of the Langthwaite Smelt Mill. Charles Bathurst, Lord of the Manor, held the mining rights here for much of the 18th century. The CB Inn near the road junction is really The Charles Bathurst, named after him in his honour.

The Walk

Our walk starts from the car park and on leaving here, turn right, then right again down into Langthwaite. Go over the bridge and continue ahead between a set of cottages. Climb up the hill and follow the lane for about ¼ miles (400m) to the hamlet of Booze. Pass the farmhouse and a stone barn and follow the track to a gate. After the gate, the track bends left, and here go straight on to a broken wall. Bear right at the wall to go past a ruined cottage, and then follow the path to the stream of Slei Gill. Walk heading upstream, go through a gate and then cross the stream using the stepping stones.

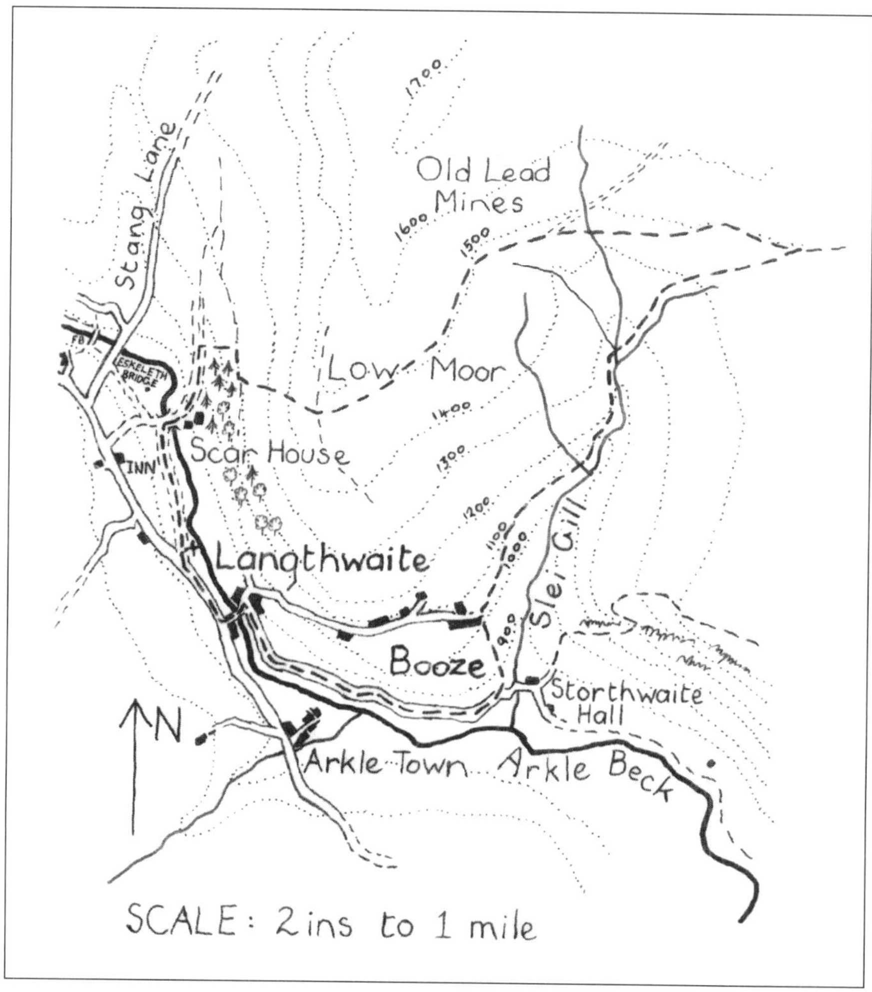

View from Booze

Walk slightly left, crossing Low Moor, to reach a wooden hut near a crossing track. Turn left along the track. At a crossing of tracks go straight on, and then at a T-junction turn left. Where the wall on your right ends, leave the track, bending right along a path and follow this down to a gate in the corner of two walls.

Follow the small gully downhill and go through a gate onto a track. Turn right along here and continue down through a gateway and on to another track by a barn. Follow this track as it bends left by a stone wall and then passes the farm buildings. Go initially through two gates to reach a third gate, white in colour.

Go through this white gate to enter the grounds of Scar House. Follow the drive as it bears right, downhill, go over a bridge and cattle grid at the bottom, then turn right. Follow the track to a road. Turn left, uphill, to a T-junction. Turn right and follow the road. After a cattle grid, turn left along a signed track which brings you up to the CB Public House. If you have timed it rightly you should be here just in time for lunch to sample the fine bar menu and excellent Theakstone's draught beer.

SWALEDALE WALK 4
Reeth

Our walk takes us over Reeth Bridge down to Grinton Bridge and then via Marrick Abbey to the small village of Marrick itself. It then returns westwards above Gornless Scar and Ince Wood to High Fremington and back to Reeth village.

Distance	5.5 miles (9km)
Ascent	500 feet (155m)
Time	2 hours
Grading	Easy
Suggested Map	OS Outdoor Leisure 30 – Yorkshire Dales – North & Central
Starting point	Grid Reference: 039993
Parking	The Green, Reeth
How to get there	Reeth is 8 miles West of Richmond on the B6270. Take the A6108 out of Richmond and turn right after about 3 miles onto the B6270
Terrain	Moorland tracks initially and then riverside path

Reeth

Reeth is often classed as the principal settlement of Swaledale. It is situated at the junction of the two most northerly of the Yorkshire Dales: Swaledale and Arkengarthdale. It was a small settlement before 1,000AD but grew after the Norman invasion and was listed in the Domesday Book.

As Reeth grew, it became important for two industries – hand knitting and lead mining, the village being the administrative centre for the whole of

Swaledale for the latter. It was, and still continues to be, a major agricultural centre for the dale.

Most of its 18th century houses and hotels are situated around the green in the centre of the village, unusual because of its triangular shape and surrounded by cobbles. The village has three pubs all of which are situated adjacent to the green. They are the Black Bull, the King's Arms and the Buck Hotel. The view from the centre of the village looks out to the nearby fells of Fremington Edge and Calver Hill.

Reeth has always played a major role in Swaledale as it controlled the important route westwards from Richmond. Reeth was granted its market in 1695 and sheep were, for a long time, the basis of Reeth's prosperity. There are still annual sheep sales each autumn, as well as the important Reeth Show at the beginning of September.

Reeth has had an important knitting industry over the years which this wool was used for, and both the men and women of the village would click away with their needles making stockings and other garments. Reeth was also the main centre in this area for the lead mining industry, which extended up Arkengarthdale and then over Marrick Moor. Its lead mining history can be traced in the Folk Museum, which houses exhibits illustrating the life and traditions of Swaledale. Reeth was the capital of this industry, with a population of nearly 1500 in its heyday. However, in the mid-19th century cheaper foreign imports were coming in and by 1885 virtually all the mines had closed and the area was reverting back to the idyllic farming community that we see today.

Reeth Bridge, reached by following the Leyburn road from the village centre by the Green, has suffered over many years from the effects of the swollen River Swale and has had to be replaced on a number of occasions. The present bridge dates from the early 18th century, replacing one washed away in 1701, and built after its predecessor succumbed to the raging torrents in 1547. The path the walk follows takes us alongside the river to Grinton Bridge. Nearby is Grinton church, once the centre of a huge parish that took in the whole of Swaledale, making very long journeys necessary for marriages and funerals as there was no other consecrated Church in the Dale at one time. Coffins had to be transported twelve miles down the dale from Keld and similar distances down the subsidiary valley of Arkengarthdale.

Marrick Priory

Marrick Priory, 2½ miles (4km) to the East of Reeth and 2 miles (3km) from Grinton is often referred to as one of the most important churches in the Dales. Marrick in the Middle Ages was home to a group of Benedictine Nuns.

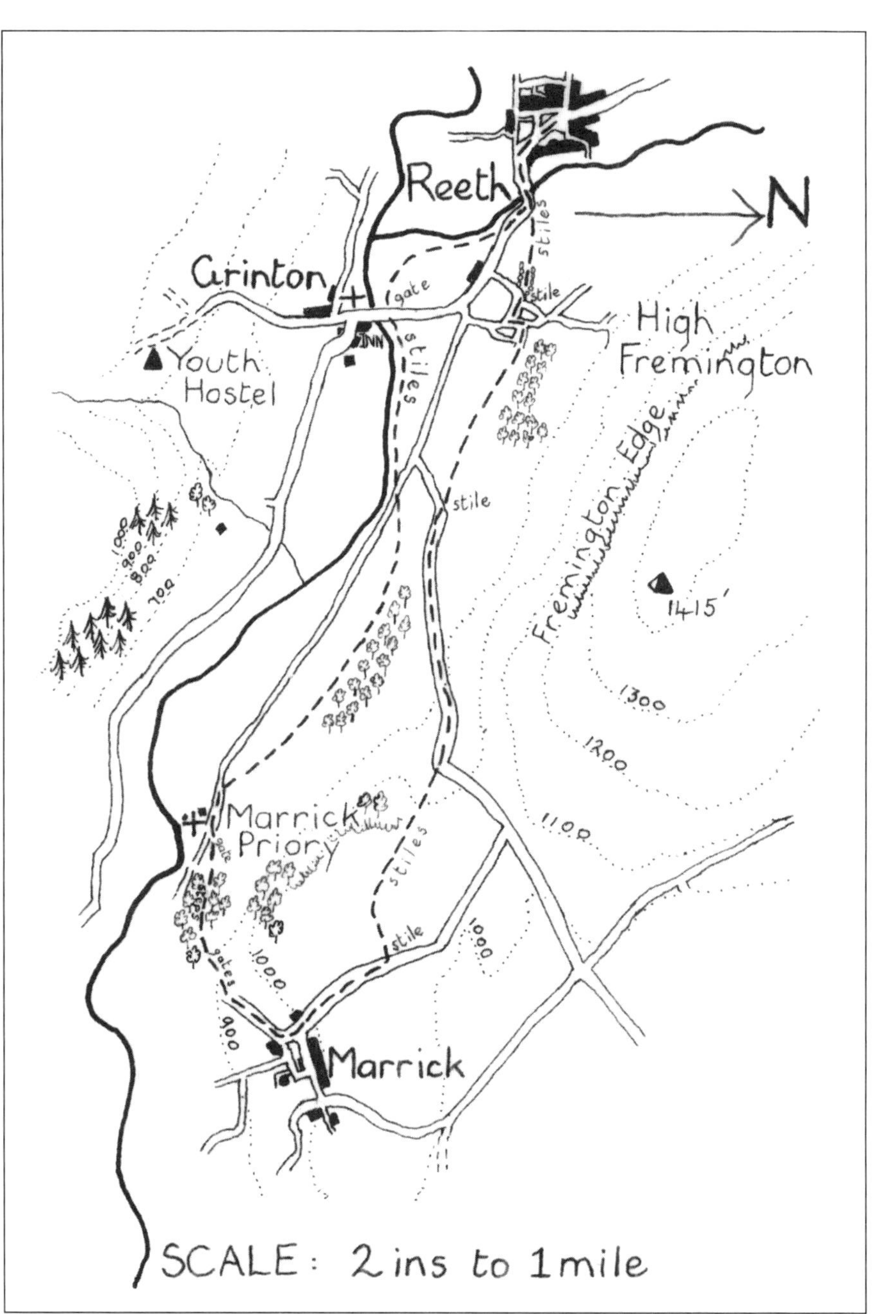

Reeth
N
Grinton
gate
stiles
stile
Youth Hostel
High Fremington
INN
stiles
stile
Fremington Edge
1415'
1300
1200
1100
Marrick Priory
gate
stiles
stile
1000
gates
1000
900
Marrick
1000
SCALE: 2 ins to 1 mile

The Priory was founded by Roger de Aske, who's descendent, Robert, was one of the leaders of the Pilgrimage of Grace. Hilda Prescott's novel *The Man on a Donkey*, about Robert Aske and his Pilgrimage, is partly set in Marrick. Today the nuns' buildings are either partially demolished or have been converted into farm buildings.

After Marrick Priory the path climbs steeply uphill on rough stone steps called the 'Nun's Causey' – a corruption of causeway. Now used as part of the Coast to Coast Walk, this is said to be the route that the nuns from the Priory built in order that they could reach the Richmond road that ran along the summit of the hill. The original 365 steps have now been broken up and removed but whilst walking the path it is easy to experience somewhat of a suitably medieval atmosphere as little else has changed over the last five centuries. Fremington, towards the end of the walk is split into Low Fremington which is built along the B6270 and High Fremington which is a scattering of houses running up towards Fremington Edge.

The Walk

The walk commences in the centre of Reeth from the Green and starts downhill heading in the direction of Leyburn until you reach Reeth Bridge. Cross over the bridge and continue along the road where it bears right for about 100yds (90m) until you reach a footpath sign to Grinton Bridge where you need to turn right.

Follow the path through the gate and go across several fields, the track being fairly distinct throughout. Upon arrival at a set of steps ascend these and go through a gate onto the bridge itself. If you wish to visit the church at Grinton, turn right and head up into the village where you will see the church on your right. Retrace your steps back down to the bridge, cross it and turn right to take a track alongside the bridge.

The path now continues along the side of the river and over the next ½ mile (900 metres) or so you will cross over four stiles, eventually reaching a metalled lane. Turn right here and follow the lane for nearly a mile (1.5km) to reach Marrick Abbey. Go past the abbey buildings, cross over the cattle grid, and then turn left through a gate signed to Marrick. Continue along the track, go through a wooden gate and follow the paved path heading for a wooded area in front. Pass through another gate, continue up the path and pass through three more gates. Upon reaching Harlands House turn left opposite this heading up a metalled road, and then turn left again at the T-junction to bring you into Marrick village.

The famous breeder of racehorses, William Blenkiron was born in Marrick in about 1807. He was originally brought up as a farmer, but he abandoned

Moors above Marrick

that pursuit, and moved to London in 1834, and began business as a general agent in Cheapside. He then turned his attention to racehorse ownership. As a breeder of stock he had few equals. Blenkiron bred Hermit, the Derby winner in 1867, and Gamos, which won the Oaks in 1870.

From the village centre, initially follow the road for ¼ mile (400m), and then at a footpath sign turn left over the stile. Go across the field until you reach a gated stile, cross this and turn right and then follow the wall, to reach a second gated stile. Go over this and then continue over a final stile located by a metal gate, and head for a second metal gate which brings you onto a road.

Turn left here and follow the road for approximately ¾ mile (1.2km). At the point where the road bends left, turn right and go through a stile signed to Fremington. Follow the path across the fields, passing through a gate, to reach another stile, and then continue along the path to reach a lane. Immediately here turn left and when you reach the houses ahead turn right. As the lane bends left, go ahead to a stile by the gate. Keep close to the wall on the left, and continue along the path through four more stiles to arrive back at Reeth Bridge. Cross the bridge and follow the road back to the centre of the village.

There are plenty of places for refreshment in Reeth at the end of the walk including the Black Bull Inn dating from 1680 with its unique upside-down inn sign. There is a fascinating tale behind this. Bob Sykes, a previous landlord of the Black Bull was more than surprised when National Parks officials took exception to his attempts to tidy up the exterior of the public house. He removed the render from the outside of the hotel to expose the original 250-year-old walls. The work was partly carried out to comply with English Tourist Board accommodation grading requirements. But Mr Sykes also feared at the time that the crumbling render was a potential danger to the public.

However, Park officials threatened legal action if the render was not replaced. The Authorities argued that the building would originally have had some form of render. Shortly after the render was removed, some local pranksters turned the sign upside down in protest at the Authorities attitude. The sign has moved now but still remains upside down.

SWALEDALE WALK 5
Willance's Leap from Richmond

This walk from the centre of Richmond takes us on a 400 year old history journey to see where Robert Willance on his horse leapt over the edge of Whitecliffe Scar, fell 212 feet and survived!

Distance	6.5 miles (10km)
Ascent	500 feet (155m)
Time	3 hours
Grading	Moderate
Suggested Map	OS Outdoor Leisure 30 – Yorkshire Dales – North & Central
Starting point	Grid Reference: 171015
Parking	Richmond town centre
How to get there	Richmond is 4 miles west of the A1. Take either the A6108 from Scotch Corner or the B6271 from Catterick
Terrain	Footpaths out of the town followed by farm track and field paths

Willance's Leap

This walk takes us from the centre of Richmond to the famous point of Willance's Leap. In 2006 the people of Richmond celebrated the 400th anniversary of the unique event of Willance's leap. The tale of this is as follows: Robert Willance, a prosperous entrepreneurial Richmond draper who also had interests in lead mining on the land at Clints, a few miles west again of the stone, was riding his horse on the moors at night. The pair leapt from the edge of Whitcliffe Scar, their destination invisible in the mist. He would often of a whim ride alone up the Dale, in both fair and foul weather. On a day in November, 1606, he may have been alone on such an excursion or he may have been hunting with friends. It is one of the delights of our folk ballads that old stories change with the telling. Robert's true tale has many variants in its detail.

Somewhere in Swaledale thick mist enveloped him and he tried to return to Richmond. Tales tell that he counted back the ditches that he knew where to cross but he went astray. Others tell that his horse panicked and leapt three successive bounds of 24 feet each. One thing we know for certain is that the pair leapt from the edge of Whitcliffe Scar, their destination invisible in the mist. They fell 212 feet, as evidenced by the Ordnance Survey contours. Robert survived the fall, but with one or both of his legs broken. It is told that he placed his legs inside the dead horse's belly. One leg later had to be amputated. Robert had a stone erected at the place, inscribed with the words "1606 – Hear Us. Glory be to our Merciful God who miraculously preserved me from the danger so great".

The stone was replaced in 1734. A fragment of that stone rests on his grave in St. Mary's Church in Richmond. Robert became an alderman in 1608. A door was constructed direct from his house in Frenchgate to St. Mary's church and he passed through that door every week to attend church. In 1615 he was carried through it for the final time to be laid to rest.

At Whitcliffe Scar the stone was renewed in both 1815 and 1843. An obelisk was erected to mark the 1906 tercentenary. On 16th September 2006, people of Richmond with their mayor and many other mayors and people from afar walked the few miles from Richmond to Willance's Leap. There a new stone was dedicated for the 400th Anniversary and John Wilson, a local folk singer, sang a song he had written to tell the remarkable story of Robert Willance to those gathered. A special beer was also brewed to mark this anniversary by the Darwin Brewery.

Willance's Leap Monument

Richmond

Richmond was founded in 1071 by the Breton Alan Rufus on lands given to him by William the Conqueror. Richmond Castle was completed in 1086, consisting of a keep with walls. The castle overlooks the River Swale and is a major tourist attraction. The nearby cobbled market place is one of the largest in England with The Green Howards Regimental Museum being based in the old Trinity Church in the centre of the market place. Also in the town is located the Richmondshire Museum.

The market town prospered as the centre of the Swaledale wool industry in the late 17th and 18th centuries and also with the growth of the lead mining industry in Swaledale and Arkengarthdale. During this period much of the town's attractive Georgian architecture was built, the most notable examples being located on Newbiggin and in Frenchgate.

Nearly 200 years ago some soldiers found an entrance to a tunnel near the castle keep. They could not fit into the tunnel so they elected to send a regimental drummer boy. The boy was asked to walk along the tunnel and beat his drum so that above ground the soldiers could follow the noise. They did

Richmond Castle

this for three miles before the sound stopped unexpectedly. This was never explained and today a stone marks the spot the noise stopped. More confusingly the entrance can also not be found. Today schools celebrate this local legend with children marching through town annually. Legend claims that on some cold nights you can hear the faint sound of the drummer boy still.

The Georgian Theatre Royal was founded in 1788 by the actor, Samuel Butler, and is located just off the market place. It was closed in 1848 when theatre became less popular and it was used as a warehouse for many years. The theatre was restored and reopened in 1963 and a theatre museum was added in 1979 and a further extension added in 2003

The Walk

Start the walk by the Tourist Information office in the centre of Richmond. Standing in front of the building turn right and go along the road past the cricket field. Take the third road on the right, called Westfields, by the shop. Walk uphill to house numbered 19, cross the road and enter the field in front through a gate. Turn right uphill to cross the open field of Westfields, continue past the seats along the top of the field with the property Bellside above you on the right. Keep right over brow of the hill and leave by the gate.

Turn left into a tarred lane, go past two entrances on the left and right and reach the gate across the lane at High Leazes Farm. Cross over the stile to the right and enter into the field. Bear left and head for the brow on the hill ahead joining an animal track and keeping above the quarry. Follow the track to the end of the trees with a dyke located on your left hand side. From here if you turn round you will get a good view of Richmond and the castle. Continue on the track bearing slightly left. Gorse bushes will soon appear on your left hand side and you need to keep these on your left all the way to the brow of the hill. As you reach the brow of the hill the panorama of the River Swale opens up in front of you. Reach a fence, turn right and follow the fence to a stile in the corner of the field. Go over the stile onto a narrow path where you have now reached Willance's Leap. Here is you will see the various monuments and the obelisk.

With the wall to your right continue along the top of the escarpment, dropping and ascending a few small valleys, perhaps where Robert made his preliminary leaps. As mentioned earlier, Robert Willance's family had lead mines at Clints, beyond here, located between Marske and Marrick. Follow the wall round a long slow curve right, until you see the TV aerial ahead. Go left down the bank to reach a tarred track where you need to turn left and follow this down to the cattle grid. Do not cross the grid at this point, but instead turn right. The path now goes down over a stile and becomes an old green

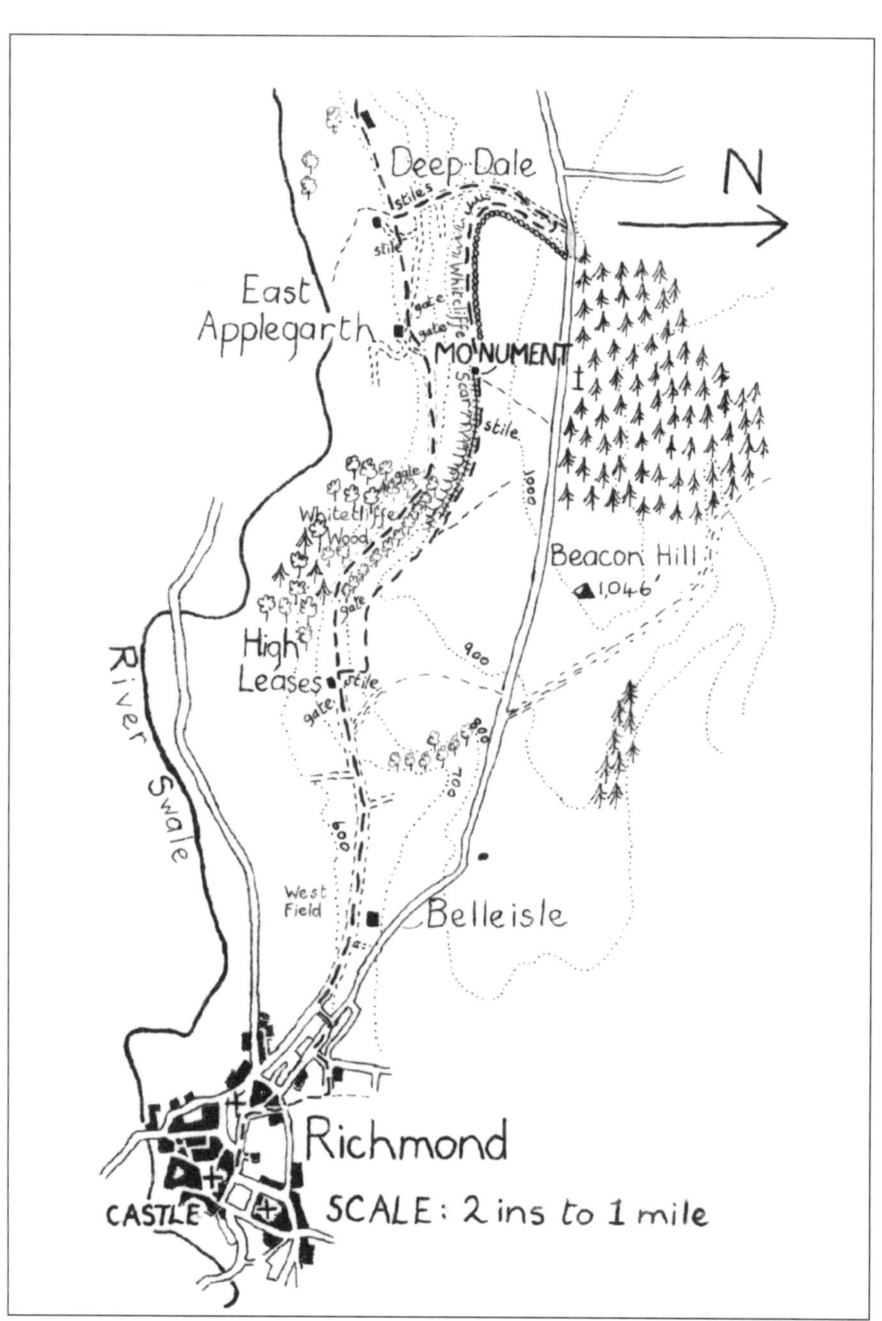

N
Deep Dale
stiles
stile
East
Applegarth
Whitcliffe
gate
gate
MONUMENT
Scar
stile
1000
gate
Whitcliffe
Wood
Beacon Hill
1,046
High
Leases
gate
stile
900
gate
800
700
600
West
Field
Belleisle
River Swale
Richmond
CASTLE
SCALE: 2 ins to 1 mile

lane. Very soon you go over another stile on your left, and at this point you join Wainwright's Coast to Coast Walk.

Cross the farm track ahead and go over the stile into the field. Bear slightly left across the field and pass a stone trough. At this point go over the stile in the wall. Continue ahead and cross over a farm track. Go through either the gate or over the adjacent stile into a field. Pass to the left of East Applegarth Farm and go through the gate at the far side of this field. Here the track bears left and leads into a rough field. Willance's Leap is now high above you on your left at the top of the scar. Continue on the track as it leads towards Whiteclifffe Woods. During the spring this field can be abundant with primroses. Go over the stile by the gate and follow the track up through the woods to exit them via another gate. Here there is an open field off to your right. Stay on the track and return to the gate by High Leazes Farm again. Go round the gate and then it is simply a matter of retracing your steps from earlier in the walk to go back across to Westfields and the town of Richmond.

There are numerous places for refreshment in Richmond including an excellent fish and chip restaurant in the Market Place. No wonder as a fervent lover of fish and chips that Wainwright made Richmond one of his overnight stops on the Coast to Coast walk.

APPENDIX – ACCOMMODATION

Below is a list of accommodation for each of the Dales for this series of walks. The list is sorted by type of accommodation and by location. However, this is only correct at the date of publishing (2015) and it is best to check in advance before leaving home regarding the availability of this accommodation. This is only a limited selection of the accommodation in each of the areas and local tourist information centres and the Internet are good sources of up to date information.

Airedale Walks

B & B	Lindon House	Airton	01729-830418
B & B	Ford House Farm	Baildon	01274 584489
B & B	Tudor House	Bell Busk	01729 830301
B & B	March Cote Farm	Bingley	01274 487433
B & B	Midland Hotel	Bingley	01274 551408
B & B	Prospect House	Bingley	01274 562313
B & B	The Cornrake	Cracoe	01756 730205
B & B	Apothecary Guest House	Haworth	01535 643642
B & B	Ashmount Country House	Haworth	01535 645726
B & B	Heathfield B & B	Haworth	01535 640606
B & B	Rosebud Cottage	Haworth	01535 640321
B & B	The Thyme House	Haworth	01535 211860
B & B	Woodlands Grange	Haworth	01535 646814
B & B	Ye Sleeping House	Haworth	01535 645992
B & B	Angel Inn	Hetton	01756 730263
B & B	Beck Hall	Malham	01729 830332
B & B	Lister Cottage	Malham	01756 749364
B & B	Miresfield Farm	Malham	01729 830414
B & B	River House	Malham	01729 830315
B & B	High Trenhouse	Malham Moor	01729 830322
B & B	Clifton Lodge	Shipley	01274 580509
B & B	Craven Heifer Inn	Skipton	01756 792521
B & B	Ponden House	Stanbury	01535 644154
Hotel	Five Rise Locks Hotel	Bingley	01274 565296
Hotel	Oakwood Hall	Bingley	01274 564123
Hotel	Ramada Jarvis	Bingley	0844 815 9004
Hotel	Premier Inn	Keighley	0871 527 8134
Hotel/Inn	Newfield Hall	Airton	0845 4707558
Hotel/Inn	Old White Lion	Haworth	01535 642313
Hotel/Inn	The Fleece Inn	Haworth	01535 642172
Hotel/Inn	Lister Arms	Malham	01729 830330
Hotel/Inn	The Buck Inn	Malham	01729 830317
Self Catering	Ellis Barn	Airton	01729 830253
Self Catering	Eshton Lodge	Eshton	01756 749364
Self Catering	Oak Cottage	Eshton	01729 830217
Self Catering	Benchmark Cottage	Haworth	01535 642040
Self Catering	Bottoms Farm Holiday Cottages	Haworth	07769 860600
Self Catering	Higher Scholes Cottage	Keighley	07769 860600
Self Catering	Mill Top	Kirkby Malham	01729 830866

Self Catering	New Close Farm	Kirkby Malham	01729 830240
Self Catering	Bull Barn	Malham	01756 749364
Self Catering	Hill Top Cottage	Malham	01729 830320
Self Catering	Lister Cottage	Malham	01756 749364
Self Catering	Old Barn Flat	Malham	01729 830486
Self Catering	Pikedaw Cottage	Malham	01729 830317
Self Catering	Rose Cottage	Malham	01756 790458
Self Catering	Town End Cottages	Malham	01729 830902
Self Catering	High Trenhouse	Malham Moor	01729 830322
Youth Hostel	Haworth YH	Haworth	01535 643324
Youth Hostel	Malham Y H	Malham	01729 830321

Nidderdale Walks

B & B	Bewerley Hall Farm	Bewerley	01423 711636
B & B	Bailey Motte Cottage	Knaresborough	01423 860340
B & B	Ebor Mount	Knaresborough	01423 863315
B & B	Gallon House	Knaresborough	01423 862102
B & B	Hermitage Guest House	Knaresborough	01423 863349
B & B	Holly Corner	Knaresborough	01423 864204
B & B	Kirkgate Guest House	Knaresborough	01423 862704
B & B	Market Tavern	Knaresborough	01423 868533
B & B	Newton House	Knaresborough	01423 863539
B & B	Teardrop Cottage	Knaresborough	07944 395886
B & B	The Groves	Knaresborough	01423 863022
B & B	The Mitre	Knaresborough	01423 868948
B & B	Watergate Heaven	Knaresborough	01423 864627
B & B	Crown Hotel	Lofthouse	01423 755206
B & B	Crown Hotel	Middlesmoor	01423 755204
B & B	Foxfield	Pateley Bridge	01423 711685
B & B	Lyndale	Pateley Bridge	01423 712657
B & B	Roslyn House	Pateley Bridge	01423 711374
B & B	Talbot House	Pateley Bridge	01423 711597
Hotel	Bay Horse Inn	Knaresborough	01423 862212
Hotel	Dower House Hotel	Knaresborough	01423 863302
Hotel	George & Dragon	Knaresborough	01423 862792
Hotel	The Royal Oak	Knaresborough	01423 865880
Self Catering	Blayshaw Farm	Lofthouse	01423 755399
Self Catering	Kirklea Cottage	Lofthouse	01423 755228
Self Catering	Studfold Farm Caravan Park	Lofthouse	01423 755084
Self Catering	Abbey Holiday Cottages	Middlesmoor	01423 712062
Self Catering	Ashfield House	Pateley Bridge	01423 711491

Ribblesdale Walks

B & B	Bank House	Dent	01539 625322
B & B	George & Dragon	Dent	01539 625256
B & B	Stone Close	Dent	01539 625321
B & B	Broad Croft House	Horton	01729 860302
B & B	Horton Women's Holiday Centre	Horton	01729 860207
B & B	The Willows	Horton	01729 860200
B & B	Bridge End	Ingleton	01524 241413
B & B	Dales Guest House	Ingleton	01524 241401
B & B	Gatehouse Farm	Ingleton	01524 241458

B & B	Hollin Tree	Ingleton	01524 241251
B & B	Holly Grange	Ingleton	01524 242543
B & B	Ingleborough View	Ingleton	01524 241523
B & B	Inglenook	Ingleton	01524 241270
B & B	Riverside Lodge	Ingleton	01524 241359
B & B	Burn Lodge	Settle	01729 823118
B & B	Littlebeck Country House	Settle	01729 822330
B & B	Oast Guest House	Settle	01729 822989
B & B/SC	Old Sunday School Studio	Dent	01539 625329
Hotel	Craven Arms	Giggleswick	01729 825627
Hotel	Harts Head	Giggleswick	01729 825627
Hotel	Golden Lion	Horton	01729 860206
Hotel	The Crown	Horton	01729 860209
Self Catering	Blindbeck Cottage	Horton	01729 860396
Self Catering	The Byres	Horton (Selside)	01729 860367
Self Catering	Beech Tree Cottages	Ingleton	01524 241828
Self Catering	Greta Cottage	Ingleton	01524 274205
Self Catering	Ingleton Holiday Cottages	Ingleton	01524 242405
Self Catering	Laburnum Cottages	Ingleton	01943 873809
Self Catering	Little Storrs	Ingleton	01524 241843
Self Catering	Tryst Cottage	Ingleton	07516770799
Self Catering	Sunnybeck Cottage	Settle	01729 893031

Swaledale Walks

B & B	The CB Inn	Arkengarthdale	01748 884567
B & B	The Ghyll	Arkengarthdale	01748 884353
B & B	Home Farm	Fremington	01748 884878
B & B	Brow Hill Farm	Gunnerside	01748 886067
B & B	Oxnop Hall	Gunnerside	01748 886253
B & B	Rowleth End	Gunnerside	01748 886327
B & B	School House	Gunnerside	01748 886874
B & B	Birkdale Farm	Keld	01748 886044
B & B	Butt House	Keld	01748 886374
B & B	Pry House	Keld	01748 886845
B & B	Muker Village Store	Muker	01748 886409
B & B	Swale Farm	Muker	01748 886479
B & B	Arkleside	Reeth	01748 884200
B & B	Cambridge House	Reeth	01748 884633
B & B	Hackney House	Reeth	01748 884302
B & B	Hillary House	Reeth	01748 884171
B & B	School House	Reeth	01748 884284
B & B	Springfield House	Reeth	01748 884634
B & B	The Black Bull	Reeth	01748 884213
B & B	The Old Temperance	Reeth	01748 884401
B & B	Walpardoe	Reeth	01748 884626
B & B	Abbey View	Richmond	01748 822233
B & B	Arandale	Richmond	01748 821282
B & B	Easby Cottage	Richmond	01748 826541
B & B	Frenchgate	Richmond	01748 823421
B & B	Fryers Cottage	Richmond	01748 823344
B & B	Millgate House	Richmond	01748 823571
B & B	Old Brewery	Richmond	01748 825561
B & B	Skeeby Lodge	Richmond	01748 850750

B & B	Victoria House	Richmond	01748 824830
B & B	West Cottage	Richmond	01748 824046
B & B	Westend Guest House	Richmond	01748 824783
Hotel	Keld Lodge	Keld	01748 886529
Hotel	Buck Hotel	Reeth	01748 884210
Hotel	The Burgoyne	Reeth	01748 884292
Hotel	Kearton Country Hotel	Richmond	01748 886277
Hotel	Kings Arms	Richmond	01748 884259
Hotel	Talbot Hotel	Richmond	07908 618468
Hotel	The Punch Bowl	Richmond	01748 886233
Self Catering	Pretoria Cottage	Gunnerside	01223 894434
Self Catering	Strands Farmhouse	Gunnerside	07921 218166
Self Catering	Keld Bunkhouse	Keld	01748 886549
Self Catering	Intake Cottage	Reeth	01748 821322
Self Catering	Orchard Caravan & Camping Park	Reeth	01748 884475
Self Catering	Abbey House	Richmond	01748 825311
Self Catering	Old Cello Workshop	Richmond	01748 825525
Self Catering	The Old Sweet Shop	Richmond	01228 406701

Wensleydale Walks

B & B	Holmedale	Askrigg	01969 650910
B & B	Heather Cottage	Aysgarth	01969 663229
B & B	Marlbeck Guest House	Aysgarth	01969 663068
B & B	Stow House	Aysgarth	01969 663635
B & B	Yordeale Guest House	Aysgarth	01969 663423
B & B	The Old Hall	Bainbridge	01969 650038
B & B	Crosby House	Hawes	01969 667322
B & B	Ebor House	Hawes	01969 667337
B & B	Laburnum House	Hawes	01969 667717
B & B	Thorney Mire Barn	Hawes	01969 666122
B & B	Clyde House	Leyburn	01969 623941
B & B	Dales Haven	Leyburn	01969 623814
B & B	Eastfield Lodge	Leyburn	01969 623196
B & B	Greenhills	Leyburn	01969 623859
B & B	Domus	Middleham	01969 623497
B & B	The Priory	Middleham	01969 623279
B & B	Waterford House	Middleham	01969 622090
B & B	Yore View	Middleham	01969 622987
B & B	High Blean	Raydaleside	01969 650205
B & B	Fox & Hounds Inn	West Burton	01969 663279
B & B	The Grange	West Burton	01969 663348
Hotel	George & Dragon	Aysgarth	01969 663358
Hotel	The Wheatsheaf	Carpeby	01969 663216
Hotel	Bulls Head	Hawes	01969 667437
Hotel	Black Swan	Leyburn	01969 622221
Hotel	Street Head Inn	Leyburn	01969 663282
Hotel	Richard III Hotel	Middleham	01969 623240
Hotel	White Swan	Middleham	01969 622093
Hotel	The Punch Bowl	Richmond	01748 886233
Hotel	Stone House Hotel	Sedbusk	01969 667571
Hotel	Fox & Hounds	West Burton	01969 663111
Self Catering	Old Goat House	Aysgarth	01969 663716

Self Catering	Westholme Lodges	Aysgarth	01969 663268
Self Catering	Country Cottage Holidays	Hawes	01969 667654
Self Catering	Country Hideaways	Hawes	01969 663559
Self Catering	Crown Court Cottage	Leyburn	01969 624448
Self Catering	Jonas Centre	Leyburn	01969 624900
Self Catering	Lilac Cottage	Sedbusk	01244 352108
Self Catering	Cowstonegill House	Walden	01539 433434
Self Catering	Grange House	Walden	01969 663641
Self Catering	Stable Cottage	West Burton	01969 663348
Self Catering	The Grange	West Burton	01969 663348
Self Catering	West Burton Cottage	West Burton	01244 357703

Wharfedale Walks

B & B	Croft	Addingham, Ilkley	01943 830400
B & B	Arthington Lodge	Arthington	01423 734102
B & B	Scaife Hall Farm	Blubberhouses	01943 880354
B & B	Glebe Barn	Burnsall	01756 720680
B & B	Manor House	Burnsall	01756 720231
B & B	Wharfe View Farm	Burnsall	01756 720643/720415
B & B	Bondcroft Farm	Eastby	01756 793371
B & B	Craven Cottage	Grassington	01756 752205
B & B	Grassington Lodge	Grassington	01756 752518
B & B	Kirkfield	Grassington	01756 752385
B & B	Lythe End	Grassington	01756 753196
B & B	Town Head Guest House	Grassington	01756 752811
B & B	Raines Close	Grassington	01756 752678
B & B	The Beamsley Project	Hazlewood, Ilkley	01756 710255
B & B	Howgill Lodge Barn	Howgill	01756 720655
B & B	Archway Cottage	Ilkley	01943 603399
B & B	Briary Retreat Centre	Ilkley	01943 607287
B & B	Friendly Dove	Ilkley	01943 463777
B & B	Roberts Family	Ilkley	01943 817542
B & B	Westwood Lodge	Ilkley	01943 433430
B & B	Chevin End Guest House	Menston	01943 876845
B & B	Chevin End	Menston, Ilkley	01943 876845
B & B	Dowgill House	Otley	01943 850836
B & B	Langerton House	Thorpe	01756 730260
B & B	Ling House	Threshfield	01756 752342
B & B	Station House	Threshfield	01756 752667
B & B	Timble Inn	Timble	01943 880530
B & B	Springroyd Housel	Skipton	01756 752473
Bunk Barn	Barden Tower Bunk Barn	Barden Tower	01756 720616
Hotel	Hopper Lane Hotel	Blubberhouses	01943 880191
Hotel	Devonshire Arms	Bolton Abbey	01756 718111
Hotel	Britannia Hotel	Bramhope	0845 3738540
Hotel	Devonshire Fell Hotel	Burnsall	01756 729000
Hotel	The Red Lion	Burnsall	01756 720204
Hotel	The Foresters Arms	Grassington	01756 752349
Hotel	Craiglands Hotel	Ilkley	01943 430001
Hotel	Dalesway Hotel	Ilkley	01943 605438
Hotel	Rombalds Hotel	Ilkley	01943 603201
Hotel	Chevin Country Park Hotel	Otley	01943 467818
Hotel	Horse & Farrier	Otley	01943 468400
Self Catering	Burnsall Holiday Cottage	Burnsall	01244 357703